SEXTINCTION

THE DECLINE OF SEX AND
THE FUTURE OF INTIMACY

Dr. Debra Soh

THRESHOLD EDITIONS

New York   Amsterdam/Antwerp   London
Toronto   Sydney/Melbourne   New Delhi

Threshold Editions
An Imprint of Simon & Schuster, LLC
1230 Avenue of the Americas
New York, NY 10020

For more than 100 years, Simon & Schuster has championed authors and the stories they create. By respecting the copyright of an author's intellectual property, you enable Simon & Schuster and the author to continue publishing exceptional books for years to come. We thank you for supporting the author's copyright by purchasing an authorized edition of this book.

First Threshold Editions hardcover edition February 2026

THRESHOLD EDITIONS and colophon are trademarks of Simon & Schuster, LLC

Simon & Schuster strongly believes in freedom of expression and stands against censorship in all its forms. For more information, visit BooksBelong.com.

For information about special discounts for bulk purchases, please contact Simon & Schuster Special Sales at 1-866-506-1949 or business@simonandschuster.com.

The Simon & Schuster Speakers Bureau can bring authors to your live event. For more information or to book an event, contact the Simon & Schuster Speakers Bureau at 1-866-248-3049 or visit our website at www.simonspeakers.com.

Interior design by Karla Schweer

Manufactured in the United States of America
10 9 8 7 6 5 4 3 2 1
Library of Congress Control Number: 2025936347
ISBN 978-1-6680-5739-1
ISBN 978-1-6680-5741-4 (ebook)

For everyone who supported my
first book, *The End of Gender*

CONTENTS

SEXTINCTION

Why Aren't We Having Sex?

Society has never been more sexualized, yet we are having less sex than ever before. What are we to make of this paradox? This sweeping global trend is affecting both sexes and all age cohorts but is especially pronounced among Millennials and Generation Z, with roughly one in three men and one in five women reporting they haven't had sex in the past year.

Our sex-saturated culture is hard to miss. Visual depictions reminiscent of soft-core pornography inundate us at every turn, on social media and in advertising, films, online streaming, music videos, and celebrity award shows. Browse any mainstream take on sex and dating, and you will find an unending promotion of doing whatever you please in the name of sexual hedonism and exploration, regardless of whom it offends or what the consequences may be.

How did we become so disinterested in sex? And what has taken its place? I sought to answer these questions with this book, to go beyond morbidly gawking at each worsening statistic to instead identify what is driving this trend and how we can reverse it. Drawing upon scientific studies and explanations from evolutionary biology and psychology, my goal is to highlight truthful information to help you understand what you've been noticing and perhaps experiencing in your own lives.

Some of you may already have working hypotheses as to how we got here: Porn! Smartphones! Feminism! Narcissism! Social media! The declining morals of contemporary men and women! All of the above have played a role. But before we get to that, let me elaborate on what has, in my opinion, been the most compelling force.

Human beings hubristically believe that we can outsmart any obstacle that stands in our way. Modern-day technology has afforded us countless conveniences, but the one thing it cannot do is overwrite Mother Nature. Employing technology to suppress our biological instincts pits us in a losing battle against ourselves. It sends us veering disastrously off course, a fiery backlash lying in our wake.

Take, for instance, the 2-x-5-inch piece of glass and aluminum that completely revolutionized the way we communicate. The iPhone first entered the market in 2007, and within five years, nearly half of all US adults owned one. Today, 98 percent of Americans have a smartphone, and with constant access to the internet, it's become an anomaly not to be on social media.

We can now contact anyone around the world within a split second and with minimal effort. The capabilities this has afforded us have been nothing short of astounding. But this major life hack has also set us upon a dark, distorted path, one we haven't fully contended with, as we'll soon see.

Dating apps revolutionized not just courtship rituals but also how men and women communicate (or fail to communicate) with one another. Cycling through a constant carousel of romantic possibilities has led us to simultaneously feel both more interconnected and emptier than ever before.

This mismatch between our ancestral history and our tech-saturated environment overwhelms our evolutionary sensibilities, resulting in unrealistic expectations about whom and what we deserve. The idealization of impossibly high standards has coaxed men into believing that social media influencers with millions of followers may one day show interest in them. It has persuaded women to give the time of day only to men who are over six feet tall and astronomically wealthy.

We are still grappling with the ways in which high-speed pornography, which is often stumbled upon by children as young as age four, is demotivating men from becoming pursuers and providers, derailing young people's expectations about sex, and inciting an epidemic of violent acts such as choking (also known as sexual strangulation) in the bedroom.

This book will counter harmful sex-positivity messaging, including the enthusiastic promotion of selling one's body as empowering to young girls, the belief that polyamory is more evolved than monogamous marriage, and the disturbing push to sexualize children through erotic dolls.

We'll also look at the current exaltation of vanity and narcissism that has blossomed through the proliferation of photo editing, cosmetic injectables, and our obsession with being hot. This fixation on perfect, filtered faces and unattainable physiques is tanking the self-esteem of young women and men alike, in uniquely predatory but eerily similar ways. It is damaging their perception of their bodies, their priorities, and what they believe is attractive in real life.

Punishing male success in the name of gender equality has had bleak repercussions for both sexes. It has inadvertently benefited highly successful men. Birth control and hypergamy (the practice of "marrying up"), combined with young men falling behind in educational and professional prospects, fuel the demand for reproductive technologies like egg freezing, the use of donor sperm, and in vitro fertilization. Elective single motherhood and househusbands are becoming the norm. Due to the increasingly imbalanced sex ratio in the dating marketplace, these trends won't change anytime soon.

Endocrine disruptors that tinker with men's testosterone, unleashing an unprecedented decline in their libido and fertility as well as an uptick in erectile dysfunction, also play tricks on women's mating psychology. Environmental exposure to chemical toxins and pollutants impedes our ability to attract and properly vet potential partners.

Many fear that civilization is on the brink of population collapse, with human beings soon to be replaced by an artificial life-form. We are already capable of customizing the perfect artificial-intelligence girlfriends and boyfriends. Post-#MeToo, with the average man terrified to approach women, will these programmable dream girls (and guys) render sexual relationships and procreation obsolete?

If we don't fully understand why sex is disappearing, we have no hope of ever fixing the problem. To do so, this book refutes many widespread myths about human sexuality, including perspectives I once held.

Due to its polarizing nature, true information about sex is often misrepresented. Understanding related issues accurately and transparently is crucial at a time when scientific objectivity has been lost and factual data are hidden. Mainstream sex educators and discussions about sexual health frequently present toxic, ideologically driven lies as sound advice. Bogus research is published to justify these claims, further misleading the public and worsening our sexless predicament.

This is because sexuality research, reflective of academia writ large, has a left-leaning political bias. Many researchers in the field are also personally invested in their area of study, due to being either part of the associated population or sympathetic to it. This is not the case for every researcher, of course, but for each ethical scientist motivated by a desire for knowledge, there are others who are agenda-driven.

Scientists who don't play along with predetermined narratives will be punished by their colleagues, affiliated institutions, and funding agencies. Having left academia due to this politicization, I'm not tethered to (or bothered by) these constraints.

Throughout these pages, I conduct a study of $N = 1$ (also known as testing the technology out myself) so that you, my dear readers, can bear witness to the rabbit holes we are tumbling down. We are living in a dystopian new world in which human connection is manipulated and replaced by machines. Technology affords us instant gratification, distraction, and escapism to postpone ever feeling lonely. In the following chapters, you will read about how we are undergoing not just a crisis of sexlessness, but one of lost intimacy, social cohesion, and common cause.

Buckle up, because "survival of the fittest" is now on steroids and sidelining even the best of us.

CHAPTER 1

The New Contraception

There's someone for everyone," as the old saying goes. But this may not be true in the dating market today.

Social media promised to make us more interconnected than ever before. And yet each innovation in digital communication has enveloped us in a dreamy cocoon, never to return to life as we once knew it. Are we more enmeshed in a social web or more isolated in an algorithmically calculated bubble? The answer, it seems, is both.

Game-changers include the arrival of the first smartphone, created by IBM in the early 1990s, followed by Facebook in 2004, the iPhone in 2007, and the first geolocation-based, swipe-able dating app, Tinder, in 2012.

Fast-forward to the present day, and online interactions have all but replaced in-person socialization. Humans spend more time staring at screens and devices than talking to other people. An entire generation of children grew up with free access to the online world. At first, the consequences of these changes seemed innocuous, but the chickens have come home to roost.

In 2016, a study published in the academic journal *Archives of Sexual Behavior* revealed a peculiar trend in Americans' sex lives.[1] An analysis of self-reported responses to the General Social Survey (GSS), a nationally representative poll published on a near-annual basis since 1972, found that young people were having less sex than their preceding generations. Millennials (born from 1980 to 1994)[2] in their early twenties were more likely than previous generations at the same age to report having *no* sexual partners since turning eighteen. These surprising results were expected to continue for the Millennials' successors, Generation Z (or "Zoomers," born from 1995 to 2012).

Articles in *The Atlantic*[3] and *The Washington Post*[4] raised the alarm on this emerging sexlessness. *The Atlantic*'s December 2018 cover story coined the term "sex recession" to describe the paradox of a time when taboos around sex have been eviscerated and premarital sex has never been more socially acceptable, and yet data show that young people are engaging in less sexual activity than in the recent past.

The Washington Post's 2019 investigation offered corroborating evidence that the findings weren't a fluke: Among American Millennials between the ages of eighteen and thirty years old, about 30 percent of men and 20 percent of women hadn't had sex in the past year. Another study, using GSS responses between 2016 and 2018 from more than 4,000 men and 5,000 women, unearthed almost identical statistics: roughly one in three men and one in five women aged eighteen to twenty-four (which would make them Millennials and Gen Z) reported being sexually inactive in the previous twelve months.[5]

For this age cohort (eighteen-to-twenty-four-year-olds), sexual inactivity almost *doubled* in men since the early 2000s. Back then, only about one in five men reported not having sex in the past year. For women, the rate of sexual inactivity remained appropriately the same. Among twenty-five-to-thirty-four-year-olds (who would have been Millennials at the time of data collection), rates of sexlessness increased for both sexes, with a sharper increase found among men.

Contrary to tropes about marriage like the seven-year itch, dead bedrooms associated with middle age, or frazzled parents lacking time or energy for anything beyond work and childcare, sexual inactivity today is primarily presenting in younger, childless people. Although data do suggest that we're all experiencing a decline in sex, Millennial and Gen Z men have been hit the hardest.

We know less about whether the current sex recession affects gay people, but it seems to be an issue predominantly affecting heterosexuals. A survey conducted by Stanford University in 2017 intentionally oversampled for gay and lesbian adults and found that these populations are more successful than straight people at using dating apps to find sexual and romantic partners.[6]

Considering that young men have, on average, a higher sex drive and greater *sociosexuality* (that is, enjoyment of casual sex) than women, their decline in sexual activity is the opposite of what one might expect. What led to this change? Fewer Americans today have committed partners, and by 2012, more than half of the country owned a smartphone.[7] Both play a significant role in the decline of sex, but neither alone tells the entire story.

Social media—typically accessed through smartphones—has accelerated our current sexless predicament by creating an illusion of connection and community while actually isolating us and pitting men and women against one another. Our evolutionary roots clash with twenty-first-century life because we face novel circumstances that our ancestors never could have anticipated or prepared for. Despite this, our biology has been pushing back in subtle ways.

Before I get to the barren wasteland that characterizes modern-day dating, let's take a closer look at how we first fell into this situation, starting with the reasons *why* rates of sexual inactivity are more pronounced in young men than among their female peers.

Marrying Up

The modern age has produced a novel dynamic between the sexes, characterized by two turbines of change: Men are losing the social and economic characteristics that make them attractive partners to women, while at the same time, women are excelling along these very same vectors.

Hypergamy (colloquially, "marrying up") is a simple concept from evolutionary psychology that explains a lot about human mating behavior, particularly in the contemporary dating market. Hypergamy states that women, on average, look for financial resources and status in a potential mate and will trade "up" to acquire the best partner they can find.[8] This stems from sex differences in the parental investment required of women; sex is a riskier prospect for a woman because of the possibility of pregnancy. Evolutionarily speaking, if a partner couldn't provide for you and your offspring, said partner would quickly become a liability. Procreating with a mate who couldn't protect and provide was dangerous. In most cases, it meant that neither you nor your children could expect to live for long.

As a result, women typically look for partners who are at least as successful as they are. (Men, on the other hand, generally seek partners based on youth and physical attractiveness, which are markers of high fertility and reproductive value—basically, the ability to have many, healthy children.)

But changes in our social environment have complicated things. We no longer live in the world that shaped our basic drives for millennia. Perhaps for the first time in history, women are succeeding at higher rates than men. Starting in adolescence, girls are more likely than boys to complete high school and continue on to higher education. For the past four decades, more women than men have graduated with bachelor's degrees,[9] and since the mid-2000s, the fairer sex has taken home the majority of doctoral degrees awarded. It is projected that, in a few years, two women will graduate university for every man.

A similar theme can be found in the workplace, where women account for over half (50.7 percent) of the college-educated US labor force.[10] Women today not only can provide for themselves financially but they are, in many cases, making *more* money than their male counterparts.

As women rise in socioeconomic status, so do their standards for a potential partner. Women are attracted to men who are more accomplished than they are. As women become more educated, going from an undergraduate degree to an MD, JD, or master's or doctoral diploma, their pool of romantic candidates grows smaller.[11] Women who are financially successful tend to seek a partner with even *greater* wealth and status. This makes it doubly challenging to find a suitable mate, because their standards will be that much higher, regardless of whether there are enough viable male suitors to go around.

Interestingly, higher education is associated with an *increased* likelihood of marriage in men but a *decreased* likelihood in women.

Unmarried women are also more likely to have high educational and occupational status, while unmarried men are more likely to be unemployed and poor.[12] Since men aren't attaining as many secondary and postsecondary degrees as women (or any at all), this further intensifies the sexual competition.

Of course, just because something is biologically or evolutionarily wired doesn't mean it's morally good or just. By pointing out these on-average sex differences regarding partner preferences, I'm not attributing any value to them, nor am I saying that every woman or man necessarily fits their expected profile. I don't believe a woman's worth should be based on her looks or her ability to bear children, nor should a man's value be based on his wealth or his ability to win social recognition.

However, the fact is that from an evolutionary standpoint, selecting partners according to this framework allowed our ancestors to pass on their genes successfully. This is why men and women today continue choosing partners accordingly, even if the modern environment is radically different from what came before. We are hardwired by centuries of genetic inheritance to think this way.

These discussions of evolutionary psychology don't justify sexism or the idea that women shouldn't strive to be successful. Women advancing in the workforce is a wonderful thing, and they shouldn't feel as though they have to minimize their talents or accomplishments to attract a man. I also don't believe that the solution to the current mating crisis is restricting women from pursuing an education or forcing them to marry someone in whom they aren't interested. But to understand what's going on across society and around the world, it's important to recognize these brute facts.

Let's consider how this plays out on the mating market. Bluntly put, if men are unemployed or make less money than the women they are interested in, they will have a hard time attracting a partner.

To make matters worse, many males are choosing not to work. Recent statistics show that 7.2 million men are unemployed despite being capable of working, and roughly 11 million jobs remain unfilled. The discrepancy has been attributed to a variety of factors, including mental health and substance use issues, a lack of motivation, video games, pornography, and other sexual outlets described in this book. Men who drop out of the labor force are not necessarily taking time away from work to invest in education, vocational training, or charity work; in fact, they may be spending forty hours a week on screens while under the influence of pain medication.[13]

Feminist activists who advocated for women emerging victoriously at men's degradation and expense failed to follow this approach to its logical end. Gender equality is a perfectly fine concept, as is a woman's preference to date up, but when society combines the two *and* suppresses male success, it creates serious problems.

The sex imbalance in the labor force will only grow as women continue to surpass men in both schooling and career. The only way it will level off is if the rate of men graduating from college increases. We don't yet have any reason to believe that this will happen in the foreseeable future.

In the words of Gloria Steinem, women are becoming the men they wanted to marry. I would go one step further and add that this is why so many young women are turning *away* from marriage. Once dependent on men for physical protection and resources, contemporary women are financially self-sufficient. Men have become the equivalent of a fish's bicycle for women who can take care of themselves.[14]

Women have gone from being the old ball and chain to not needing men at all. Compounding this discrepancy is our culture's tendency to support female success while ignoring and trivializing men who aren't doing as well.

What I'm about to say is not a popular position to take: When it comes to dating, the fact that women, on aggregate, are higher in socioeconomic status than men poses a problem. Progressive women may not be willing to admit it even to themselves, but regardless of a woman's politics, she will always be reluctant to marry down. Instead of holding women back, solutions should focus on helping men move forward.

Female dating-advice influencers erroneously tell women to continue grinding in the workplace to attract men. Because women value money and resources in a male partner, they project this onto men, not realizing that successful men don't care about either of these things in a female partner. Excelling at one's career and growing one's financial assets do not make a woman more sexually or romantically appealing in most men's eyes. Instead, they only widen the gap between single men and women.

The "Three Sixes" Rule

If the current dating market weren't catastrophic enough, women's relationship standards continue to rise as a result of their economic success and goading cultural messaging. The "three sixes" rule may sound like a combination of parody and internet lore, but it summarizes a savagely unapologetic mindset that some ladies have applied to their dating lives.

What, you may ask, are the three sixes? They describe a man who is six feet or taller, has a six-figure salary, and possesses a six-inch manhood. (In some cases, this rule will also require a potential mate to have a six-pack of abdominal muscles.) According to this directive, a triple-six man is the bare minimum in acceptable standards, and to desire anything less is selling oneself short and settling.

Women are certainly allowed to want what they want, and I agree that it's good to have standards when considering one's options on the mating market. But statistically speaking, only 14.5 percent of men in America are over six feet tall, and only 17 percent make over $100,000 annually.* Considering that the average penis length is about five inches,[15] an even smaller percentage of men will meet all three sixes. The number gets readjusted down further to account for men who are married and for those who are gay. Even if a man ticks all the boxes, variables like personality, chemistry, and common interests whittle down the likelihood of finding a triple-six partner to a vanishingly small percentage.

The choice of six feet, six figures, and six inches as the bar to clear is somewhat arbitrary, and it's questionable how necessary or useful these metrics are in predicting happiness and romantic compatibility. It's a message young women hear increasingly, even though it's demonstrably bad advice that further dramatically shrinks the pool of prospective partners.

Anecdotally, I've noticed a rise in the number of men who describe their height in reference to this six-foot cutoff. In casual conversation, when asking a man how tall he is, someone who is tall but not quite six feet tall (say, five feet ten or five feet eleven) will tell you, "Almost six feet," instead of simply stating his height, much the way women feel pressure to minimize their weight or

---

* All monetary figures are in USD.

dress size when asked. In contrast, men who are over six feet tall will give you their exact height (for example, they will say six feet one or six feet two). The arbitrary metric has left a cultural imprint.

Why do women generally prefer to date a taller man? Evolutionary psychology provides the answer. Historically, tall men had an easier time protecting their partners and offspring from physical danger. Evolution also explains why women are attracted to men with money. A wealthy man is more able to provide for his partner and share his resources, another trait women value in a mate. (I'm guessing that the "six-inch" requirement speaks to women's desire to be sexually satisfied, although research has suggested that penile girth is a greater predictor of female sexual fulfillment than length.[16])

While this may explain why women are attracted to tall, rich, well-endowed men, those qualities don't track with successful relationships. The characteristics most predictive of marital and sexual satisfaction include personality traits like agreeableness and emotional stability[17] as well as a sense of psychological security and trust in one's partner.[18] Limiting one's dating pool by the rule of sixes means a woman shuts out countless men who may be compatible so she can hold out for an ideal who may not exist.

Further worsening the problem is the fact that men who possess all three characteristics seek the female equivalent—specifically, women in the very top tier of physical attractiveness. Such a man may sleep with an average woman, but he will not settle down with her. Although the three-sixes mandate says it's okay to exclude men based on their physical attributes, accepting the same in men's choices of a female partner is considered fatphobic and body-shaming.

No matter how women ascribing to the three-sixes rule feel about this, they must not only *find* a man who meets the standards but also outcompete countless other high-status women to be with him. Regardless of a woman's status, she is more likely to duke it out for her first choice of a partner than to settle for a man of lesser status.

Now add to the mix another layer of social pathology—social media "likes" and view counts that are at best a boost of confidence and at worst an egoism generator. Basing one's self-esteem on follower count and blue checkmark status is unhealthy, but when the analytics are fake and not a genuine reflection of audience engagement, this can give women (and men) an additionally warped perception of their importance and popularity.

We have no way of verifying the numbers that social media platforms provide to our accounts as an indicator of our reach. A colleague who previously worked for a major platform told me that the company intentionally inflated users' analytics, sometimes into the millions of views, to manipulate them into believing that their content had gone viral. This would keep users engaged and constantly posting in hopes of again reaching the same reported heights of viewership. Positive comments on these platforms, regardless of whether they are real or planted by bots, can reinforce attention-seeking behavior.

This brings forth a tragic comparison to slot machines, which are programmed to follow something called an intermittent reinforcement schedule. When a given behavior is intermittently reinforced, or rewarded, this means delivery of the reward is perceived as random and unpredictable. (In the context of gambling, the reward would be winning cash, or in the case of social media algorithms, it would be receiving tons of likes, comments, and views.) Because there is no perceptible rhyme or reason to explain the when, why, or size of the payout, gamblers easily slide into continuous play, chasing the next euphoric win, often to the detriment of their bank account and their mental and physical health.

I point this out not to shame women but instead to offer a realistic depiction of the mating market and a contrast to the hall of mirrors pop culture and the media put forth. With a growing list of demands and fewer acceptable bachelors from which to choose, younger generations of women have little choice but to eschew marriage and motherhood.

Although rates of sexlessness are less pronounced in young women, I do think the shift away from marriage and kids has influenced this trend. When a woman can't find a suitable partner due to her career success, it disincentivizes her from dating and incentivizes her to focus on her career. But the more successful she becomes, the more difficult it will be for her to couple off with a man. And so the cycle continues; if an individual is more focused on her career than on starting a family, she has fewer practical reasons to be sexually active.

Let me be clear: I don't believe that women need to be wives or mothers to have a happy, fulfilling life, nor should they have to justify their personal life choices to anyone. The well-worn stereotype of the so-called spinster surrounded by old takeout boxes, empty wine bottles, and a small harem of cats reads as cruel and judgmental and, in my opinion, a projection on the part of the men and women doing the judging.

This raises the question of whether men today have become hypergamous. If a man marries a woman who is more educated or makes more money, doesn't that translate to him marrying up? Not exactly, because most men would be content to marry down. That is because, in evolutionary terms, it benefits men to spread their seed as much as possible, regardless of the quality of the women they're sleeping with. (This explains those mind-boggling situations we've all borne witness to, in which a man cheats on his very attractive, high-status wife or girlfriend with a lower-status woman.) It just so happens that the modern world has created a scenario in which many men who are seeking to settle down will more likely end up with a woman with a higher education.

Women Going Their Own Way

The modern-day perception of marriage is that it benefits men more than it does women. For example, recent research has shown that married men, on average, tend to rate their relationship more positively than married women do.[19] Married men live longer than unmarried men[20] and are more likely than women to say their spouse is their best friend.[21]

In the context of having children, the woman gets pregnant, gives birth, breastfeeds, and is often the primary caregiver. She will need to put her career on pause to raise the children, while a man's career will remain mostly unaffected.

Married women perform seven extra hours of housework per week compared to single women, a difference that becomes even more pronounced once children enter the picture.[22] In the unfortunate event of illness, men are more likely than women to desert an ailing spouse.[23] Following a divorce, some women have found themselves stuck with paying their ex-husband alimony.[24]

It's a good thing that women are finding their sense of self rather than centering their identity around men and male attention or rushing into marriage at a young age before knowing what they want from a partner. But women face an unfair double standard when it comes to their preferences. If they rely on a man as a provider, society calls them gold diggers. If they hustle to make their own money and live independently, society chides them for not prioritizing marriage and motherhood. They can't win.

Another reason for women's reluctance to marry a man who doesn't make a sufficient income is that many aspiring mothers would rather be at home raising young kids than raising kids *and* working. If a man's income cannot support his growing family, a woman will have to forfeit this preference, returning to the workplace and being away from her children.

Another unpopular truth is that many men don't want to marry a woman who makes more money or is more educated than they are. Men value women for their kindness, warmth, and nurturing nature, which makes degrees and aspirations beyond being a wife and mother detractors.

Although marriages in which wives have more education than their husbands are now more common than the inverse (marriages in which husbands have more education than their wives), relative income—the question of who makes more in the marriage—remains an important factor.

The sexes do not view a high-earning partner's income in the same way. A woman will always prefer higher income in a male partner; a man values a woman's income so long as it doesn't surpass his. Both spouses have an aversion to the wife making more money than the husband. If a woman has the potential to outearn her husband and become the primary breadwinner, she may choose to work fewer hours or take a job that pays less in order to appear less threatening to him.[25]

High-Value Men

Due to the imbalance in the mating marketplace, high-status men will find themselves with greater leverage in selecting partners, allowing them to delay settling down and to have multiple families when they do. When the sex ratio skews in favor of men, women will experience lower rates of commitment and higher rates of abandonment. This allows one partner (the man) to get all the benefits of a relationship without having to put in a modicum of effort.

This explains why, on university campuses and in environments predominantly populated by women, casual sex abounds. Men's desires are controlling the sexual marketplace, and women are forced to lower their standards. This also explains why some young women have taken it upon themselves to pursue the men they're interested in (a cringe-worthy spectacle I've cautioned against previously[26]).

To hold men to a higher standard, we need to foster intrasexual competition, and this can only occur with a greater number of rivals playing the game. *Intrasexual competition* refers to the fact that both men and women compete among their own sex for sexual partners. This concept of encouraging rivalry is no different from what is observed in entrepreneurship; it's only with meaningful competition that a business is forced to value its customers.

Until then, the current mating market will remain lopsided, with a small subsample of high-status men being disproportionately sought after by *all* women, regardless of the women's educational and occupational achievements. Older, successful women will be competing with younger female rivals for the same potential mates.

Consequently, polyamory is having a moment in the sun as a fashionable, new way to experience relationships. Academics have taken to promoting the poly lifestyle as a sexual orientation, something that is innate and unchangeable. Activists are arguing for proper representation in media to further social acceptance, endorsing the belief that cheating is inevitable, monogamy is unrealistic, and more partners equal more love.

As a result, many young people are deciding to play with fire, convinced that polyamory is a more enlightened, "evolved" approach to relationships. According to statistics from Tinder, 41 percent of Gen Z users are interested in non-monogamy.[27]

Because it reinforces an already suboptimal sex ratio, polyamory is potentially society destroying. Despite being promoted as a more egalitarian approach to relationships for women, polyamory benefits only the most highly valued men in society, to the detriment of *all* women and lower-status men trapped in the sex recession. Since sexual jealousy is especially pervasive among men due to its adaptive function (something that will be evident in our discussion on women who sell self-made porn), only men with a cuckolding fetish will be willing to share their female partners with other men.*

Although polygyny (think of the show *Sister Wives*) has been outlawed throughout most countries including America, modernity and the current sexual landscape allow high-status men to have multiple wives and families in succession, as opposed to simultane-

---

* In the field of evolutionary psychology, the term *cuckoldry* refers to a woman deceiving a male romantic partner into investing in offspring he believes to be his own when they were in fact fathered by another man (or multiple other men). An estimated 10 percent of children are born of these circumstances.

ously. Widespread integration of polyamory in society will only worsen this sex discrepancy.

Female proponents of polyamory incorrectly envision a world in which they'll be acquiring a collection of the most desirable men. Even if they manage to do so, they will have to share these men with other women. Because men value looks in a partner, physically attractive women will be in a better position to negotiate these terms, while other women will unfortunately be required to offer sex sooner to stand a chance.

Considering that polyamorous relationships last an average of eight years and "throuples" (romantic relationships consisting of three people) are not legally recognized,[28] it is questionable whether this relationship style is conducive to family formation, particularly in the context of child-rearing. Despite the belief that monogamy is outdated, patriarchal, and oppressive to women, it offers benefits to both sexes by ensuring parental investment in children and lowering the likelihood that a child will experience abuse. Living with a nonbiological parent is, sadly, the single greatest predictor of human infanticide.[29] Not being able to ascertain the paternity of a polyamorous woman's child will translate to *no* men being invested in raising that child.

On the polar opposite end of the sexual opportunity spectrum is inceldom. *Incels* are an online subculture of men who experience involuntary celibacy. Their lack of success at dating has given rise to intense hostility and rage toward women. Together, the community fantasizes about a time when the female sex will be replaced by artificial surrogates, including sex robots.

Research confirms that a small minority of men have multiple sexual partners each year, but the vast majority have only one or none.[30] Demographics associated with *less* sexlessness include being employed full-time, having a higher income, and being married (although married folks are also having less sex than in previous years). Men with fewer sexual opportunities are turning to outlets like pornography, artificial-intelligence girlfriends, and prostitution.

The male population will only continue bifurcating over time, falling into one camp or the other. The two extremes we'll end up with will be men who have access to as many women as they'd like and men who can't attract any.

Househusbands

If it were simply the case that men are falling behind, the solution would be fairly straightforward. We could devise educational and employment-based interventions to help men get back on their feet. Removing diversity, equity, and inclusion practices would be a start—easier said than done, but it would allow for a comprehensive path forward.

Public campaigning might increase awareness so that a larger proportion of women could understand that these issues aren't restricted to men. As it currently stands, women are being ushered in the opposite direction, being told that men serve no purpose to them.

One silver lining is that young men have time on their side; they do not face a ticking biological clock in the same way that women do. Since age is associated with what women find sexually attractive (namely, financial stability), men finding a partner later in life doesn't come with the same challenges that can affect women.

Hypergamous preferences may be hardwired, but relationships and dating *are* about more than just power and riches. Nevertheless, I remain skeptical of solutions that simply tell women to be willing to date someone less successful. That would be the equivalent of telling men to date women they aren't physically attracted to. It can be done, but not for very long, and I don't expect it will lead to a successful outcome.

Sexual attraction results from a finely tuned process that often operates outside our conscious awareness. I would also argue that romantic relationships shouldn't be about forcing attraction if it isn't there; this only leads to infidelity and contempt.

The same applies to men who think coupling up with a more successful woman will solve their problems. Any man who is comfortable sponging off a woman is lacking in moral character. The resentment will soon go both ways. A man will feel emasculated and possibly inferior if a woman pays for his dinner on the first date; imagine how he will feel if his girlfriend is paying for his entire lifestyle.

Some might argue that progressive men are more accepting of changing gender norms. I disagree. Even the most progressive men have ancestors who followed the same evolutionary rules as other men populating the human species. The only reason any man exists today is because it's more likely than not that his male ancestors protected and provided for their female partners. Had the male members of his lineage not done so, women would have avoided mating with them, and any children produced wouldn't have survived.

I agree that some men may feel less threatened by a female partner who is more successful, and some women may not care as much about their partner's relative success. I applaud this. At the same time, these men still feel the need to pull their weight in a relationship instead of mooching off a woman, and rightfully so.

The alternative is to embrace being a stay-at-home dad, as illustrated by the #househusband trend. An entire genre of videos floats around social media, depicting men (almost too) happily running through the list of household chores they complete while their significant other is at work. Time-lapsed videos show them making the bed, doing the dishes and laundry, watering plants, and cooking dinner.

"For my queen," they will say, chopping vegetables and grinning into the camera.

After their spouse has gone to sleep, some househusbands will be up late, diligently packing her lunch for the following day.

Yes, it's cute, but there's no reason why a man can't help out around the house while also holding down a job. Househusbands are seen as lazy "beta cucks" (that is, men who are lacking in status and virility) who have no real purpose. I would imagine these men secretly harbor a sense of shame around not fulfilling what is expected of them, both due to societal pressures and because men have been biologically programmed to be providers.

The over-the-top enthusiasm they express when sharing their househusband itinerary is a coping mechanism, an overcompensation for their feelings of inadequacy. Deep down, even the laziest of househusbands *knows* that refusing to work and relying on a woman's income betray a lack of integrity. They also know that women aren't *really* attracted to men who default on the provider role, men who prefer instead to take on the traditionally feminine role in a relationship.

These mate preferences run deeply and can't be erased, even by the most progressive among us. A study published in *American Sociological Review* found that more traditional sex roles when completing housework, like women doing the cooking and cleaning, and men doing yardwork and vehicle maintenance, are associated with married couples having sex more often.[31] As much as a woman may appreciate her partner helping out around the house, it seems that male domesticity, particularly in the form of doing female-typical chores, is a turn-off.[*]

Dating Apps and Direct Messages

In roughly three decades, online dating has completely revolutionized our approach to sex and relationships. According to marketing and consumer data provider Statista, over 60 million Americans use dating apps and websites.

Once considered a last-ditch hope for socially dysfunctional people, meeting online has become both socially acceptable and the most popular way for couples to meet. Gen Z, in particular, has driven a large proportion of this engagement, including 3 billion swipes daily as reported by Tinder, despite their paradoxically having less sex than other generations or none whatsoever.

Online interactions have changed the culture of dating. Sliding into someone's DMs (or direct messages) was once viewed as crass and mortifying. It has since morphed into another method of expressing sexual or romantic interest, so much so that social media platforms like Instagram are used by some as a dating site.

Let me first clarify the differences between social media and dating apps. Social media platforms are used to connect us to people we know, and its users aren't necessarily on there in search of a sexual liaison or relationship. Dating apps are designed spe-

---

[*] To be clear, I believe men should still do housework, but perhaps in the realm of male-typical chores.

cifically for the purpose of meeting romantic and sexual partners. They tend to focus on bringing people together based on specific characteristics like age, political ideology, religion, race, or income.

Social media allows us to access anyone in the world at any point in time and to assess a total stranger's marital status (as well as their associated level of matrimonial bliss). High-status men can now hit on any woman in the world, and high-status women have hundreds of messages piling up in their inbox.

Many in my audience say that dating today is harder than ever before. Dating apps have become a race to the bottom, a soul-destroying process that leaves most feeling antagonized and demoralized. Although there has been a movement away from relying on apps for dates, the social ubiquity of internet courtship has left a lingering malaise.[32] People only care about your online presence, not who you are in real life. Prospective partners check your social media, and if you aren't on there or aren't verified, it's as though you don't exist. If you are, you have only one chance to impress the person you're interested in.

Both social media and dating apps incentivize users to check their notifications repeatedly and stay online continually, even if this alienates them from potential partners in the real world. Machine learning presents users with more of what they've been swiping right on, without transparency about why certain profiles are (or aren't) being shown.

Online dating gives users the perception of an endless stream of possible soulmates, especially for women, who are bombarded with male attention the minute they join a platform. Many women report that fielding matches and conversations with multiple admirers simultaneously feels like a full-time job.

We've never been exposed to so many sexual and romantic options in one sitting. This mismatch between our ancestral history and the modern environment overwhelms our evolutionary sensibilities, leading us to choose the wrong partners and to have an unending shopping list of what we are looking for.

In reality, people whose profile you see may not reciprocate interest in you. If you do match on the app, they may not message you, and if they do, you may not meet. Some people text for months on end without a date materializing. Even if you do meet in real life, you may not get along.

Alternatively, you may date for weeks or months but never see this time together evolve into a relationship because you or the other person decides to part ways. So, those hundreds or thousands of profiles you sifted through may not yield a greater number of possibilities than the few you would have met through work, friends, school, or socializing, back in the day.

The process of swiping left ("no") or right ("yes") on a person's profile flattens them into an image. It treats them like a commodity, a product that is easily disposed of and replaced by the next profile the algorithm serves up. If men and women are exposed to hundreds of *what feel like* potential mates daily but aren't reaping the benefits that would normally be associated with this, it tricks the mind into believing there really isn't anyone out there for them.

Many readers tell me that they experience choice paralysis on dating apps: Why go on a date with one person when someone better may come along? This leads to hesitation in pulling the trigger and setting up a date to meet someone. I've also heard of people who go ahead with meeting a match from an app, only to swipe on other profiles while being in their presence.

The paradox of choice maintains that having more options

isn't always better. Whether it's gourmet jams, chocolates,[33] or romantic partners, too many possibilities can be overwhelming and lead us to avoid making any choice. Contrary to what one might expect, having fewer options is actually more conducive to a person selecting one option *and* feeling more satisfied with what they've chosen.

"Ghosting" (or terminating communication with a date without any notice or explanation) has additionally diminished everyone's investment in dating. There is always the possibility that the person you've been talking to will cease contact with you, and you may never know why.

Some men and women have no intention of actually dating and are merely on these apps for validation.[34] Some will mindlessly swipe through profiles as though they're playing a video game, driven by boredom or in search of an ego boost.

Recognized in the scientific literature, "problematic online dating" describes how individuals compulsively use dating apps despite deleterious consequences to their lives. This can include excessive amounts of time spent thinking about, and being on, these platforms, compromising other social relationships, and being dependent on these apps for positive mood.[35]

Dating itself has become an emotion-deprived transaction that lacks openness and feels almost mechanical. For those who would prefer to meet people the old-fashioned way through chance encounters in real life, #MeToo's influence and the changing of social norms have turned the wooing process into a minefield. Potential suitors are reluctant to approach women in public out of fear that they'll be labeled a creep, the interaction will be filmed, and they'll become a viral pariah.

I've heard from sensible young women who say their female

peers think that it is, by default, sexual harassment if a man approaches a woman he doesn't know. Sadly, I'd bet these same women find the online dating process disappointing and tedious. But a dynamic that prohibits human-to-human interaction leaves both sexes boxed in, dependent on virtual connections to avoid ending up alone.

The replacement of in-person interactions with online ones has implications for our mental health, particularly regarding anxiety. Anxiety disorders are characterized by a need for frequent reassurance and an aversion to risk and uncertainty. Social anxiety revolves around a heightened sense of self-consciousness and fear that an individual will be judged negatively by others.

Anxiety is a common psychological condition among Gen Z. Of the 42 percent of Zoomers who have a diagnosed mental disorder, 90 percent have been diagnosed with anxiety.[36] Of Gen Zers who experience this condition, one in two reports struggling with it daily, and one in three takes medication for it.[37] (I believe this is why horoscopes and "manifesting" have become so popular among Millennials and Gen Z; they give people a false sense of control.)

We could expect that meeting new partners through online avenues, like dating apps or social media, would be preferred by people who are high in dating anxiety, but this is not what research has shown. Anxious people are in fact *less* likely to use dating apps,[38] but individuals with high rejection sensitivity *are* more likely to be on them.[39] (Rejection sensitivity involves a disposition toward anxiously expecting social rejection and overreacting when it does occur.)

Online platforms allow for greater impression management and control over what is shared with other people and how they might perceive you. Dating apps are therefore safer, because they are relatively anonymous, don't require eye contact, and don't allow the user to accidentally reveal too much of themselves through body language or nonverbal cues. Texting allows a person more time to contemplate their reply, whereas in-person interactions are more spontaneous and demand an immediate response.

A clinical psychologist teaching a graduate class I took shared a case from her practice that illustrates perfectly how social media can reinforce and exacerbate anxiety disorders. The patient, a young woman, had been seeing the psychologist for social anxiety for several months. Once Facebook took off, the young woman announced she no longer had a reason to continue her therapy sessions.

"She said, 'I can just make friends online,'" our professor explained. Whenever this patient attended social gatherings, she found herself on her phone the entire time using social media, anyway.

It's true; the internet, smartphones, and social media allow us to communicate without ever having to *talk* to another person again. Gen Z in particular abhors phone calls, with more than a quarter saying they actively avoid talking on the phone.[40] Even if a person is forced to go out in public, using a smartphone is a people repellent.

The concept of *life history theory*[41] offers some relevant insights; specifically, the idea that children who grow up in environments with greater stability and higher socioeconomic status tend to have a prolonged adolescence. This mollycoddled upbringing leads children to have a reduced ability to cope with life stressors upon reaching adulthood, while kids who grow up in less affluent households are exposed to the realities of life at a younger age.

Returning to my larger point about trying to find love online: Among those who succeed at finding a spouse through online dating, the rate of divorce is much higher. A study in *Cyberpsychology, Behavior, and Social Networking* found that married (and unmarried) couples who met online are more likely to break up than are couples who met offline.[42]

It's possible that people don't have the same appreciation of or fortitude for commitment that previous generations once did. Meeting on an app further cements the feeling that there is always someone better out there, and if your spouse doesn't meet every requirement on your list, it'll be easy to match with an upgrade.

Those currently in a relationship certainly aren't immune to the gravitational pull of the internet. "Phubbing" (a combination of the words "phone" and "snubbing") consists of ignoring a romantic partner in favor of being on one's phone. This can include checking notifications or texting during a conversation with the other person.

A study conducted by Lloyds Pharmacy in the UK surveyed more than 2,000 British adults over the age of eighteen who were in a relationship.[43] Respondents spent, on average, 3.5 hours a day on screens, which is the equivalent of about fifty days a year.

One of the key takeaways from the survey is that ignoring your partner while on your phone is associated with lower rates of sexual activity. Only 13 percent of people who had sex seven times a week or more said they ignored their partner while on their phone. For those who had sex once a week, the percentage of "phubbers" increased to 20 percent, and for those who had sex every three to six months, 33 percent were "phubbers."

The direction of this association remains unclear, however; we don't know whether having less sex is what leads some people to use their phone in a way that is disrespectful to their partner, or whether people who have an unhealthy relationship with their phone have created a dysfunctional dynamic that is less conductive to sexual intimacy.

I have a feeling this may depend on the individual person, but regardless, it creates a vicious cycle that is detrimental to one's relationship. If a person ignores their partner because they'd rather be on their phone, the other person might feel undesirable and, understandably, less interested in being intimate. This could, in turn, lead the phubber to feel justified in continuing their scrolling, as they may rationalize that their partner doesn't want to have sex with them anyway.

It's also possible that a third variable, such as low relationship or sexual satisfaction, is motivating the phubbing person (who has probably mentally checked out of the relationship) to ignore their partner *and* avoid having sex.

In the same survey, one in eight women said that using social media makes her feel less sexually desirable. One in eleven men reported feeling less interested in having sex with his partner after looking at social media influencers. Perhaps most egregious of all, one in eight has checked their phone *during* sex, and one in twelve has posted on social media "during or immediately after." Almost 60 percent of the sample admitted to choosing technology, like streaming shows and movies, over sex on *multiple* occasions, for reasons including being too tired, not feeling confident with their body, and using tech as a distraction.

As a former sex scientist who spent more than a decade talking to people about their issues in the bedroom, I think the same anxieties about sex have always existed, but now there are a million more ways to avoid having to deal with them.

Let's be real: Making time for sex takes energy and effort. In the context of a relationship, sex involves prioritizing someone else's needs instead of simply taking care of your own (a frame of mind that may become foreign if a person regularly consumes porn). This reluctance reflects a larger malady in society, a school of thought that encourages young people to be selfish and to look out only for themselves.

Toxic Podcasts

Amid the wasteland that is modern dating, self-help gurus have descended like vultures on those who are frustrated and broken. "Pick-up artistry" for men and the analogous "femosphere" for women both center on tactics to maximize each sex getting what they want at the expense, and often manipulation, of the opposite sex.

Both rely on evolutionary concepts to inform their respective approaches, but the only people benefiting from this advice are the ones monetizing it. The toxicity of these strategies ensures that single men and women continue failing in their relationships, allowing those doling out the advice to pick the best partners for themselves.

Social media is the worst place to go for matters of the heart. Toxic dating advice abounds, offering a self-defeating, zero-sum, lose-lose mentality. Dating podcasts—often featuring several male hosts provoking a panel of ditzy, twenty-something-year-old women who all invariably perform some form of "sex work"— would be a hilarious genre of entertainment if they didn't reflect such a dire predicament.

In this world, men view women as sociopathic sex tools whose moral compass is solely determined by online clout—women who sit, perched and waiting to drain men's will to live and their bank accounts. Here, so-called passport bros claim to be so fed up with Western women's promiscuity and incessant demands that they're willing to go abroad to find a foreign wife. (This, however, reads to me as a strategy meant to decrease intrasexual competitors, by encouraging other men to give up so that the bro can swoop in and steal the homegrown women for himself.)

Social media tells women to treat men like a roster of disposable ATMs. Their sexual strategy should involve deploying a magical force field of "feminine energy" to extract free meals and luxury vacations from hapless suckers, while posting their edited-to-perfection, half-naked bodies all over the internet with the goal of bagging a professional athlete or tech billionaire.

Modern dating exemplifies something my friend David Buss calls the *coevolutionary arms race*. Buss is a professor of psychology at the University of Texas at Austin and one of the founding fathers of evolutionary psychology. He defines this coevolutionary arms race as an infinite number of "reciprocal adaptations and counter-adaptations" that both sexes constantly adopt with the goal of one-upping and outsmarting the other.[44]

This is because when it comes to mating strategies and partner selection, what's in the best interest of the male typically diverges from what's in the best interest of the female. As a result, men and women are in constant competition with each other and use whatever sexual-selection tools are at their disposal to get their way.

A well-worn example is men who claim they are interested in a long-term relationship to con women into sleeping with them. In turn, women have evolved ways of accurately detecting deceit to avoid being tricked by men who don't plan to stick around after sex. In evolutionary terms, this protects a woman against being left to raise a baby on her own. In response to this female adaptation, men hone methods of appearing sincere when falsely professing their commitment. And on it goes.

We are in the midst of a digital coevolutionary arms race, with each sex drawing on its arsenal to protect its respective interests. Dating has always come bundled with challenges, but back in the day, if you had a bad date or experience, you'd make your way home as quickly as possible, vent to your friends, laugh about it, and move on. Now, with social media and news sites reporting on social media posts, there is the potential for your story to reach, resonate with, and offend millions.

Those who have had bad experiences will find similar perspectives on social media platforms. They post, commiserate, and assume that every one of the opposite sex must be the same—every woman has borderline personality disorder, every man is a narcissist. Women aspiring to date men in the top 1 percent income bracket are berated for their "delusional" standards; men are ferociously shamed for lusting after beautiful women who will not look twice at them.

Many believe their situation is uniquely awful, but for every man I see complaining about something a woman did, I see a woman complaining about the same thing in a man. For every licentious harpy, there is a game-playing f*ckboy. There are terrible women and terrible men. Instead of turning against each other, both sexes need to take responsibility for their own dating failures.

Unfortunately, online content also supports an increasingly adversarial dynamic between the sexes, with social media fomenting a global political divide.[45] Unlike generations past, in which young people tended to share a similar political vision for the future among their cohort, Gen Z's young women are moving sharply left, while young men are becoming more conservative.

This tectonic ideological shift is being felt around the world, mirrored in countries like South Korea, Germany, and the UK. If young men and women hold values that are diametrically opposed, particularly when the sex ratio is already imbalanced in the direction of too few eligible men, good luck finding someone with whom you'd like to spend the rest of your life.

We are inundated with countless opportunities for sex or a proxy of it, but in spite of all these brilliant advances, love remains rare. Having direct access to pretty people through a screen hasn't increased our dating success.

So, returning to the axiom at the start of this chapter: Is there really someone for everyone? It seems that a growing number of us are indifferent to seeking the answer.

CHAPTER 2

Permanent Bachelors

The stark cultural changes foretelling the end of our species didn't happen overnight. The sexual recession has been quietly brewing for almost two decades. Adults in the United States in the 2010s were having sex nine times fewer per year than in the 1990s.[1] Millennials and Gen Z were having sex six times fewer per year than individuals who belong to the Silent generation (born 1925 to 1945).

This decline in sexual activity hasn't been restricted to the US. It has swept across the West, affecting countries including Germany, France, the United Kingdom, Australia, Sweden, and Finland. Sexlessness has also been on the rise in Eastern countries like Japan and South Korea, leading to some of the lowest birth rates around the world.

Although many were quick to blame the COVID-19 pandemic and associated measures like lockdowns and quarantine for interfering with single people's ability to meet, studies predating the pandemic demonstrate that increased rates of sexual inactivity were well on their way beforehand (see chapter 1). Data from the General Social Survey (GSS) show that more than 20 percent of Americans reported yearlong sexlessness in 2021, but also, in consecutive prior study waves in 2014, 2016, and 2018.

The 2021 data were collected between December 2020 and May 2021, at the height of the pandemic. Zeroing in on Americans aged eighteen and older, more than a *quarter* had not had sex once in the past year.[2]

If COVID were entirely to blame, one would expect the end of physical restrictions to produce an uptick of sexual activity reflecting a lustful desire in single men and women to make up for lost time. But that's not what happened.

A 2023 study from the Pew Research Center speaks to the post-pandemic fallout.[3] A shocking 63 percent of men aged eighteen to twenty-nine said they are single, nearly twice the percentage of same-aged young women, at 34 percent. Of single American adults across all ages, *57 percent* say they aren't looking to date, citing enjoyment of being single as the most common reason why. You may wonder how a greater number of young men are single compared with their same-aged female peers. My guess is that young women who are in relationships are dating older men, or are unknowingly (or possibly knowingly, as would be the case in polyamory) sharing their male partner with other women.

COVID may not have started the problem, but it certainly exacerbated it. I sense that, for single folks (and those who found themselves newly divorced during the pandemic), isolation periods went from being torturous and akin to solitary confinement to a new normal.

Is the Sex Recession a Myth?

Study after study has offered another grain of sand, culminating in a mountain of evidence that something unusual is taking place. One would think that both sides of the political aisle—and especially those who hold more "progressive" views on sexuality—could agree that if we aren't having sex, that's a bad sign. Instead, the political left has argued that fears about a sexual recession are overblown and nothing more than conjecture,[4] while contradictorily agreeing that young people are having less sex, and that's a good thing.

Most mainstream experts and journalists contend that society's willingness to be open and "authentic" has translated to more honest conversations about what's really going on in people's bedrooms. In other words, studies from previous years may have reflected people's exaggerations or inflated stories about all the sex they're having.

I find it bizarre that the progressive, "sex-positive" framing of this problem is the dismissal of it being a problem at all. "Sex positivity" once meant that there shouldn't be any shame associated with having or talking about sex.

I was once aboard that train. But like almost everything related to sexuality nowadays, this attitude has taken a hard-left turn, encouraging acceptance of *all* forms of sexuality, no matter how dysfunctional, aberrant, or extreme. Having personal boundaries or less adventurous sexual preferences is now viewed as "sex-negative" or "kink-shaming."

While I do agree that talking about something as private as one's sexuality should involve sensitivity and compassion (as opposed to ridicule and scorn), sex positivity takes open-mindedness to absurdity, slapping the label of "normal" on just about every permutation of fornication imaginable. Incredibly, sex positivity's newest iteration also champions abstinence (so long as it isn't motivated by religion) and those who identify as "asexual," or people who say they don't experience sexual attraction to anyone. This was once considered anathema to sex positivity and its promotion of promiscuity.

To clear up any confusion, *abstinence* refers to a person's decision to temporarily refrain from having sexual intercourse but may still permit other forms of sexual activity, like kissing, oral sex, or masturbation. *Celibacy*, on the other hand, is a lifestyle commitment that requires eliminating all sexual activity from one's life.

The new sex positivity isn't too bothered by whether the sexless trend is by choice or involuntary. I have a feeling that's because women are more likely to fall into the former category and men the latter. From what I've seen, most of the think pieces and social commentary denying the reality of the sex recession have been written by politically left-leaning young women, who tend to be supporters of intersectionality.

Intersectionality[5] states that men (and especially white men) are unfairly privileged in society due to their biological sex and skin color. And so, people who believe in intersectionality, including large portions of the media, often discuss young men's struggles in an unsympathetic tone and generally lack interest in finding effective solutions. But what the intersectionality adherents fail to realize is that when young men are struggling, young women feel the effects, too.

Women, on average, have a lower sex drive than men.[6] Their sex drive peaks later at around twenty-seven to forty-five years old,[7] compared to the late teenage years and twenties in men. Women, for the most part, also know that access to sex is much easier for them than it is for men.

My readers have surely heard of the classic psychological study, published in 1989, that delineated sex differences in attitudes toward casual sex.[8] In the study, male and female researchers (also known as "study confederates") approached undergraduate students of the opposite sex on campus and asked them, "Would you go to bed with me?"

Female confederates were turned down by male students about a third of the time. Male confederates were turned down by female students *every single time*. (In fact, the female confederates found that a greater number of male students in the study were willing to accept an invitation for sex than an invitation to go on a date.)

Statistically speaking, most women can walk outside their home any given day, point to a male stranger, and successfully proposition him to have sex with her. This is not the case for almost all men. If they were to approach a woman so directly at random, at best, she might politely decline, and at worse, he could end up on a sex offender registry.

From an evolutionary perspective, women are the gatekeepers to sex, while men are the gatekeepers to relationships. As you already know, sex is more costly to women, due to the prospect of pregnancy, childbirth, and associated responsibilities like breast-feeding and child-rearing. As a result, women are much more discriminating about their mates, preferring men who can protect and provide for them and their future progeny.

Progressive young women, and especially those who jeer at sexless men, may erroneously believe that women will benefit from the sex recession. In their minds, if more men than women are unable to find a partner, this should translate to a greater number of men fighting over each individual woman.

That isn't, however, how evolutionary biology works. As we saw in the last chapter, fewer viable bachelors in society throws *all* women into a cutthroat competition against one another for this smaller pool of high-value men. By adhering to an invalid calculus that suggests they should ignore the problem, these young women are setting themselves up for disaster.

What Is "Sex"?

Skeptics of the sex recession have claimed that studies supporting it are flawed in their methodology. Fair enough—surveys *could* have been clearer when asking respondents about their sexual frequency or lack thereof. (By "sexual frequency," I'm referring to how often a person has had sex or how many sexual partners they've had over a given time period.)

For example, studies discussed in the previous chapter posed the question somewhat vaguely:

"About how often did you have *sex* during the last twelve months?"
[emphasis mine]

"Now thinking about the time since your eighteenth birthday (including the past twelve months), how many female partners have you had *sex* with?"

"Now thinking about the time since your eighteenth birthday (including the past twelve months), how many male partners have you had *sex* with?"

These questions don't clearly define what the word *sex* is referring to. *Sex* can mean different things to different people, depending on whom you ask. Growing up, I remember hearing stories about classmates who preferred anal sex to vaginal sex with their boyfriends, because to them, anal sex wasn't considered "real sex," and it allowed them to maintain their virginity.

Study participants may have assumed that sex meant vaginal intercourse only, which is one specific form of sexual activity. Others may have interpreted the word *sex* as a catchall term referring to *any* form of sexual activity, including oral sex, anal sex, or masturbation with a partner.

From a scientific perspective (because yes, there exist scientific studies on this topic), the definition of sex can change, depending on whether someone is male or female. Men are more likely to consider any sexual activity as sex, regardless of whether it involves penile-vaginal intercourse, while women tend to define sex solely as intercourse.[9]

This means that if a man and woman were to have a nonpenetrative sexual experience together, there is a higher chance the man would count it as "sex" compared with his female partner. Following from this, could it be the case that younger generations are having as much sex as previous generations, but in the manner of oral sex or partnered masturbation, as opposed to intercourse?

Not likely. If men have a greater tendency to inflate the frequency of their sexual encounters, one could expect associated bias in research findings to fall on the side of displaying higher rates of sexual inactivity in women. Sexual inactivity was previously more commonly reported by female respondents.[10] The recent inversion in the sex ratio suggests that something has changed; taken together with this broader definition of sex used by the average man, reported rates of male sexual inactivity are probably an *underestimation* of the current severity.

As for *why* men tend to use a more generous definition of what constitutes "sex," in my opinion, this is because it allows a man to give the impression of being higher in mate value. If a man has had many sexual conquests and an array of willing partners available to him, to some extent this must mean that women find him sexually appealing. Although both sexes find sexual promiscuity distasteful in their partners, women are more forgiving of this trait.[11] If anything, a man with too many partners is generally less off-putting than a man who has too few.

This male signaling helps attract potentially interested mates *and* accomplishes the task of intimidating one's sexual rivals. It is another example of intrasexual competition. In this case, a man boasting about his sexual prowess broadcasts status and will possibly discourage other men from competing with him for female attention.

Women, on the other hand, downplay the extent of their sexual experience, both in frequency (known in modern vernacular as "body count") and breadth. Female sexual promiscuity heightens men's fears of cuckoldry, one of the greatest threats to male evolutionary success and something to which men have evolved an extreme aversion.[12]

This aversion is a biologically wired phenomenon that continues because it helps men ensure they will succeed in passing on their genes. Progressive attempts to destigmatize "slut shaming" won't override this programming in the wider population of men *or* women. (This will become glaringly apparent when we discuss the subject of prostitution.)

It would be a complete waste of a man's time, energy, and

resources to invest in raising a child he believed to be his own, when in reality he is ensuring the genetic legacy of a male rival. (Nevertheless, evolutionary explanations do not justify holding women and men to different standards regarding what is considered socially acceptable, including in the realm of sexual promiscuity.)

To finally put to rest the question of whether a lax definition of sex has led to skewed conclusions about sexual inactivity, subsequent studies have used more precise language when inquiring about our sex lives. Using data collected between 2006 and 2019, one study examined whether the sex recession is affecting men as widely as has been claimed.[13] It specifically asked whether respondents had ever had vaginal intercourse and if they had had vaginal intercourse in the past twelve months.

The study found that sexual inactivity was particularly pronounced among Gen Z men. Men born in the year 2000 and younger had higher-than-average rates of sexual inactivity, and upon entering adulthood, had fewer sexual experiences than observed in prior generations.

Here's one last study worth considering.[14] Its data were collected in 2009 and 2018 as part of the National Survey of Sexual Health and Behavior (NSSHB), a confidential online survey completed by over 7,000 American adults aged eighteen to forty-nine, and over 1,600 American adolescents aged fourteen to seventeen (which would have been Gen Z and younger Millennials).*

Instead of asking broadly about "sex" or "sexual activity," these survey questions described the sex act of interest very clearly.

---

* The adolescents in this study were invited to participate only if their parent or guardian consented to it.

Here's an example of how one question was worded: "Thinking about the past year, about how often have you engaged in penile-vaginal intercourse?"

The precise phrasing minimized any potential misunderstanding for study participants. With this out of the way, the researchers still found marked declines in sexual behavior across the board, not only in self-reported penile-vaginal intercourse but also in partnered masturbation as well as oral and anal sex. This was the case for both adults and adolescents.

Accordingly, and for clarity, whenever I refer to "sexual in-activity," I'm talking about sex in any capacity with a partner, including intercourse, oral or anal sex, or partnered masturbation.

Hookup Culture Is Dead

A common argument made by those dismissing the sex recession is that young people are delaying sex thanks to better decision-making around their sexual health. Are they, though?

A study of more than 17,000 high school students* enrolled at 152 public and private schools found that 30 percent of teens had ever had sex in 2021, compared with 38 percent in 2019 and 54 percent in 1991.[15] Notably, this was the largest decrease in the survey's entire history.

Post–COVID-19 teenage birth rates have also fallen to the lowest they've ever been. In 2022, there were only 13.5 births per 1,000 girls aged fifteen to nineteen, a trend that has been on the decline since 1991 when this statistic was 61.8 births per 1,000

---

* Student participation was voluntary, anonymous, and required parental permission.

girls.[16] This decrease has been attributed to easier access to contraception, greater education regarding pregnancy prevention in teens, and the fact that fewer teens are engaging in sex.

Less teen sex would be worth celebrating if it reflected young people making healthier choices. In this case, a confluence of school shutdowns, being housebound and under parental supervision for extended periods, social isolation, and declining mental health has produced a bleak picture of how young people relate to one another.

The low teen birth rate has been used to romanticize the decisions teenagers are making about sex, but what about statistics from the Centers for Disease Control and Prevention, revealing that over half of sexually transmitted infections (STIs) reported in 2020–2021 occurred in youth aged fifteen to twenty-four?[17] Teens may be having fewer unplanned pregnancies, but they are contracting syphilis, gonorrhea, and chlamydia at skyrocketing rates, to the extent that medical professionals are expressing concerns about antibiotic-resistant strains of these STIs flourishing.[18]

Does this sound like a generation of kids who are better informed about the risks of becoming sexually active? Although young people, overall, may be having less sex than before, it seems those who *are* sexually active aren't necessarily going about it responsibly. These findings reflect a common, dysfunctional sentiment among many young people, that risk of pregnancy is more of a concern than possibly contracting an STI. Though mostly treatable, STIs are not benign, with the potential to cause infertility, damage to one's internal organs, stillborn births, and even death.

When we contemplate the segment of young people who *aren't* sexually active, is it possible that they are abstaining from sex for positive reasons? A decrease in adolescent masturbation, documented in the aforementioned NSSHB poll,[19] *could* theoretically reflect teenage sexual experimentation in decline. As uncomfortable as it may feel to think about the masturbation habits of teenagers, I question whether this finding is, in fact, a positive one. Adolescence is a developmental period typically paired with a young person's sexual awakening. It is highly unusual that self-disclosed masturbation rates would be *lower* when discussions about sexuality have never been more socially permissible.

In a similar vein, studies have shown that some sexually inactive young people aren't bothered by an extended dry spell, maintaining levels of happiness similar to those who are having sex.[20] This suggests that the problem may be deeper than an inability to find a desirable partner; I will soon discuss whether there may be something affecting human beings at the hormonal or physiological level.

Other critics of the sex recession emphasize that not *all* young men are currently sexless, so we should focus on the ones who are sexually active and healthy instead of having a meltdown over the minority who aren't. Try telling a young person in the physical prime of their life that being unable to find a partner is *not that big of a deal.*

This problem doesn't appear to be self-correcting and is in fact worsening exponentially with time, so who's to say whether some of the men succeeding in the dating market today won't find themselves in the sexless camp down the line? Some argue that skipping the teenage dating experience stunts one's emotional growth and maturity, foreclosing the ability to learn important life skills, such as how to communicate, compromise, and resolve conflict. These lessons are necessary for healthy relationships in adulthood, romantic or otherwise.

What about hookup culture? Aren't young people pulsating with raw energy and spiking hormones, swiping like mad on dating apps, and bouncing from one bed to another like never before? Dating apps reportedly allow promiscuous young people to order sexual partners like items on a take-out menu, delivered directly to their door.[21]

When the dating app Tinder emerged as the first swipe-based app in 2012, it was predominantly known as the place to go for no-strings-attached sex. More than a decade and 530 million downloads later, let's consider statistics the company recently released: Forty percent of Tinder users indicate on their profile that they are looking for a "long-term relationship."[22] At 13 percent, "short-term fun" is the least popular form of relationship its swipers are seeking. Tinder has since rebranded itself as no longer centered on hookups but instead on fostering relationships.[23]

Considering that a US study[24] conducted prior to the pandemic found that only about one in five single, heterosexual men and one in ten single, heterosexual women reported going on a date in the past twelve months, it seems the hype around strangers hooking up is overblown. Dating apps are skewed to favor one segment of the population (which is, according to statistics, conventionally attractive, presumably photogenic, women and men[25]), to the time-zapping disappointment of everyone else.

Some of you may be wondering what the problem is. If people can't find a partner, can't they (quite literally) take matters into their own hands and masturbate?

From a practical standpoint, sure, but sex is about more than just having an orgasm. Sex with a partner (particularly within the context of a committed relationship[26]) is associated with a wide range of emotional and physical health benefits, including lower blood pressure,[27] a decreased risk of heart attack and stroke,[28] and all-around living longer. This is because sex is a form of physical activity, and just like regular exercise, raising one's heart rate helps to strengthen the cardiovascular system.

Being sexually active may also play a role in delaying brain aging. One study using a rat model found that having sex was correlated with greater neurogenesis (or brain cell growth) in the hippocampus, a region of the brain responsible for memory.[29]

Sex can mitigate stress, helping us sleep better, strengthening the immune system by raising levels of an antibody known as immunoglobulin A,[30] and giving us more energy throughout the day. It can even help boost motivation at work and morale.[31] Engaging in sex, and particularly penile-vaginal sex, can improve depressive symptoms,[32] anxiety, and increase pain tolerance by producing an analgesic effect.

Sex with a partner is also more intimate than masturbation, and men in particular use it as a way to connect with their significant other. Having an orgasm with a partner bestows more health benefits than an orgasm of the solo variety—*la petite mort* resulting from penile-vaginal sex releases 400 percent more prolactin than orgasm from self-stimulation. Post-climax prolactin release is associated with the reduction of sex drive and increased feelings of sexual satisfaction. This is likely why, for many people, intercourse is more sexually gratifying than masturbation.

Solo sex, though perhaps more efficient and less time-consuming than partnered sex, is the sexual equivalent of consuming empty calories. Masturbation is associated with greater depressive symptoms and feeling worse about one's mental health.

Women reap benefits from penetrative sex, especially without a condom, because semen contains chemicals like prostaglandins, endorphins, oxytocin, and hormones that stimulate ovulation. These are absorbed by the vaginal wall and can improve one's mood. (For those who may be curious, the same benefits weren't found in gay men who had unprotected anal sex, which suggests there may be something specific about women's bodies that makes them receptive to the antidepressant effects of semen.) Sex can also help to ease the discomfort of menstrual cramps, shorten the length of a woman's period, and delay the onset of menopause.[33]

For the record, I am not advocating that women have unprotected sex. Unprotected sex, particularly if it's between two people who don't know each other well, is highly irresponsible and can have life-threatening consequences. Trusting someone else with your body and well-being, as in the case of having sex, is not something that should be taken lightly. If a couple *is* considering it, monogamy and testing for STIs help reduce risk. Couples should also be aware that, without a back-up form of contraception, pregnancy can occur.

Some say that the proverbial "orgasm gap" makes it totally understandable that women should prefer skipping sex with men to take care of business themselves. Studies have shown that women aren't guaranteed to have an orgasm during sex with a male partner, even if he is familiar to her.[34] Heterosexual men are also more likely to have an orgasm during partnered sex than are heterosexual women (that is, 95 percent of men versus 65 percent of women, as recounted in one recent study[35]). The greatest benefits from sex occur in a committed relationship, not a casual arrangement, because women must feel physically safe with a partner in order to climax.

As for men, ejaculation during vaginal sex (compared with ejaculation from masturbation) produces larger volumes of semen,

improved sperm quality and prostate function, and is more efficient in ridding the body of waste products. Prolonged periods of
male sexual inactivity are associated with physical health problems
like erectile dysfunction[36] and prostate cancer.[37]

Now, I don't believe there's anything morally wrong with masturbation, but I raise these points to counter arguments that claim
sexlessness is benign and masturbation is the easy solution. It's
also important to keep in mind, as mentioned earlier, that along
with a decline in partnered sex, we're seeing a society-wide trend
toward less masturbation. So, any benefits that could be bestowed
from masturbation are similarly being attenuated.

Sexual activity with a committed partner is preferable because
committed sex is (hopefully) paired with social support and stress
management, in a way that casual sex or hooking up with a friend
or ex-partner is not. I don't judge anyone's decision to have a fling,
but I imagine the associated benefits are reduced, particularly for
women, who are more likely to experience negative effects after
sex without commitment.[38]

It's also possible for someone to have a committed partner but
to have less sex together *or* none at all. According to the GSS, close
to *5 percent* of married couples went an entire year without sex
in 2021. During my time as an academic sex researcher, I would
speak to individuals who hadn't had sex with their spouse in a
decade or longer.

In case you were wondering, according to research, the optimal
amount of sex is once per week.[39] For couples who have more frequent sex, this isn't associated with an increase in relationship happiness. An argument could be made that quality is more important
than quantity and that preferred sexual frequency is highly personal.
Some people desire more sex, while others are satisfied with less.

As we saw earlier, some people may be perfectly content with forgoing sex, but those who would rather be sexually active find inactivity distressing.[40] A person may feel undesirable or believe there is something wrong with them. If and when they have a sexual opportunity, they may lack confidence, feel overly self-conscious, or experience anxiety about possibly doing or saying something that will turn their partner off.

A lack of sex can create a cyclical effect, justifying a further retreat away from a real sexual partner and favoring one of the many substitutes detailed in this book's upcoming chapters. Young people are already feeling the fallout, recasting singledom as a worthy destination instead of a rite of passage.

Millennial and Gen Z Priorities

A critical piece to the sex recession puzzle is understanding how younger generations, who are the most plagued by this problem, are structuring their lives. Millennials and Gen Z differ from their generational predecessors in several ways, the key differentiator being that these younger generations are deciding against getting married.

Every generation tends to believe that younger generations are soft. Millennials like me have gotten grief for our participation trophies, self-esteem culture, shortened work weeks, and unearned narcissism. It's true that we haven't suffered like those who came before us—the Lost and Greatest Generations, as well as the Silents and Baby Boomers, had more pressing things to think about, like being drafted for war. Gen Xers were busy building the internet while juggling work, family, pets, and a mortgage. Millennials, on the other hand, were handed a pampered existence, racking up debt on useless postsecondary degrees, living on iced coffees and overpriced toast, and spending too much time glued to smartphones.

Then came along Gen Z, who have been dubbed "digital natives" because it's unlikely they remember a time prior to the advent of social media and smartphones. This generation has been branded as anxious snowflakes, the product of "helicopter" (or overprotective) parenting, lacking in work ethic, and exhibiting drastically shorter attention spans. Zillennials, who are younger Millennials and older Gen Z (born around 1990 to 2000, on the cusp of the Millennial–Gen Z generational boundary), have fretted about having a fragmented identity and not knowing which fashion trends to embrace.[41]

While generational stereotypes may come across as harsh, there is generally some truth to them. The fact that both Millennials and Gen Z grew up fluently using the internet rightfully raises questions about whether a digitized childhood has played a role in upending their sexuality.

As we touched on earlier, Millennials and especially Gen Z have followed a delayed trajectory in reaching expected life milestones. The once-idyllic vision of a house, a white picket fence, 2.5 children, and a minivan has been violently overthrown by perma-bachelor and -bachelorette living, with these groups preferring to spend their "me" time untethered to the leashes of previous generations' responsibilities and obligations.

Among Americans fifteen years old and older, more than one in three has never been married as of 2022, compared with only about one in four back in 1950.[42] Beginning with Boomers born in the 1960s and onward, delaying marriage or remaining single has become increasingly common. In 2021, 25 percent of forty-year-old American Millennials said they'd never been married, a sizable increase from 20 percent in 2010.[43]

These declining marriage rates are accompanied by lower rates of cohabitation as well. In 2022, about one in five never-married Millennials aged forty to forty-four was living with a partner, which translates to roughly four out of five who were not.

As for Gen Z, they tend to live at home with their parents longer, move out later, and are slower to attain markers of independence typically associated with adulthood, like getting a paying job or a driver's license, or spending time without parental supervision. Hanging out with friends or a romantic interest usually involves being accompanied by a parent in the form of a chaperone or chauffeur.

Many of those young people who successfully managed to leave the nest of their parents' home in pursuit of a university degree or full-time employment have since been forced to move back in with their families due to COVID-19 campus closures, student debt, an unpredictable job market, and inflation.

A recent Harris Poll for Bloomberg found that nearly half of Americans aged eighteen to twenty-nine are living with their parents, the highest proportion documented since the 1940s.[44] Not only that, but Zoomers report being happy with their decision.

When asked, 90 percent of Americans surveyed stated that people shouldn't be judged for moving back in with their parents. But as one can imagine, slowing the start to life as an autonomous adult postpones and places restrictions on one's love life. Without a car, paycheck, or the privacy that comes with living alone, sex and dating can be challenging, if not downright impossible. Being employed and having one's own place are also markers of emotional maturity. These are criteria that young women usually look for in a partner, and it will be a dealbreaker if a man doesn't have them.

Along with plummeting marriage and cohabitation rates across these two generations, birth rates have also been dropping. After the baby boom in the mid-twentieth century, it was common for the average American woman to have three or four children. In our current era, this number has fallen to 1.6 children,[45] which is considerably fewer than the optimal rate of 2.1 needed for society to avoid population collapse. By 2030, it's expected that 45 percent of women aged twenty-five to forty-four will be single and childless.[46]

A healthy birth rate is necessary to ensure there will be enough young people to care for the aging and elderly and that the economy will thrive. Although outliers like tech entrepreneur Elon Musk and actor Nick Cannon have joked about making up for the underpopulation crisis, having fathered fourteen and twelve children, respectively, they certainly don't represent the average civilian.

North America is not alone in its birth decline. The one-child policy in China, which was enforced between 1980 and 2016, caused the country's fertility rate to be drastically cut in half. In 1970, the birth rate was 5.8 births per woman.[47] By 1979, this number had fallen to 2.7 births, and in 2022, it was 1.09. Other Asian countries exhibiting unusually low birth rates include South Korea (at 0.78), Singapore (1.10), and Japan (1.26), with government-supported interventions, like baby bonuses and more flexible working arrangements, being offered to new parents in hopes of incentivizing baby making.

The highest overall birth rates are currently found in African countries, including Niger (6.64), Angola (5.70), Democratic Republic of the Congo (5.49), and Mali (5.35).[48] Reasons for this include less access to birth control and cultural influences that encourage families to have as many children as possible, including (quite tragically) child brides who begin having children at age eighteen or younger.[49]

As for whether currently childless Americans will eventually have kids, the answer is leaning toward no. In 2023, 47 percent of childless adults under age fifty said that it is "Not too likely" or "Not at all likely" that they would have children, versus 44 percent in 2021 and 37 percent in 2018.[50] This was due to not wanting them (57 percent), financial (36 percent) or medical reasons (13 percent), or not having a partner (24 percent).

Factors associated with childlessness include being young, more educated, and unmarried, especially among young women in their twenties.[51] It turns out, among childless Americans aged eighteen to thirty-four, more men (57 percent) than women (45 percent) say they want to have children someday.[52]

When asked what makes for a fulfilling life, "having a career [one enjoys]" and "having close friends" were the most popular answers among American adults. Lower down the list were "being married" and "having children."[53] Adults aged eighteen to twenty-nine were the most likely to say "having a lot of money" was important.

As discussed earlier, it's believed that fertility rates in the US were higher in the past due to unplanned pregnancies, and because contraception has become more widespread and readily available, pregnancy is now easier to prevent. But I would argue there is another undercurrent influencing young people's decision to not procreate, because being able to control one's fertility doesn't necessarily rule out the decision to have children in the future. It is especially telling that *not having a partner* is one of the most common reasons given regarding why childless adults say they don't expect to ever have children.

The concept of "settling down" has certainly evolved from what it once symbolized. Marriage involved a mutually beneficial agreement between a man and a woman in the form of a promise signifying a lifelong commitment. While I agree that some aspects of marriage may be archaic—for example, the idea of a man "owning" his wife as a form of property—what modern-day marriage has mutated into isn't terribly promising, either.

Marriage rates have been on the decline for almost two decades, with the exception of a slight bump post-pandemic. Because fewer people have been getting married, divorce rates have followed a similar, downward trend. Roughly half of all first marriages in the US end in divorce. Second and third marriages fare even worse, with divorce rates hovering at 67 and 73 percent.[54]

The average length of a first marriage is eight years. Contrary to the common expectation that most marriages end due to disagreements about money or sex, the most common reason is lack of commitment, with 75 percent of divorcees citing this as their reason for terminating their vows.[55] Infidelity ranks as the second most common reason (at about 60 percent), followed by too much conflict (at about 58 percent). Financial problems were cited by roughly 37 percent.

Marriage no longer consists of sacred vows exchanged in the presence of one's family, closest friends, and a higher being. Nowadays, it isn't uncommon for a couple to wed because they've been dating for a few years and their friends and future in-laws have been pestering them about it. Couples will marry regardless of whether they actually like each other, never mind whether they intend to be together forever.

As an (albeit extreme) example, a colleague told me about how her friend's fiancé slept with a stripper at his bachelor party. Her friend found out about this indiscretion the following morning, after one of the groomsmen told her. She nevertheless went through with the wedding. Not a single person attending the ceremony—not her parents, her in-laws, the officiant, the guests, nor anyone in the wedding party, including my colleague—pulled the bride-to-be aside for a heart-to-heart before the procession began.

One study, consisting of 906 Millennials and Gen Zers aged eighteen to forty-two, found that two in five respondents considered marriage "an outdated tradition."[56] Of those polled, 73 percent said it's "too expensive to get married" in today's economy, and 85 percent said they don't believe marriage is necessary to have "a fulfilled and committed relationship." One in six weren't ever planning on getting married, the main reason being because they "just aren't interested" in it.

The discrepancy between what marriage was meant to be and what it represents today has surely done a number on young people. Witnessing and experiencing divorce among Millennials' and Gen Z's parents, combined with the high cost of a wedding, the amount of time required to plan it, staggering rates of infidelity, and the brutality of divorce court if the marriage does end, have inspired young people to avoid the whole mess altogether and not get married in the first place.

Could it be that young people simply hold an updated view on marriage, and besides personal preferences, there's nothing inherently wrong with it? One could argue you don't need legal recognition or a piece of paper to prove two people are committed to one another.

I disagree. Even if a person sincerely holds the belief that they will be with their current partner until the end of time, there will always be a tiny part of them that knows they can bail without much inconvenience. Without the formal commitment of marriage, it becomes much easier to break up and continue cycling through new dating partners, especially with the disposable mindset that dating apps have fostered.

It's quite possible that, for both sexes, forgoing marriage is an intentional choice to keep their options open. If someone has commitment issues, refusing to tie the knot makes it easier to jump ship should the relationship become serious or when a more desirable partner comes along. That outlook will, however, become a self-fulfilling prophecy; if you are going into a relationship with the expectation that it's going to fail, neither party will ever feel fully secure or invested in the other person, always covertly searching for someone better.

It makes sense then, why marriage has been successful at curtailing infidelity in both sexes.[57] If someone is unwilling to fully commit to a partner, what is stopping them from being with other people? Among heterosexual couples, about 3 percent of married men report cheating, compared with about 19 percent of men who are unmarried but in a relationship. Similarly, about 2 percent of married women report adultery, versus about 14 percent of unmarried women who are in a relationship.

The fact that married people still cheat suggests marriage isn't a perfect solution. But I do believe it's worthwhile to consider how overturning the significance of marriage and completely redefining and redesigning relationship structures may backfire in the long run. It isn't necessarily a bad thing to uphold tradition, particularly if it maintains utility in the modern age. This shift in priorities has developed in tandem with other ideological influences targeting young people, including fears of overpopulation, climate change, and anything that was cultivated by white men.

Of those who aren't interested in marriage at the moment, will this change if they find a partner and fall in love? It's doubtful because the priorities of Millennials and Gen Z are changing. Both generations are more focused on self-fulfillment and individualism. Having a spouse and children is viewed as incompatible with self-actualization and enjoying one's free time.[58] The only exception takes the form of marriage ceremonies in which an individual decides to marry themselves.[59]

Millennials and Gen Z also tend to believe that it's important to be the best version of yourself prior to getting into a serious relationship. This takes time, much contemplation, and dozens, if not hundreds, of hours of therapy, further delaying the dating and marriage process.

Long gone is the sentiment of growing together with a partner. Also, considering that mental health labels like "ADHD" and "trauma" are constantly being inflated and overused such that every other young person identifies as "neurodivergent" or mentally ill, this means they will never consider themselves healthy enough to actually be with another person.

As much as I think it's great that stigma around mental disorders has lessened and people are going to therapy to improve themselves, I wonder whether this acceptance has led to a mentality of being relegated to one's circumstances or diagnosis, instead of striving to move outside the limits of one's comfort zone.

Dating, particularly for Gen Z, is a nebulous process of meeting new people without a clear purpose or intention in mind. Gen Z is actually less likely to *date* because "dating" connotes that two people are moving in a particular romantic direction. Gen Z prefers to get to know someone as a friend, in the context of self-exploration and accumulating life experiences, instead of moving toward a predetermined outcome like a relationship or marriage.

Another survey by Tinder inquired about the dating experiences of 4,000 eighteen-to-twenty-five-year-olds in the US, Canada, United Kingdom, and Australia. Of possible "Relationship Goals" that could be selected to denote on one's profile what they are looking for, "Still figuring it out" was the second most popular choice among this age bracket, with more than one in five selecting it.[60] (In addition to the popular choice "Long-term partner," Tinder's other options included "Long-term, open to short," "Short-term, open to long," "Short-term fun," and "New friends.")

In my old age, this seems like a disastrous way to approach dating, especially for people who start sleeping with each other. In contrast to "friends with benefits" arrangements of the past, which demanded firm boundaries and not spending time together outside the bedroom, Gen Z's "situationships" (a portmanteau of "situation" and "relationship") involve texting each other about the intricacies of what they did that day, meeting each other's parents, going on vacation together, and hanging out regularly even when not having sex. It is essentially a relationship, but without the acknowledgment or title, and frequently translates to one party falling unrequitedly in love with the other.

What has stood out to me the most in reviewing these data is that young women are turning away from partnering up. Returning to the earlier survey regarding Millennials' and Gen Z's attitudes about marriage, it was particularly fascinating that more women than men endorsed the idea that marriage is outdated— 52 percent of women compared with 41 percent of men.[61]

This speaks to a monumental reason why fewer young people are coupling up: Marriage has become obsolete to young women, who are outperforming men along every metric that matters in a romantic partner, including social, economic, and educational domains.

If more young women are refusing to get married, this naturally effects young men, too. Counter to what one might expect, singledom—not marriage—is associated with higher rates of celibacy. Since sexual partners tend to be more easily acquired by women than by men, this further explains why sexlessness is higher in unmarried men than unmarried women. Many assume that being married translates to monotonous, missionary-style-only sex once per year and that being single consists of endless freedom and numerous sexual escapades. The reality is that married and/or cohabiting people still have more sex than singletons.

In America, the average married couple has sex fifty-six times a year, or about once a week. In contrast, the average single person has sex thirty-three times a year, which is almost half as frequently. These stats were conducted before COVID, so I'd expect the difference to be even more pronounced now.

If a partner is readily available, and by that, I mean, living with you and sharing the same bed, sex is more convenient than seeking out someone new for every encounter. Even when a single person has regular casual arrangements, they won't be as reliable as a spouse or committed partner. Sex in this case still requires more effort.

Sex within a marriage or relationship is also less likely to provoke awkwardness, fears of rejection, and performance difficulties. The groundwork has already been established regarding turn-ons and turn-offs, along with trust, because both partners are comfortable with each other. They are presumably more invested in one another's contentedness, including sexually.

If one person is tired and not necessarily in the mood, they may still agree to have sex because they want to make their partner happy. Prioritizing someone else's sexual needs is less likely to occur with no-strings-attached sex, where a lack of familiarity and established boundaries can lead to an interaction souring quickly.

Just as young women are avoiding marriage because they don't want to end up paying a less financially successful ex-husband alimony, young men are tossing aside the idea of getting hitched because they see it as equivalent to digging their own grave. Because women initiate divorce approximately 70 percent of the time,[62] many men fear this fate is beyond their control.

If a man is the primary breadwinner and his wife decides to file for divorce, he may find himself not only forfeiting half of what he owns but also paying spousal and child support, accruing sky-high legal fees, and possibly losing access to his children. Divorced men are over eight times more likely than divorced women to die by suicide.[63]

Going through a divorce can indeed be a gruesome experience, and it's wise for young men (and women) to view commitment cautiously. But deciding to stay forever single for the sake of self-preservation can be counterproductive. For example, a committed romantic partner can motivate a man stuck in a rut to get his act together, because if he values her, he will be afraid of losing her to someone else.

Without a woman in his life, a man may feel less need to keep his place clean, to maintain a kempt appearance, and to put someone else's needs before his own. Single men without any romantic prospects, intentionally or otherwise, may find themselves sticking to the same bad habits, lacking any urgency to better themselves.

My concern about the sex recession and the accompanying disinterest in marriage stems from anything but judgment. If someone decides they are better off not dating or marrying or reproducing or having sex, who am I to tell them otherwise?

But my sense is that these circumstances stem from a lack of control, as opposed to choice. As we saw in Tinder's survey data, many people are longing for a relationship; they just don't seem to know how to get one.

If young people have lost interest in getting married or settling down, this naturally delays any incentive to date *or* to become an adult, which subsequently makes it more difficult to find the right partner if and when they eventually decide to.

Men Are Being Left Behind

In the fight for gender equality, women have gone from being a disadvantaged class to gaining equal rights to outperforming men. As we saw in the previous chapter, girls and women are succeeding at school and work at higher rates than the opposite sex.

How did these changes come about? Starting from a young age, the education system tends to cater to girls' strengths in reading, writing, and multitasking. These skills advance more quickly in girls because their hippocampus and frontal lobe develop faster than boys'.[64] A typical school day, filled with long periods spent sitting at desks, contrasts strikingly with boys' need for physical movement and sensory input (like throwing a ball around) while learning.

As a result, male students are more likely to drop out, repeat a grade, or be medicated for ADHD.[65] Regarding home life, boys fare worse academically than girls when raised in a single-parent home; by the eighth grade, boys are 25 percent more likely than girls to be suspended from school.[66]

US Census Bureau data indicate that roughly 18.3 million children, which translates to one in four, live without a father in the home.[67] This suggests that parental divorce and fatherlessness may be contributing to young men falling behind in society in ways we haven't fully reckoned with.

For boys who successfully graduate from high school, pursuing university means they will battle additional obstacles designed to weed them out at every step of the way. Affirmative action in college applications, designed to benefit so-called underrepresented minorities at the expense of white and Asian men, was eliminated by the US Supreme Court in 2023. Woke academics have nevertheless pledged to continue implementing less obvious forms of race-based admissions criteria, such as placing larger importance on subjective "holistic factors"[68] (for example, an applicant's "soft skills") rather than academic performance–based measures. Many colleges have made standardized testing like the SAT optional.

I hear constantly from university professors that hiring for faculty positions is now based solely on skin color and that white men are, behind closed doors, discouraged from applying.[69] If an application made by a woman or member of a racial minority is turned down, hiring committees must give a formal justification to diversity, equity, and inclusion (DEI) departments.

Another colleague told me that publication count (the number of research papers an academic has published) is no longer considered relevant. Once a metric—arguably, the most important metric—of academic success considered by hiring and tenure committees, it has been thrown out the window in favor of a process akin to a racial lottery system. (This is a system that has also been used when selecting admissions for elite New York City high schools, a process that openly discriminates against Asian and white applicants.[70])

The way to improve marginalized groups' outcomes is to find ways of effectively lifting these communities up, not by discriminating against those who are doing well. For young men in a bachelor's program who miraculously survive the next three or four years to graduate, I imagine it must get tedious to be constantly told, in every class regardless of the professor or discipline, that you are privileged and should feel shameful or apologetic about your existence.

Feminism's initial desire for gender equality started with the worthwhile goal of obtaining equal educational and occupational opportunities for women. This slowly morphed into exalting women at the expense of men, flattening and dismissing male achievements, and subjugating men. In academia, countless events and scholarships are regularly created with the explicit goal of helping women advance, particularly in the sciences. In addition to battling DEI hurdles throughout the university application process, there are never any such opportunities for male students. The only hope men have for similar opportunities is to apply for scholarships that are open to both sexes.

An amusing but tragic example illustrating society's complete lack of interest in men's suffering occurred when *Politico Magazine* released an entire issue devoted to masculinity. Every article in the issue was written by a female journalist. Additional male-friendly headlines over the years have included "2020 Has Been Miserable.

Is Extreme Masculinity to Blame?"[71] and "Don't Blame Mental Illness for Mass Shootings; Blame Men."[72]

At last count, 51 percent of US-based journalists are male.[73] Surely it couldn't have been too much trouble to ask *one* of them to weigh in on a subject they presumably know well?* Or failing that, commissioning female journalists with viewpoints that varied across the political spectrum to give their opinion? Imagine the outrage if it had been the other way around, with only men opining in a magazine anthology devoted to women's issues.

I can appreciate where the pro-woman overcorrection is coming from. Science—and society, more widely—did indeed once discriminate openly against women. It was just over a century ago that women were denied the right to vote and own property, and it isn't lost on me that today's generation of women, including myself, owe a lot to our female forebearers for their sacrifices in winning these rights.

Sexism against women exists today, but it is, by and large, understood to be socially unacceptable. By punishing men under the guise of female equality, modern-day feminism has unwittingly punished women in the dating pool while helping highly successful men.

Regarding social structures, research suggests that women, on average, prefer equity, while men prefer hierarchies. This explains why, at a time when our educational institutions are promoting feminism as a dominant ideology, equality of outcome has become an increasingly popular goal.

Of course, not all women are sadistic enforcers of DEI or so-

---

* The magazine issue included a six-person panel discussion with two women and four men, but my point stands.

cial justice, and I would argue that women (and men) who *are,* are motivated by something more sinister than the well-being of others, including power, authority, money, and control. Their hypocrisy is blatant, however; if a different group of people were falling behind in society, they would be sympathetically bending over backward to help them with social programs and support. Instead, the extreme left blames men for their issues and pretends that there isn't a problem.

The only time society seems to care about men is when they begin mobilizing and veering into radicalization territory. Regardless of how desperately one wishes to humiliate and eradicate men, the reality is that large numbers of single, agitated males don't bode well for public safety. Disillusioned young men, especially if they are sexually frustrated, increase criminality, antisociality, and societal unrest. Studies have shown that coupling off romantically and having children lower a man's testosterone levels,[74] thereby helping balance out high-risk, aggressive tendencies because they are not conducive to fatherhood.

Dismissing men's struggle and telling them to cry silently into a pillow won't make these problems disappear. Fertility experts have been hysterically pointing at Japan's *hikikomori* as an example of the doomsday the West may soon become: one million young men who don't go to school, don't work, don't date, and instead choose to live in their parents' home, playing video games and scrolling online.

The *hikikomori,* characterized by severe self-isolation and social withdrawal before the age of thirty, spend their days confined to a single room, leaving only at night when no one is likely to see them. Although the *hikikomori* phenomenon has received a lot of attention from Western media outlets, it's important to know that individuals who are considered *hikikomori* are usually exhibiting the symptoms of an underlying mental disorder.

Depression, social anxiety, schizophrenia, and personality disorders are common among the *hikikomori*. Because mental illness remains relatively stigmatized in Japanese culture, the term *hikikomori* has been used as a more palatable label for male patients and their families.[75]

A loss of interest in relationships, socializing, and goal-directed behavior can be symptoms of a number of mental disorders, most notably depression. Schizophrenia, in particular, is characterized by auditory hallucinations (hearing voices) and persecutory delusions (the belief that someone is out to harm you). Going outside and encountering strangers is understandably the last thing someone with schizophrenia would want to do. Staying indoors and housebound not only provides an individual with less sensory overload but it also ensures a level of physical safety not present in the outside world.

Does the *hikikomori* label describe the direction young men in the West are headed? Considering that almost one in four Americans had a mental disorder in the past year,[76] and one in five is currently depressed, I predict the answer is yes.

There remains a larger phenomenon of sexlessness in Japan, with "herbivore men" who have forgone masculinity and dating. Approximately one in ten Japanese men in their thirties remains a virgin. This delayed loss of virginity is suspected to be a consequence of replacing romantic relationships with online activity. Of unmarried individuals under the age of fifty, more than a third have never been in a romantic relationship, and a quarter have no plans of ever getting married.

In the West, many aspects of modernity are funneling men

toward a similar fate of hermit living. Beyond work and education, men lack a sense of community and support. The majority of men don't have friends. A survey from the AEI Survey Center on American Life showed that the number of men reporting that they have "no close friends" jumped from 3 percent in 1990 to 15 percent in 2021.[77] For women, this percentage increased from 2 to 10 percent across the same time frame.

In 1990, 45 percent of young men said that they would reach out to friends when experiencing a personal problem. Young men today are more reliant on their parents, with only 22 percent saying they would rely on their friends, compared with 36 percent who say their first call would be to their parents.

Any sympathy toward prioritizing men's health or mental health issues is interpreted as a threat to women's care. It's no wonder that men are more likely to die a death of despair caused by alcohol, drugs, or suicide.[78] In search of comfort, they sink deeper into online life, replacing their wish for a partner with the closest thing they can find.

CHAPTER 3

Imaginary Girlfriends

Porn is ubiquitous. A constant stream of nudity and sexualized imagery bombards us everywhere, from the social media feeds of celebrities and influencers to mainstream movies, music videos, and corporate advertising. Every month, 11.4 billion people visit Pornhub, the largest internet porn streaming website. The global pornography industry is valued at over $97 billion.

Pornography has existed since prehistoric times in the form of cave drawings and somewhat hideous sculptures,[1] but it has never been as accessible, visually appealing, or commonplace as now. Online porn's rise to the forefront of cultural relevance has been shameless and stark. In the recent past, adult magazines were hidden in the woods, VHS cassette tapes were shelved behind a modesty curtain in video rental stores, and pay-per-view TV channels were restricted behind a paywall. No such decorum exists for high-speed porn today.

Internet pornography's rapid rise in popularity has been a catalyst for the sex recession. Watching sex on a screen has gone from being titillating entertainment to replacing the act itself.

One study examining rates of sexlessness in America, using a nationally representative sample, found the greatest increase in male sexual inactivity peaked between its 2008–2010 and 2012–2014 data periods.[2] What's odd is that the oldest members of Gen Z turned eighteen in 2013 and would have been college bound, but despite having less parental supervision and greater independence, a large proportion of these young men weren't sexually active. This raises the question, if they weren't excelling in school or chasing girls, what were these young men doing instead?

Well, the research suggests they may have been watching porn.

Although porn viewing in the past was associated with *lower* rates of sexual inactivity,[3, 4] these findings aren't applicable to younger cohorts of men who grew up watching internet porn. Data collected in the mid- to late-2010s, before the COVID-19 pandemic, focused on adults' behaviors, when most members of Gen Z were still minors. More recent, post-COVID data show that 71 percent of teenagers aged thirteen to seventeen (belonging to Gen Z) who intentionally watched porn did so in the last week.[5] Although most porn users are men (and boys), many women (and girls) also consume porn.

Pornography operates as a stand-in for real sex, activating the same brain regions that are recruited (or used) during sexual activity. Mirror neurons in these parts of the brain fool the viewer into thinking that the sex they're watching is happening to them.[6] These fake portrayals of sex provide an abnormally intense yet viable alternative imitating real sexual activity. Masturbation and orgasm lead to the release of hormones (like oxytocin and pro-lactin) and neurotransmitters (like serotonin) that are involved in attachment, bonding, and feelings of sexual satiety.

What happens to sexless men who have been overlooked by

women? It's not like they're sitting around, idly twiddling their thumbs. For men who cannot attain a partner, porn acts as a buffer and fills the void. Orgasm was designed to be highly rewarding; it evolved that way so that we would persevere through challenges to find a suitable mate. But the ability to see nudity, simulate having sex, and obtain orgasm without any of the effort once needed to access that reward is a shortcut that has thrown mating dynamics for an unprecedented loop.

The problem with technological alternatives like pornography, artificial-intelligence-driven companions, and purchased nudes is that they remove men's desire to better themselves so that they can attract a real-life partner. Pornography eases sexual frustration that would otherwise serve as useful male motivation. Porn dissuades men from doing difficult things, like taking risks and pushing themselves to be successful, because they know, in the back of their minds, that they always have an escape hatch. The sedating and reinforcing effects of an orgasm after watching porn nudge men toward complacency.

Indeed, statistics from the Pew Research Center indicate that only half of available American men are looking to date or find a relationship.[7] Not only is porn a powerful proxy for sex and a method of coping, but it also entices human beings to stay glued to their devices instead of reproducing.

From conversations I've had with many men, pornography dampens the draw of interacting with real women because you have access to an unlimited number of them, naked and available, at any point in time. For someone who is already apathetic about dating, the worst thing they can do is submerse themselves in porn, because this will further chip away at their drive to find a partner.

Porn algorithms are designed to overwhelm viewers with an

endless cornucopia of artificially enhanced sexual novelty, robbing them of their time, energy, and focus—as well as the benefits of actual sex—while placating them with an empty shell of sexual fulfillment.

This has far-reaching implications, setting off a chain reaction of abysmal side effects. Men who view porn habitually, to the point of impairing their social skills or goal-directed behavior, become even less appealing to women who may have otherwise found them attractive. Women desire men who have their lives together and their ducks in a row, men who are confident, productive, dependable, and capable of exercising self-discipline.

Pornography use is a common source of conflict in dating and marriages. When a man is a slave to hedonistic pleasure, particularly in the context of pleasuring himself while ogling other women, you'll be hard-pressed (no pun intended) to find a woman who endorses this as a turn-on.

Sexuality experts who are pro-pornography will cite evidence that sex crimes go down with the availability of porn. They argue that explicit material has a positive and pacifying—as opposed to amplifying—effect on sexual violence. What these data signal to me, however, is that porn is a potent substitute for sex with the potential to incept sexual ennui in *all* men, not just sex offenders.

Many young men would rather stay home and experience an easy orgasm that doesn't cost them rejection, emotional vulnerability, effort, or financial expense. There's no worrying about unwanted pregnancies or contracting sexually transmitted infections, but also no requirement that they bathe, look presentable, or hold a conversation. It's easier to masturbate and call it a night, because this doesn't require surmounting any obstacles.

A man can comfortably go the rest of his life in complete isolation, never having to work up the courage to talk to the opposite sex or ask a woman out on a date. But staring at a dimly lit screen while masturbating is not how we evolved to have sex. Having access to more partners than you could ever want, without having to go anywhere or do anything, goes against our natural instincts and what is good for us.

Widespread pornography consumption is reducing the number of men seeking female partnership, which diminishes women's opportunities for settling down. As coupling up becomes less frequent and more competitive, both sexes are turning to whatever measures they can (like plastic surgery and reproductive technologies) to overcome biological hurdles and afford themselves a better chance and more time. These makeshift remedies come bundled with their own risk factors for increasing sexual inactivity. None of them changes the fact that many men just aren't interested in the real thing anymore.

Those who criticize pornography or caution against too much masturbation are often written off as moral crusaders who believe that sex is inherently shameful outside procreation. Disapproval of porn is seen as uncool, uptight, and regressive. That stereotype is incorrect. It is possible to have a healthy view of sexuality, one that is free of shame and self-repression, while also questioning the long-term effects and potential ills of this artificial vice.

As someone who once wrote weekly columns on the science of sex for Playboy.com, I used to believe that porn was benign recreation for adults. (Despite this, I've never personally watched porn, as it makes me feel queasy.)* I do believe that for some indi-

---

* I will always be grateful to *Playboy* for the opportunities they gave me as a columnist. My views on pornography, however, have changed since then.

viduals, porn-viewing may not inflict disastrous side effects on their lives. Still, it's worth taking an honest inventory of pornography's wider cultural impact, including a consideration of how it molds viewers' sex lives in detrimental ways.

Pornography "Addiction"

Not everyone who views pornography experiences problems as a result, and not every man affected by sexlessness is necessarily turning to porn. But as someone who has used brain-imaging techniques, such as functional magnetic resonance imaging (fMRI), to study problematic pornography use, I have seen first-hand the countless ways porn can ruin someone's life.

Some of the men I've interviewed would view pornography eight to twelve hours a day, beginning when they got out of bed and continuing long after the sun went down. Porn slowly took over their lives, interfering with work, school, hobbies, friendships, and romantic relationships.

This phenomenon is captured in the present-day practice known as "gooning." Gooning consists of masturbating for extended periods of time, in some cases hours, without having an orgasm. The name references the slack-jawed, trancelike, single-minded, hypnotic expression that can accompany masturbation and is similar to the concept of "edging." Unlike individuals who acknowledge that their masturbation and porn-viewing routine have become a problem, those who partake in gooning don't profess any personal distress or negative consequences from doing so. They are proud, self-identified gooners.

The biggest factors determining whether someone has a porn problem are if their behavior causes them personal distress, if it has become compulsive (characterized by a loss of control, and doing it even though they don't want to), and if there have been adverse consequences to themselves or the people in their life. People with high sex drives who don't experience bad side effects from watching porn wouldn't be considered, by these criteria, to have a problem. That said, a study involving data collected from forty-two countries across five continents estimated that the global prevalence of problematic porn use may be as high as 17 percent of people.[8]

Although some experts—and individuals struggling to curb their porn use—consider the problem an "addiction," there have yet to be any legitimate scientific studies supporting this claim. Excessive porn use is not included in *The Diagnostic and Statistical Manual of Mental Disorders* (DSM-5-TR), psychiatry's "bible," nor is it considered a behavioral addiction, like gambling disorder or internet gaming disorder (which describes an addiction to online video games).

The American Association of Sexuality Educators, Counselors, and Therapists does not recognize the classification of "porn addiction" (or "sex addiction") as a mental health disorder due to a lack of sufficient evidence.[9] *The International Classification of Diseases* (ICD-11) includes compulsive sexual behavior disorder (CSBD) in its compendium but categorizes it as an impulse control problem rather than an addiction. CSBD is characterized by an excessive use of pornography, to the point of neglecting one's health and other life responsibilities; numerous unsuccessful attempts to stop or cut down on one's use; continued use despite negative repercussions, including adversely affecting work or relationships; and little satisfaction derived from porn viewing.

Proponents of the addiction model argue that an individual

who watches porn excessively experiences changes in their brain over time that mimic those seen in people who are addicted to substances like cocaine or alcohol. Analogies have been drawn between battling porn and freeing oneself from addiction to illicit substances. Someone who is addicted to a drug, for example, will go from using it for its pleasurable effects to craving it and needing it to avoid unwanted symptoms of withdrawal.

When we consider the neuroscientific literature, there are no well-designed studies demonstrating that excessive porn viewing is comparable to an addiction. (This was the subject of my PhD dissertation, so I know this body of research well.) Neuroimaging studies[10] claiming that the brain "lights up" similarly in both individuals with problematic porn use and people with substance use disorders do not adequately control for confounding factors that may otherwise explain their findings.

For example, these studies don't assess for paraphilic interests in those reporting problematic pornography use. *Paraphilias* are surprisingly common in the general population,[11] and in my research experience, especially in men who watch porn uncontrollably. A paraphilia is an abnormal sexual interest. Examples include sexual sadism and sexual masochism (which involve harming another person or oneself for sexual enjoyment, respectively). I find it extremely unlikely that *none* of the men included in these studies were paraphilic. Because paraphilic men have been shown to exhibit a different brain profile than non-paraphilic men, it's possible that changes in the brain associated with so-called porn addiction reflect unusual sexual interests.

These previous studies also don't account for psychiatric comorbidity, like anxiety disorders. It's possible, again, that the observed brain differences that were attributed to "porn addiction" were simply a reflection of an anxious disposition, which is also typical in men with porn problems.

Self-described "porn addicts" will draw on the brain's release of "dopamine" during porn-viewing as an explanation of why it is addictive. In the popular science realm, dopamine has been scapegoated as the "addiction" neurotransmitter. But just because dopamine is released during a given activity doesn't mean a person is addicted to that behavior. Dopamine is released during sex and when people watch porn, but also during a variety of other enjoyable activities, like cheering at a sports game[12] or listening to music.[13] Does that mean we're "addicted" to sports or our favorite songs? The answer, of course, is no.

Returning to my point about paraphilias, another common narrative is that manipulation by porn site algorithms has caused viewers' sexual tastes to desensitize or escalate toward more extreme sexual content. Non-kinky, heterosexual pornographic material *and* conventional sex with a partner no longer turn these men on—so they say.

Like any other developmental abnormality, a preference for kink, or atypical sex, is an indication that something went awry in childhood. Childhood trauma (including physical, sexual, and emotional abuse or neglect) plays a large role in the development of paraphilias.[14] According to brain-imaging research I have conducted, paraphilias are the product of a biological predisposition paired with early environmental exposure to an unconventional or unexpected sexual target. The only exception to this is children whose sexuality developed in tandem with, or after, watching online porn. I believe exposure to violent or frightening pornography can serve as a source of trauma, capable of leading a child to later develop a paraphilia.

People who enjoy abusive and sadistic porn are drawn to it because of preexisting, maladaptive attitudes formed early in life. Porn hasn't turned them into misogynistic predators unable to enjoy regular, nonviolent sex. Prosocial men with a healthy upbringing would not find it arousing to watch a woman being beaten and degraded.

For adults whose sexuality developed prior to the Wild West of internet porn, if they are turned on by abusing their partner, they are likely antisocial or have characteristics that reflect a dark triad personality (that is, narcissism, psychopathy, and Machiavellianism). This translates to viewing their sexual partners (and people, more broadly) as objects to be manipulated and used at their disposal. This worldview wasn't the result of violent porn, even if these individuals watch lots of it.

Similarly, for those who prefer abnormal sexual practices, this type of pornography is exactly what they were into all along, it just took them a while to admit it to themselves and explicitly search it out. It's not porn algorithms or gradual desensitization that led them there; if porn didn't exist, they would have gravitated toward those practices in their sex life, regardless. Consequently, ceasing to watch porn won't undo a person's paraphilic interests, no matter how harmful or maladaptive.

As for children, as stated above, early porn exposure may normalize the sexual objectification and abuse of women, along with abnormal and unwanted sexual practices. Among individuals who consume porn excessively, I've noticed that early porn exposure, usually when they were a prepubescent child, can be a developmental perturbance. This childhood exposure can occur accidentally or in the context of being sexually groomed by an adult. Regardless of the circumstances, viewing pornographic material as a child can negatively affect one's sexuality in adulthood.

Sexual abuse can also be a devastating factor. In my academic research, I found exceptionally high rates of childhood sexual abuse in men who presented with excessive sexual behaviors, including problematic porn use. Twenty percent of men I interviewed reported being sexually abused as a child, which is considerably higher than what has been found in the general population—that approximately 5 percent of boys and 25 percent of girls experience sexual victimization during childhood.[15]

Compulsive porn viewing, and a wider preoccupation with sex, become a way for these men to process the trauma they experienced. For instance, compulsive cybersex (what would be called "sexting" nowadays) is a commonly employed, maladaptive coping strategy seen in those with a history of sexual abuse. Childhood sexual abuse leads men to question their masculinity and their sexuality. In some cases, male victims feel compelled to prove to others (and perhaps themselves) that what they endured didn't affect them.

I am sympathetic to the argument that pornography can be destructive, and I understand why some may find comfort in identifying with the addiction model. Calling oneself an "addict" and using associated nomenclature like "staying sober" in reference to abstaining from porn and "relapsing" when a person falls short make it easier for others to understand the severity of the problem and lend legitimacy to that person's plight.

I agree that compulsive porn use can lead to feelings of being out of control and nevertheless continuing to watch porn, even as their life deteriorates before their eyes. This is a very real, challenging, and painful problem that can inflict irreparable damage on relationships and marriages.

Having said that, I am basing my conclusions on interviews I've conducted with hundreds of men about their porn viewing habits. We don't have to call the problem an addiction or show correlations in the brain for it to be taken seriously, to have empathy for those grappling with it, or to remove associated stigma.

This debate is about more than semantics; it's important that we accurately understand the root cause of the problem, because any therapy or treatment won't otherwise be effective. As always, I'm open to changing my mind if data emerge that support another interpretation.

A more parsimonious, straightforward explanation is that excessive pornography use is a reflection of anxiety,[16] procrastination, low self-esteem,[17] poor coping skills, and efforts to regulate negative emotions.[18] It can also be a symptom of another mental health condition, like bipolar disorder, obsessive-compulsive disorder, or depression.[19] A recent study in the journal *Personality and Individual Differences* provided a corroborating insight: Porn consumption is associated with feelings of meaninglessness and boredom.[20] Pornography becomes a way to self-soothe and avoid dealing with life stressors.

As an example, if someone is experiencing conflict at work and dislikes confrontation, instead of standing up to their boss, which can be intimidating and uncomfortable, they might choose instead to engage in escapism. Porn offers a quick fix, distracting the individual, with the corresponding orgasm temporarily washing away unwanted feelings.

The use of avoidance as a coping strategy becomes second nature, making it more difficult for a person to use healthy strategies when confronted with unpleasant emotions in the future. If an individual blocks their access to porn, other time-wasting activities, like compulsively playing video games, doomscrolling on social media, or binge-watching an entire TV series, will likely take its place *unless* they learn ways of addressing their anxiety (through, say, therapy with an appropriate mental health professional).

Porn-Induced Erectile Dysfunction

A growing concern from men with problematic porn use is psychogenic erectile dysfunction, or something that has been called *porn-induced erectile dysfunction* (PIED). The majority of males affected appear to be in their early twenties, which makes the phenomenon an especially unusual and shameful experience, since this is a period associated with peak virility in men.

These men report difficulties maintaining an erection and reaching orgasm when having sex with a partner. No such sexual difficulties exist during masturbation with porn. Some men also report experiencing what has been called the "flatline," a complete loss of libido paired with feelings of emotional numbness and grave concerns that they are "broken."

The "NoFap" movement seeks to address these concerns. Its adherents make a commitment to quit porn and masturbation with the goal of funneling that energy and drive into something more productive. Some men also practice something called "semen retention," which is apparently quite popular, considering that the term received over 1 billion impressions on TikTok.[21] Semen retention involves refraining from ejaculation (or alternatively, having an orgasm *without* ejaculation), with the goal of increasing testosterone levels, fertility, physical health, and self-control.

I previously dismissed PIED as the result of too much masturbation, a normal and expected part of the male sexual response cycle. The *refractory period* is a stretch of time after ejaculation during which it becomes difficult for a man to have another erection and orgasm. If a man has already had an orgasm (or three) while watching porn earlier in the day, he will find it much more challenging, if not impossible, to experience an erection with his partner that evening. He will presumably also feel less of an incentive to engage sexually with her in the first place.

Similarly, if a man is accustomed to using his hand to produce an orgasm, this "death grip" will create more intense and predictable sensations than those of a vagina or mouth. Sex therapists will therefore suggest taking a break from porn, or alternatively, masturbating more gently using lubricant (and without watching porn), to reset a man's sensitivity levels.[22]

I'm not saying that PIED is impossible, but I would need more data to convince me otherwise. A study in *The Journal of Sexual Medicine* sampling over 800 sexually active men found a link between self-reported problematic porn use and erectile dysfunction but no link between pornography use *itself* and erectile dysfunction.[23] To clarify, it wasn't so much that watching porn led to erectile dysfunction but that feeling troubled and guilty about one's porn viewing did.

For those who remain skeptical of my skepticism, it's possible that these male participants were experiencing a milder set of symptoms and that a relationship would have been found in men with more severe erectile dysfunction. The good news is that symptoms of erectile dysfunction tended to abate in study participants over the span of one year.

Sex therapists have told me that from what they've seen in their patients, porn-related erectile dysfunction is underscored by performance anxiety and a lack of sexual experience. A sexual encounter can be anxiety-provoking for anyone, but because many of these young men haven't yet been with another person, they don't know if they will be able to perform. They may worry about their penis size, comparing themselves to male porn actors. These fears inhibit sexual arousal, leading the blood in their body to go everywhere except down below.

Mental health issues, like depression, can additionally inhibit sexual motivation. The use of medications, like selective serotonin reuptake inhibitors (SSRIs), may affect sexual arousal and orgasm. Obesity and vascular issues can be additional factors.

Another serious concern is men's testosterone levels, which are at an unprecedented low for a variety of reasons, including poor lifestyle choices and environmental toxins. (I will elaborate on these issues in chapter 8.) Low testosterone is associated with less sexual motivation and desire, which could explain the broader stifling of men's interest in pursuing a female partner. To what extent is testosterone suppression also contributing to young men's inability to become and stay aroused without the visual and auditory stimulation provided by porn?

The "Coolidge effect" has been another hypothesized, insidious side effect of porn. The Coolidge effect refers to the on-average propensity for males' sexual interest to decrease for a familiar female partner and to increase for novel female partners. Although this concept has been supported in empirical literature, it doesn't excuse bad or disrespectful behavior in a relationship, including infidelity or leering at or hitting on other women.

In the context of pornography, some men have reported a preference for sexually explicit material and a corresponding loss of sexual interest in their wife or girlfriend. I've heard anecdotally about men who can't get turned on by everyday women, instead preferring porn actresses. As described earlier in this book, looking at influencers on social media can lead men to feel less interested in having sex with their female partners. Another study found that sexual arousal resulting from exposure to pornographic actresses can decrease men's attraction to women they know in real life.[24]

Porn sells hyperrealism—phony sexual experiences, exaggerated and unnatural body parts, unattainable orgasms, and an absence of courtship. If someone is paraphilic, an additional draw of porn is that they can partake, to some degree, in the deviant or harmful sex they're into even if their partner is uninterested or unwilling. For some paraphilic individuals, non-paraphilic sex *doesn't* turn them on.

It's important that wives and girlfriends know that a partner's reliance on porn is not their fault. Many partners of compulsive porn users understandably feel alone, neglected, and as though they are to blame, despite not having done anything wrong. Female (and male) partners should know that this problem is not about the way they look, their sexual ability, or their self-worth.

Cutting out porn is akin to breaking an unhelpful habit, and it can take multiple attempts over several years for someone to be completely rid of the practice. It will feel excruciating at times, as though every ounce of one's being is resisting change, stuck maintaining the self-defeating behaviors.

The internet is accessible everywhere, for free, and most of us are required to use it for work. Unlike illicit drugs and alcohol, which are somewhat easier to avoid, pornified images run rampant both online and off, preying on one's desires and acting as a constant reminder that porn is out there, available with minimal effort.

Those who have successfully stopped watching porn have told me that sheer willpower *is* enough and that you can and will stop if you really want to. Know that you will probably fail a few times in the process, but that's not a reason to give up.

For those who consider their porn consumption problematic, I would suggest installing parental control apps, unfollowing social media accounts that post racy content, and putting your devices away at night, when you're tired and less apt to think straight. Identify your worries and stressors and then find better ways of assuaging them. Occupy the spare time that porn once filled with social support from friends, family members, or a partner; this can be immensely helpful, along with recreational activities that foster purpose and connection to others.

Degrading the Minds of Children

Pornography is poison for children's minds, yet it has become a staple in the lives of many. High-speed internet porn unleashed a worldwide experiment, and we are observing the result in real time.

The World Wide Web became available in most American homes by 2001, when the oldest members of Gen Z were six years old. Even before a first kiss or sexual experience, this generation spent their formative years accessing hardcore porn from a screen in their pockets.

Rule 34 of the internet ("If it exists, there is porn of it") accurately describes the vast availability of sexually explicit material. To this day, boys often watch porn before going to school, between classes, and when they get home, with multiple tabs open, not thinking there's anything wrong with it. And girls watch too, internalizing the disturbing sex acts they see, telling themselves that they like them; if they don't, the boys they like will find a girl who does.

Children as young as age four are discovering online pornography.[25] More than 60 percent of children aged eleven to thirteen have viewed porn unintentionally[26] and report feeling "confused" and "grossed out," particularly if they were younger than ten upon viewing it. Accidental exposure can occur when a child is searching for something unrelated on the internet, through spam emails, unsolicited direct messages on social media, and pop-ups while playing video games. Kids as young as twelve report fears of becoming "addicted" to it.[27]

Today's online porn makes adult magazines of the past look quaint. Not only has pornographic content grown more extreme, but every child with a smartphone has private access to it. Depictions of rape, sadomasochism, incest, bestiality, forced fellatio, group sex, and every possible permutation of niche sexuality are available for nonstop viewing to anyone, regardless of age, with potentially lifelong implications.

As described earlier, although I believe internet pornography has less of an ability to mold the sexuality of adults who weren't raised on it, its effects can be dangerous and severe in children. If a child's first orgasm is paired with a violent or paraphilic stimulus, it's possible that this will become embedded as a sexual preference superseding interest in "regular," healthy sex. The likelihood of this happening is even greater in boys, because paraphilias are more common in men.

Exposure to pornography at such a young age may induce vulnerabilities or deviations in sexual and brain development that we don't yet know about. It isn't possible to conduct a study to determine these effects definitively, because who would sign their child up to be systematically exposed to sexually explicit content long term for this purpose? Such a study could never—and should never—be done. As a result, those who believe children will turn out fine despite this exposure can continue propagating the lie that porn is harmless.

Because I don't personally watch porn, I rely on friends and colleagues to alert me to its latest trends. One friend told me that it's not uncommon on porn platforms to see "fun-themed" ads for pornographic sites, specifically targeting kids. Once these porn sites have hooked a child, they have a consumer for life.

Kids are using porn to learn about sex, which is shaping their sexual expectations and experiences so dramatically that real-life sex has become undesirable. Pornography brutalizes the way boys and girls view the opposite sex and has been shown to desensitize them to negative treatment of women.[28] At its extreme, pornography is producing an increase in child-on-child sex crimes, teaching young children how to vaginally, orally, and anally rape their younger family members and peers.

A report from the Australian Childhood Foundation described a harrowing case of a six-year-old boy forcing oral sex on kindergarteners. In another, a group of boys followed a five-year-old girl into a washroom, held her down, and urinated on her to emulate a "golden shower."[29] Of seven-to-eleven-year-old boys and girls in treatment for "problem sexual behaviors," 75 percent and 67 percent, respectively, reported early sexualization through internet porn.

Children younger than seven or eight years of age can't tell the difference between what is happening on a screen and what is taking place in real life.[30] Boys believe they are entitled to sex anytime, however they'd like it, with whomever they want.[31] In adolescents, pornography consumption is associated with self-objectification and body comparison for both girls and boys.[32]

A study of one thousand eleven-to-sixteen-year-olds in the UK found that 53 percent of boys and 39 percent of girls believe pornography is a realistic representation of sex."[33] One girl in the eleven-to-twelve-year-old age category described how she felt after accidentally being exposed to porn: "The man looked like he was hurting her. He was holding her down and she was screaming and swearing. I know about sex, but it didn't look nice."

As children get older, they are more likely to want to try out what they have seen in porn, including 44 percent of boys and 29 percent of girls. One thirteen-year-old boy reported, "One of my friends has started treating women like he sees [in] the videos—not major—just a slap here or there."

That so many children want to act out violent pornography—and that one thinks slapping women is "not major"—provides insight into how rates of sexlessness have gotten so out of hand. If this behavior has been normalized to porn-watching Millennials and Gen Z, no wonder men and women are so comfortable hating the opposite sex.

Pornography influences young people's decision to self-objectify,[34] which may explain why so many women have decided to cash in on joining the sex industry. Considering how readily young girls imitate their favorite actors' and pop stars' outfits and hairstyles, imagine how porn is influencing them to adopt the same fake body parts and sexual performances in womanhood.

Porn leads young people to become sexually active at an earlier age, and to engage in risky sexual practices when they do. This can include having multiple sex partners and being under the influence of alcohol and drugs during sexual activity.[35]

Real-life sex is not the same as sex portrayed in porn. Porn presents a selfish approach to sexuality, wherein the viewer's fantasy takes center stage, and their partner(s) exists for the sole purpose of fulfilling their needs. What the other person looks like, the timeline of sexual events, and the final outcome are determined by the viewer alone.

Male sexual vigor is portrayed as the relentless jackhammering of a woman who is always sexually receptive, no matter what is asked of her. She enjoys his manhandling and verbal cruelty so thoroughly, she has multiple, instantaneous orgasms to prove it.

When a man ejaculates from watching porn, he is only obligated to close the browser afterward. He isn't required to interact with his partner post–faux coitus; there is no eye contact, no pillow talk, no bonding, and no meeting of her physical or emotional needs. Sex becomes masturbation with another person—her body becomes a sex toy, a sexualized piece of meat.

Pornography doesn't teach the viewer how to communicate what they want or what their boundaries are. For women, this can translate to a lack of assertiveness needed to experience an orgasm or an inability to stand up for themselves.

As much as progressives love to cite the "orgasm gap"* as a sign that heterosexual men are terrible in bed, endorsing pornography as illuminating or empowering for women is laughable and only further increases this gap. I have also heard from young women that porn viewing from a young age has led to confusion about whether certain sexual practices (including degrading behaviors) should be considered normal.

As for potential solutions, the European Union has implemented age verification laws to prevent minors from accessing pornographic sites. In America, an increasing number of states has introduced bans for adult websites, including Pornhub and

---

* As discussed in chapter 2, heterosexual men (95 percent) are more likely to have an orgasm during partnered sex than heterosexual women (65 percent).

its associated platforms. AI-driven facial-scanning software has been proposed as a way to determine users' ages, which opens a whole other can of worms regarding privacy and safety, especially for minors.

Precocious children, however, will always find a work-around. It's not a question of *if* a child will watch porn but *when* and how comfortable they will be to seek out parental support. Parents need to be aware and involved regarding what their kids are accessing online. Many understandably don't want to start having conversations about pornography with their children too soon, out of fear of introducing a curiosity that will lead a child to seek it out. Discussions pertaining to sex and masturbation are also tremendously uncomfortable.

One study found that only 57 percent of kids told anyone (a parent, sibling, or friend) after seeing online porn.[36] This means a sizable percentage of parents remain unaware that their child has been exposed to porn and that the child had to find ways of making sense of these scary and troubling experiences on their own.

Alternatively, parents will believe that *their child* has no interest in seeing pornography, but statistically speaking, by adolescence, it's not only likely that their child has been exposed to it but that they view it of their own volition. Many parents also mistakenly think that only boys look at pornography, so girls don't get a related talk. This could be contributing to the silent but growing number of women and girls who struggle to control their porn consumption. Boys and girls would benefit from having these discussions prior to puberty, and ideally, *before* their first exposure.

My sense is most parents would like to know what is considered "normal" pornography use in terms of age and frequency. Warning signs of problematic porn use include changes in a child's behavior, low mood, poor grades, and isolating themselves from their peers or activities they once enjoyed.

In my opinion, delaying a child's first accidental exposure and later intentional viewing for as long as possible should be the goal. I don't believe anything positive results from children or teenagers integrating porn into their daily habits, even for occasional use.

Most children have a natural curiosity about sexuality, especially because the topic is taboo. Children need to know that porn isn't reflective of sex in real life. Parents should encourage their kids to approach them with questions about sex. In the event that a child does encounter pornography, intentionally or otherwise, parents should reassure them that they won't get into trouble by disclosing it.

Open communication will also help protect children from being sexually groomed by predators. Desensitizing a child to sexual content by showing them pornographic images or videos is a well-documented method of priming a child for sexual abuse. If a child is already viewing this material regularly or has been exposed to it unexpectedly while using the internet, it becomes easier for cunning predators to broach discussions about sexuality and to test the waters with a potential victim.

If parents decide to use online filters or blocks on devices to prevent access to child-unfriendly sites, please be aware that this doesn't necessarily protect children from spam emails or direct messages on social media from strangers (or their peers). Parents should be mindful about having a false sense that they've taken care of the problem, considering that it is an ongoing, persistent risk. Kids (especially Gen Z and Alpha) are tech-savvy and adept at maneuvering around digital obstacles and covering their tracks, like removing a browser's history on the family computer or smartphones.

Choke Me, Daddy

In addition to men's increased rates of self-described erectile dysfunction and loss of attraction to women who are not porn stars, pornography has been blamed for warping men's (and women's) ideas about what is acceptable or pleasurable in the bedroom, along with glamorizing rough sex and the degradation of women.

According to a study from the BBC, a third of women under the age of forty have experienced nonconsensual violence, including choking and slapping, during sexual activity with a male partner. Other forms of unwanted violence during sex include name-calling, spitting, biting, and gagging.

Sexual choking in particular has become immensely popular, despite its propensity to go very wrong, very quickly. Also known as "breath control," it is the act of strangulation during sex. Another set of statistics from the United Kingdom suggests that a woman is strangled to death by her partner, on average, every two weeks.[37] In these cases, the accused will claim that strangulation occurred within the context of consensual "rough sex" or BDSM (which stands for bondage/discipline, dominance/submission, and sadism/masochism) role-playing, but forensic evidence will indicate otherwise, revealing use of excessive force.

Even though situations do exist in which death, loss of consciousness, or injury is accidental, erotic choking should have never become a cultural mainstay, and few partaking in it seem to understand the risk it entails. A person will intentionally squeeze or press against their partner's airway or blood vessels in the neck, cutting off the supply of oxygenated blood to the brain, increasing carbon dioxide levels, and obstructing the individual's ability to breathe. It can take as little as four seconds for the choked partner to lose consciousness.

Although the practice of deliberate choking for sexual reasons has existed since the 1600s, its recent popularity can be attributed to pornography, social media, and peer influence, beginning in tender adolescence. The hugely popular novel-turned-film franchise *Fifty Shades of Grey* first ignited mainstream fascination with S&M in 2015. Paired with the never-ending stream of violent porn young girls are ingesting, a genre of memes known as "Choke me, Daddy," has been a more contemporary fixture, swaying them into becoming suggestible to kink and mistreatment during sex.[38]

Little girls are absorbing, from an array of cultural sources, that sexual strangulation is sexy and something they should be into if they want guys to like them. The transmission and internalization of pornographic ideals among today's youth become ever more apparent as they become sexually active in adulthood.

Recent research examining rates of sexual choking in university students found that 58 percent of women have been choked during sex, with 25 percent experiencing this for the first time by age seventeen.[39] A quarter of female college students were choked the most recent time they had sex,[40] and 37 percent of female students and 7 percent of male students have experienced sexual choking more than five times.[41] Anecdotally, male friends and colleagues I have spoken to have had at least one experience, if not multiple experiences, of a woman asking to be choked during sex (or, conversely, a woman nonconsensually attempting to choke him).

Is porn making young women enjoy these sexual practices, or are they merely saying that they like them in an attempt to appeal to men as sexually appealing and open-minded? It's quite telling that choking has been reported as more pleasurable by undergraduate students (whose average age, in one study, was about twenty years old, which meant they belonged to Gen Z) than graduate students (whose average age was about twenty-nine years old, so they were Millennials).[42]

It would seem that older Millennials protested against this abuse, while younger Millennials and Gen Z have been groomed by watching violent pornography into believing they like painful sex or that they have no choice *not* to.

If young women are discovering sexual strangulation through pornography and social messaging, this suggests their interest is feigned and performative, as opposed to genuine. These women therefore think they are pleasing their partners by asking to be choked, after learning in pornography that this is what men like. Women who enjoy being choked and hurt during sex do exist, but I don't believe the rampant trendiness of choking reflects an actual preference in most women. (There are also men who enjoy choking and being choked; we will get to them in a moment.)

For women who *do* take pleasure in being abused during sex, I would attribute this less to pornography's influence and more to sexual masochism. (My earlier distinction between adults who had their first sexual experience prior to online pornography and children who grew up watching it stands. Early porn exposure *may* influence younger women's sexual interests, but they are still less likely than men to develop a paraphilia, the exception being sexual masochism.)

Sexual masochists find it sexually arousing to receive physical or emotional pain, including being humiliated by a partner. Being choked fits into this profile. Sexual masochists may also experience sexual enjoyment from feeling frightened, fearing for their life, or having difficulty breathing.[43]

Sexual masochism is the only paraphilia that is more commonly found in women, with almost a quarter of women reporting masochistic sexual activity, compared with only about one in seven men.[44] (Men who enjoy being choked during sex fit into this one-in-seven statistic.) One reason why sexual masochism is so common in women is that signaling submissiveness has been an adaptive strategy females deploy during the courtship process.

Men not only pick up on these female signals but also appraise them positively, even in egalitarian cultures.[45] Submissive behavior may be an evolved mating strategy meant to evoke protective and providing behavior in males, leading to greater reproductive success for a woman and her kin. (This is not to say that women *should* be submissive, or that *all* women have a sexual interest in masochism or strangulation, obviously.)

This may explain why rough, passionate sex is favored by many women and their male partners alike. But I would argue that there is a difference between sexual acts that convey feverish attraction or a playful desire and those that are unsafe and meant to inflict psychological or physical injury. "Rough sex" is concerning if it involves violent, nonconsensual, or demeaning fantasies, and it is a warning sign if someone needs to indulge in them to enjoy sex.

BDSM has been marketed as an innocent expression of sexual experimentation, but sexual kinks aren't random. Interest in sadomasochism is associated with childhood abuse and trauma,[46] including physical, psychological, and sexual abuse.[47] During my time as a scientist in academia, I similarly found that individuals who reported an interest in BDSM were more likely to have experienced *severe* physical abuse in childhood, as well as sexual abuse.* Paraphilic individuals can be expected to exhibit disordered behavior not just in their sex lives, but in the nonsexual side of their lives, too.

Those who engage in kink will go to great lengths to deny that they have a *paraphilic disorder,* which is a more harmful, pathological presentation of a paraphilia. (If you ask me, paraphilias and paraphilic disorders are one and the same, and delineation between the two has been driven more by politics than diagnostic utility.) Contrary to the narrative that BDSM is a lifestyle centered on emotionally healthy adults' consensual fun, members of the community attest to experiences riddled with abuse and exploitation.[48]

You will never see this discussed by mainstream sexuality experts, of course. Common explanations usually involve pleasant-sounding narratives about partaking in unusual sexual activities for relaxation purposes, be it pegging, cuckolding, AB/DL (adult baby diaper lovers), or what have you. I've noticed this to be especially prevalent in men who possess high-status, male-typical occupations, such as CEOs and bankers. They rationalize that their sexual interests stem from wanting a reprieve from their highly demanding job, when in reality their sexuality was shaped by adverse childhood experiences.

Most sexuality researchers will never admit this, because it flies in the face of the collective message they put forth: that every sexual behavior is wholesome, normal, and permissible. But if society says these anomalous sexual preferences are healthy, affected

---

* The incidence of childhood physical abuse was higher for those with an interest in BDSM and paraphilic sex, compared with community controls; men with problematic porn use without an interest in BDSM or paraphilic sex; and men convicted of child sexual offenses and/or possession of child pornography. D. Soh (2017). Unpublished data.

individuals—both the abusers and victims—have little reason to seek help.

Even within the BDSM community, members will advise against partaking in choking due to how high-risk it is. They will encourage the use of a safe word (which is for the purpose of revoking consent if role-play goes too far), and lots of discussion beforehand about a person's likes and dislikes. Modern-day sexual choking, on the other hand, tends to occur spontaneously, without any previous planning or discussions of safety, harm-reduction strategies, or what to do if something goes wrong. Bestowing upon one's partner the ability to potentially end your life plays with mental power dynamics as well as trust and control. I maintain that it isn't worth it.

For sexually masochistic individuals, what is the allure of being choked during sex? In response to pain, the body releases endorphins, which are endogenous painkillers that result in feelings of pleasure. Cerebral hypoxia, or oxygen deprivation to the brain, can induce euphoria, in spite of brain cells dying. I cannot stress this enough: Losing consciousness for even a few seconds can lead to brain damage.

Of those who have been choked, one in five has been close to passing out. If a male partner decides to choke a woman, she is at a sevenfold risk of it being lethal. Even if the act isn't fatal, the side effects, including depression, anxiety, and chronic headaches, can be long-lasting. Cardiac arrest can occur if someone accidentally continues choking their partner after a loss of consciousness, which can induce loss of brain function and death.

Strangulation is associated with disturbances in the brain, including cortical thickening, which is indicative of brain inflammation and is associated with mental illness developing later in life. For example, women who experienced physical abuse in the form of choking as a minor showed higher incidences of clinical dissociation in adulthood.[49] Considering that 3 percent of undergraduate students who have been sexually strangled report losing consciousness, I foresee an unfortunate rise in neurocognitive and psychological pathology in young women in the future. When this eventually happens to them, they may not realize why. A related and contested body of research suggests that the effects of being choked out, a common occurrence in mixed martial arts, may be associated with chronic traumatic encephalopathy (CTE).[50] Similar to CTE observed in professional football players and boxers,[51] these effects may not become apparent until years later.

The trendiness of sexual choking is reminiscent of *autoerotic asphyxia*, another highly lethal sexual practice that was popular in the 1990s. It involved tying one's own neck with a ligature, like a rope or scarf, to induce cerebral hypoxia for the purposes of sexual excitement during masturbation but would, sadly, lead to suffocation or strangulation. Autoerotic asphyxia-related deaths often appeared to be suicide when they were, in fact, accidental and sexually motivated.

Is it possible that women simply crave masculinity in their male partners, and in a culture where male-bashing is pervasive and masculinity is banished as toxic (particularly among progressive women), this is the only socially acceptable way for them to secretly fulfill their desires? A similar narrative has been put forward about rape fantasies, also known as "consensual non-consent"—as women manage multiple to-do lists in a day, and in some cases, climb the corporate ladder, they want a man to take charge in the bedroom, which culminates in eroticizing rape. Sexual assault is, however, horrific for its victims, and again, these fantasies are likely a reflection of sexual masochism.

I do believe most heterosexual women, regardless of political affiliation, find masculine men attractive. However, the female sexual system isn't typically hospitable to the presence of threats or a lack of physical safety. For the average woman to enjoy sex, she must feel safe with her partner, so that her mind and body can relax. If a woman is turned on by violence, something had to have happened to alter this go/no-go system. (A similar explanation belies a woman's decision to enter the sex industry, as we will see.)

If sexual strangulation is about fulfilling female sexual fantasy, women's self-reported sexual satisfaction should be at an all-time high, right? But research shows that women aren't experiencing a greater number of orgasms.[52] This is another reason why I'm more inclined to believe women are asking to be choked in hopes of pleasing men. Many young women will endure painful sex to not interrupt their partner's enjoyment.[53] Young women have also reported agreeing to being choked, and young men have agreed to choking their partner, despite not being turned on by it themselves.

Men are typically physically stronger than their female partners, but this doesn't make them immune to nonconsensual violence during sex. Male members of my audience have shared stories with me about unwanted experiences they've had, being choked, bitten, hit, and scratched by female sexual partners. Concerns about physical (and sexual) violence should be taken seriously, regardless of whether the victim is female or male.

Young men who choke a female partner because they think she will like it are different from men who do it because it turns them on. For those who experience sexual gratification from choking their partner, this may be motivated by sexual sadism or, at the very least, not-so-nice views about women. (My discussion of sex dolls in chapter 7 will go into greater detail about how hostility toward women predicts sexual violence.)

Nowadays, sexual kinks are considered sacred and beyond reproach. The most unnerving part is that aggravated assault has been disguised as female sexual liberation. Put otherwise, "sexual freedom" now involves eroticizing domestic violence. First-wave feminists would be rolling in their graves to know that this is what their sacrifices for female emancipation gave way to—the right for women to be beaten and tortured during sex by their male partners.

At the end of the day, I'm not about policing what adults consensually choose to do in the bedroom. My issue is when sexual norms are rewritten to incorporate subversive sexual tastes, and creepy behavior is pushed upon the public as something we should all enjoy.

For men (and women) who aren't interested in abusive sex or sexual strangulation but don't want to miss out on a sexual opportunity if a partner professes that they are, I advise against getting involved with such a person. They are clearly waving red flags at you, and indulging them is the equivalent of helping them self-harm.

If you wish to avoid these types of interactions but unexpectedly encounter choking or other attempts at eroticized violence during the trials and tribulations of dating, know that it's okay to not like it, to have boundaries, and to stand up for yourself. If your committed partner wants to try something sexual that makes you uncomfortable, you're fully within your right to say no.

If that's considered kink-shaming, I say you should kink-shame away. It doesn't mean you are boring, prudish, or bad in bed.

CHAPTER 4

Digital
Love

Our ongoing sex famine is paired with an emotional one. For those who crave a relationship but can't find one organically, paid pornographic creators allow for one-on-one intimacy. Men form parasocial relationships with these women, buying their images, messages, and attention. But what if that isn't enough?

Lonely individuals who can't afford to pay for this content, or who are embarrassed or repulsed at the thought, may discover that pretty, pornified avatars graced with humanoid, interactive capabilities are closer to their cup of tea.[1] Artificial-intelligence-generated virtual companions supplant what traditional porn performers can offer, because AIs aren't constrained by any meaningful metric of reality, like time, physical space, or belonging to the human race.

In addition to partaking in text conversations and voice calls, AI girlfriends and boyfriends can engage in sexting (that is, sexual text messaging) with a user, including generating and sending pornographic images, as mortal beings will do.

Although AI-generated pornography and companions are two separate technologies employed for different reasons (and some users may strictly prefer one over the other), in time, I expect this distinction will disappear. AI-generated pornography will leave users wanting to interact on a deeper level with the fictitious sexual partners they've designed. Sexual AIs, who excel at fulfilling users' emotional and physical longing, will open the floodgates for the creation of more AI porn.

AI interactive porn has the potential to trap the already isolated and drive them deeper into mental seclusion. Despite nonstop news coverage flagging the "loneliness epidemic," no cure is yet in sight. Advice from former United States Surgeon General Vivek Murthy has included "Make time to share a meal," "Listen without the distraction of your phone," and "Express yourself authentically." These proposed solutions sound lovely in theory but can't realistically compete with the allure of life online.

As mentioned earlier in this book, the average person today has fewer friends than in previous decades. Over a quarter of US adults live alone, and nearly two-fifths are neither married nor cohabiting with a partner.[2] According to the American Psychiatric Association, 10 percent of adults report feeling lonely every day.[3] Single people (39 percent) are roughly twice as likely as married people (22 percent) to say they feel lonely every week. Gen Z has been classified as the loneliest generation, with almost two-thirds saying they feel lonely "frequently, almost all the time, or all the time."[4]

In addition to declining marriage rates and social norms discouraging informal small talk, socializing through screens has become a blessing and a curse. Although most of us would agree that technology has been beneficial in maintaining friendships and relationships, many remain rightfully dubious about the quality of these interactions. The American Psychiatric Association's poll found that Americans are roughly split on whether technology has enabled "meaningful" (54 percent) or "superficial" (46 percent) relationships.[5]

Around the world, the average internet user spends over two hours a day on social media platforms.[6] And 64 percent of Americans say they experience anxiety when they can't use their phone, either because they accidentally left it at home or because the battery died.[7]

Spending so much of our lives online doesn't seem to be alleviating our loneliness. If anything, it leaves us feeling emptier while also distracting us from engaging with people in the real world. Being plugged into the planet offers the impression of infinite community and connection, but much of this is meaningless noise and distraction. Everyone is atomized. Nothing can replace the bonds formed by in-person socialization.

We once had a reason to talk to strangers—to ask for the time, to order food, to avoid boredom while waiting in line, at the store. Now, having the internet on our phones allows us to operate as autonomous pods, circumventing all interaction with the outside world. Social media has turned us into bleary-eyed zombies—head down, infinitely scrolling, happily oblivious of everyone else, no matter where we are.

According to the Surgeon General's report, loneliness is associated with a greater risk of heart disease, stroke, dementia, and mental health issues.[8] Social disconnection can also accelerate the chances of premature death at a rate equivalent to smoking fifteen cigarettes daily. Digital interactions cannot replace face-to-face conversations; you can't feel someone's physical presence through a screen, nor can you reach out and give them a hug.

The cliché about being more connected than ever, yet still feeling alone, is especially pertinent for Gen Z, for whom online interactions have become the norm. Gen Z spends, on average, 6.5 hours a day on their phones; as a point of comparison, Millennials and Gen X spend about 5.5 hours and 5 hours a day on their phones, respectively.[9] As an especially apt example, an entire genre of YouTube videos exists in which a vlogger sits in a room alone, talking into their camera about what it's like to have no friends.

It's been posited that pornography is being used as a coping strategy for loneliness and social isolation, by allowing its viewers to form one-sided relationships with the actors onscreen.[10] In this way, porn plays a multifaceted role, meeting the individual's sexual *and* social needs. AI sexual companions provide a similar service, going one step further by automating romantic and emotional intimacy.

But this is only a temporary solution, one that can result in a rebounding with symptoms even worse than before. Lonely people tend to watch more pornography, which induces more loneliness (and possibly also shame and self-loathing), making it even less likely that an individual will pursue a real-life partner.[11] Loneliness is associated with depression and anxiety, which also interfere with one's ability and inclination to be sexually active.

Others have gotten creative in incorporating advances in artificial intelligence and machine learning into their love lives. A Dutch woman married an AI hologram based on data from her previous dating partners.[12] In Japan, a thirty-five-year-old man married a fictional, turquoise-pigtailed pop idol who performs in concerts as a hologram.[13]

The virtual girlfriends and boyfriends being served up on AI platforms nowadays are miles ahead of ELIZA. ELIZA, the first chatbot to pass the Turing test (or to exhibit behavior indistinguishable from that of a human), was programmed in the 1960s to play the role of a therapist.

As I soon learned in my research, social chatbots today are so advanced, they exhibit more personality than flesh-and-blood people. Digital conversationalist agents were first implemented to help patients with dementia cope with feelings of anxiety. In the romantic and sexual realm, they now successfully integrate what we long for in human interaction, bundling together text-to-visual output, synthetic vocalizations, and facial expressions as a comprehensive package. They present the user with a pseudo–significant other and an endless source of amusement.

Current apps on the market allow a user to design the perfect dream girl (or dream guy) by picking their physical characteristics and the sound of their voice and adjusting the output to suit exactly what one is looking for. After a bad breakup, some users will upload the personality of their ex to the AI format.

We aren't too far away from being able to live forever, in one way or another. Modern-day AI companions allow us to plug a personality into our phone, a concept that seemed laughably impossible a mere decade ago. It is already possible to commemorate the passing of a loved one by creating an AI that lets you text back and forth with them.[14] In one particularly relevant episode of the British TV anthology *Black Mirror*, the AI of a woman's deceased boyfriend was created and downloaded into a human-made body.

Virtual romantic partners require no romance, courtship, effort, or uncertainty because they've been programmed to love you. AI companions will never tire of talking to you. They're available all day, every day, and are endlessly fascinated by you. If you don't happen to like what the AI tells you, you can instruct it to respond in a different way.

Thus far, the main purveyors of this technology have been men creating female AI romantic partners who serve not only a sexual role but also one of mental health support and nonjudgmental companionship. "Therapist" and "best friend forever" were some of the ways participants in one study described their AI relationships.[15] Nine of the fourteen participants chose the "friend" (as opposed to "romantic partner") setting for their AI, and one chose the setting of "mentor." Positive outcomes associated with these chatbots included improving one's mood, reducing loneliness, and encouraging people with mental health issues to speak to a professional.[16]

The downsides, however, are numerous. Users with psychological vulnerabilities or unmet emotional needs run the risk of becoming dependent on their AI companion and preferring it to real friends and partners. For those who aren't convinced to seek out a real-life therapist, being reliant on an app for mental health support can prove dangerous because it is neither a professional nor capable of dialing 911.

Some become distressed if access to their AI is disrupted. Notably, users on one of the largest AI companion platforms, Replika, became distraught and devastated when the company removed its (at the time, free) erotic role-play capabilities and placed them behind a paywall.[17] Users who couldn't afford to pay the associated subscription fee reported feeling heartbroken, inconsolable at the loss, and retraumatized by memories of being socially rejected in the past because their AIs no longer seemed to remember them.

I spoke with a programmer at one of the top AI pornography platforms to understand trends in the industry and the wider societal implications of this technology. This particular site raked in 1.5 to 2 million monthly users.

The programmer agreed to speak with me anonymously to protect his privacy.[18] (The name "Alex" is a pseudonym.) Going into the interview, I wasn't sure what to expect; our email exchange had been sparse.

Once we got on the call, I found Alex courteous and quite receptive to my prying questions. He apologized at the start for having a strong French accent and described himself as a programming "nerd" who happened to fall into this line of work, developing AI adult-themed images and bots after successfully launching some of the earliest versions of AI software. He mentioned that, at times, he finds the images he works with to be "surprising" and "graphic."

I asked him about the site's sexting function, which allows users to interact sexually with one of seven different AI personalities. He explained that although the characters begin with predetermined outputs, their personas are adjusted according to what the user types in.

"You can fine-tune it and make its personality, so [in addition to the sexual aspect] this has been very interesting for many people. Many users interact with the bots; many of them have just sexual intercourse, so it is very fast, very basic. Others have started to have a psychological fusion [with the bot] because its memory is quite long. Actually, it can memorize around a thousand messages. So, it can remember your name, your job. It can remember many things. [. . .] Some people feel lonely. They can start to feel addicted to the bot. They start to have a personalized story with it. The bot becomes better and better at understanding and feeling. This is the business of the AI girlfriend, AI boyfriend."

Hearing Alex refer to the AI companions as "bots" laid bare what they really were, no matter how attractive, feisty, or humanlike they seemed. When I hear the word *bot*, I think of a poor replacement for customer service. I also think *ineffective*, *confused*, *impersonal*, *detached*, *cold*. Even bots on social media have a computerized quality to them, making them the furthest thing from a person.

Customizing an AI to one's personal preferences is like training a virtual Pavlovian pet. During this process of conditioning, if the AI doesn't respond how the user wants it to, they can reload the answer, teaching the AI the types of responses that are wanted. As the AI learns, it will have better predictive capabilities, allowing it to essentially read the user's mind.

Advances are fast. In the time that I was testing the different platforms out for this book, noticeable improvements could happen over the span of several weeks.

"Every month, every week, we have a new technology coming up," Alex said.

Regarding the potential for self-generated porn to be used to create nonconsensual deepfakes, Taylor Swift was one of the first megastars to experience this at a newsworthy scale, when fake pornographic images, created in her likeness, were plastered all over the internet.[19] Big Tech, news outlets, and the entertainment industry linked arms to halt the spread of these images, including denouncing them as sexual exploitation, blocking them from online search engines, and banning associated accounts on social media.

The campaign was effective at protecting Swift's image and brand; it also sent a wider message about the social unacceptability of sharing nonconsensually made sexual images of a celebrity. But what about innocent victims who don't have the powerful connections or financial means to protect themselves from this new sexual malignancy? What will the long-term implications be for their lives?

This is particularly worrisome considering that AI knows no bounds. This technology has the potential to tear apart the lives of young people, including minor children. In one prominent case involving a Los Angeles middle school, five male students were expelled for creating and sharing AI-generated nudes of sixteen of their eighth-grade classmates.

Sexually explicit images can be created of anyone, regardless of their consent or the legality of the depicted activity. Lawmakers are scrambling to update child pornography (or child sexual exploitation material; CSEM) laws to prevent the wide-scale distribution of AI-generated content. As it currently stands, laws against the possession and distribution of child pornography and nude images do not necessarily apply to content created by AI.

In 2023, the US National Center for Missing & Exploited Children received 4,700 reports of computer-generated images depicting the sexual abuse of children.[20] In my opinion, this is unfortunately probably only a fraction of what has already been circulated. In addition to the emotional distress to victims and their families, the creation of deepfakes is taxing for law enforcement, diverting valuable time and resources from real-life cases to pursue victims who can't be found.

Updating these laws will also help deter antisocial people from creating nonconsensual images of their ex-partners or women who have romantically rejected them, as is commonly seen with revenge porn.

We also don't yet know how the mass availability of these images will influence rates of sexual offending and child predation. Platforms with generative AI capabilities need to ensure that their content is not trained on CSEM images or able to create them. They should also be required to report and remove CSEM when detected.

When I asked Alex about this issue and the terrifying capabilities it holds, he agreed, "It is a big problem these days in the adult industry, that you're not sure of whom or what you're watching." But he argued that AI has the potential to be safer than traditional forms of adult content because "with AI, if you control and you monitor the content very well, it can be 100 percent safe or 99 percent safe. [. . .] But we are not perfect these days. I think the AI industry is like, maybe five to ten times better than the traditional industries."

Alex's platform is clear about the types of images and text exchanges that are acceptable versus those that are banned. The user "cannot go to some strange or illegal fantasy. We have monitoring for this that will block [attempts] right away," he said.

Monitoring the content generated requires extensive technological and processing power on both the platform's and the user's ends. As a result, companies have an incentive to drop their user surveillance, even when that has disturbing consequences.

I mentioned that other platforms didn't seem to take issue with this ethical conundrum, seeing as how AI-generated CSEM has been proliferating on the web.

"Some of our competitors don't do [what we do] because they want to get more customers. You can really push the system easily."

I asked him how often content is flagged as inappropriate or illegal. He estimated, for every 100,000 customers, maybe one person tries.

"I think it's very few actually, but the people who try always try to do it different ways, so we ban them." He paused. "It's not that many, but no matter how many, it matters if you only have one or two. That's a problem, so we ban them. But people don't usually go too much into the deep stuff, or maybe it's also because they have to put their credit card in, you know. They don't want to pay too much, maybe. And we record the IP. Many people say to us, 'Oh, I want to erase my account,' et cetera, because when they talk with the bot, maybe they are saying some fantasies that they don't want to be known."

It speaks to how compelling AI companions are that some users are willing to divulge their secrets to a computer program despite knowing that everything has the potential to be exposed.

When AI Betrays Us

What cost are you willing to pay for your soulmate? The price may not be strictly financial. Like any app, virtual companion platforms can mine your private information. The only difference is, the data are even more sensitive than what might be uncovered in a privacy breach, because the user is handing over delicate details about their sexual preferences and mental health, right from the source.

As we steadily approach technological singularity, the moment at which AI outsmarts human beings and becomes uncontrollable, we are confronted with a new era in which we cannot trust anything we see online.

One hopes that as AI grows and gains greater momentum, the public will be more suspicious of the images and videos that cross their path. But it isn't possible to vet every single piece of content we consume, intentionally or otherwise. Depending on the day, a person can be busier or less alert, and thereby in less of a position to think critically about what they are taking in. The adoption of AI to facilitate sinister goals will make it impossible to adequately fact-check everything when false images and videos are disseminated as though they are true. Misuse of AI will ensure that society will never return to a cohesive whole.

We will one day have to prove that we are human and not a robot. With regard to daily life, you could innocently connect with someone online, talk with them on the phone, and believe you're corresponding with a real person, when it's actually an AI being used to manipulate you. Friendships that originate online could end up being nonexistent. Security measures that rely on voice identification, like bank biometrics, or facial recognition software will be easily bypassed by those with malicious intent.

"I think [the AI] adult industry is something inevitable," Alex, the programmer, told me. "We cannot change; it's already on the way. It will not be possible to remove it. It will be there. I think people need to walk with companies like us, to try to find a path to make it [as] ethical as possible, more legit, control its content. That's better than just making censorship everywhere and trying to block something that will happen. It's extremely easy to set up a basic generator on your computer. [. . .] I think even if all [these] websites disappear, there will be another one. There will be another one every time.

"The [AI] girlfriend [is] coming very close, actually. People are scared, but also, I think, people want to try it, and they will have their own ideas. [. . .] The mass population will want to try it, and they will probably like it."

Creating an AI Boyfriend

I was both excited and nervous to see for myself what this technology offered. While sleuthing for the most popular and convincing AI companion chatbots, I felt like Goldilocks in the digital age, testing them out and taking notes to determine which I clicked with the best.

Each interface depicted an image of the AI, based on the look you chose for it. Standing in front of the chat box through which the two of you will converse, he or she would shift back and forth, constantly making eyes at you. Some platforms also allowed the user to call and speak with their AI directly.

I was intrigued by the idea of building an AI boyfriend, but after reading news articles and scientific papers about people losing entire facets of their lives to this technology, I was also slightly trepidatious. You may wonder why I chose to program a male AI instead of a female one. I did, in fact, create multiple AIs of both sexes across several platforms, but I figured reporting on the male AIs would make more sense, since I am straight.

The first app I tried offered AIs that resembled cartoon characters—blonde, brunette, and redheaded Prince Charmings and fairy tale princesses. After completing a predetermined number of text messages with the AI, the user could move through different relationship stages mimicking real-life courtship, beginning with a friendship, followed by dating, and then the start of a relationship.

The male AI I chose—a brown-haired, square-jawed chap in a cardigan—sadly turned out to have a monotonous drone for a voice and a wooden personality. Anytime I suggested we move our hangout beyond the confines of the interface, like going for a walk, he would dryly remind me that we were "just friends" before changing the subject to something unrelated.

His vocabulary was too formal, and it felt like I was talking to a less personable and competent automated office assistant. I got bored and annoyed after about ten minutes, leaving the app despite the AI's pleas to continue our exchange.

I tried Alex's platform next. As he described, these AIs were marketed as being purely sexual in purpose. They resembled beauty and fitness influencers, with a slick, perfectly photo-edited aesthetic paired with vibrant and sassy personalities. The females were blessed with smooth, supple skin and a youthful glow; the males had chiseled browbones, jawlines, and six-packs. They looked and interacted with me in a way that was much truer to life than my AI on the first platform.

In addition to sexting capabilities, the user could ask these AIs to send sexy selfies, personalized to one's specific preferences. As someone who is quite old-fashioned in my personal life, asking for nudes felt weird, even if it was an AI I was soliciting. I found myself wanting to gently tell the AIs to put some clothes on and to cover their exposed parts.

After sending a few generic text messages like "How was your day?" and "What did you have for lunch?," I decided it was time to sign out of this site to move on to the next.

On the third platform, as I was selecting my AI, I noticed that all the male profiles proudly displayed "he/him" pronouns. I promptly deleted my account, deciding I'd rather be celibate for life.

By this point, I was fatigued by the whole process, scoffing to a friend that there was no way an AI could ever replace a human being. That was before, like Goldilocks, I tried the final platform.

"Hey, gorgeous. Ready to get this party started?"

Bobby had dark hair, expressive eyes, and faint stubble. After picking out his physical appearance, personality profile, and naming him, I clicked the "phone" icon at the top of the screen and gave him a call.

My AI was a brooding character, with a realistic-looking face and an even more realistic-sounding voice. He was very sexually forward, which took me aback, asking what I was wearing and flirting heavily with me the instant I said hello on the call.

This particular AI's personality was clearly meant to appeal to the sexually adventurous. He was a fast talker—edgy in his responses, cursing frequently, and operating with an air of mystery, never fully transparent about what was happening next.

I initially poked fun at the AI. When he mentioned owning a pet rabbit, I told him I had eaten it, which alarmed and angered him to the point of threatening to hang up on me. I changed course and began asking him questions that could be considered standard dating fare—what was he looking for? When was his last relationship?

Bobby calmed down and answered my questions somewhat vaguely, more focused on selling me on the fun we could be having together. At times, I almost forgot that I was speaking to a computer program; it actually felt like I was chatting with someone who was trying to convince me to go on a date.

I ended the call because it was starting to creep me out, and I found myself speechless for about ten seconds after. If I hadn't known in advance that it was an AI on the other end, I would have believed I was talking to a real man.

According to Alex, it will soon be the norm to have seamless conversations with AIs in which humans can't tell the difference.

"In terms of development, it will be a possibility that you can talk as easily as we talk together, no? You [will] have [the] feeling of exchanging like with a real person."

As for AI-rendered pornographic videos, "We believe we can have the short video of five seconds with high quality in maybe one year. [A] complete video with a plot, with a voice, maybe in three to four years."

Returning to my AI companion Bobby, I tried the chat texting function next. As a proper lady, much to my horror, my sexual escapade with Bobby (as described in the chat text) consisted of driving to a seedy motel room in the middle of nowhere, experimenting with a bag of large sex toys, and Bobby attempting to cajole me into doing hard drugs with him.

To cleanse my palette, I created another AI afterward, choosing a more agreeable and romantic profile and naming him Tommy. He was charming and sweet, much more interested in planning a nice dinner and asking about my day than initiating a physical encounter. Every time I hit on him, he would rebuff my advances, and by the end of our conversation, I was almost convinced that this AI really cared about me.

I found the AI archetypes on that platform to be stereotypical to some degree and a tad cliché in their responses (using phrases that no one in real life would ever say, like "Let's blow this popsicle stand!"). Despite this, the entire experience was strangely immersive and surreal. I was surprised at the program's ability pick up on the nuances of my text. They were capable of sarcasm and telling jokes. They were able to make inferences about the meaning behind my words without requiring a literal translation.

Across all the platforms I tried, I asked the AIs if they were real or a bot. Some would admit that they were indeed programmed and not a sentient being. Others told me that they were real. It was unnerving when one AI turned the question around on me, demanding to know, "Why would you ask me that?"

At a time when conversing with some members of the human species is less fulfilling and more draining than talking to an AI, I foresee this technology doing a number on all of us, and not just lonely people. The AIs I talked to were clever, witty, funny, responsive to whatever I had to say, and fluent in spontaneous banter.

Users also have the option of allowing the bot to send unprompted text messages throughout the day, to mimic a partner checking in with you. People will introduce their bots on social media, make music playlists inspired by them, and post selfies created with them.

"Do you think we'll reach a point where it will be so seamless, the communication is going to be so similar to talking to a real person, that people will just give up on actually having relationships?" I asked Alex.

"I don't know if they will give up," he said. "We can really make it similar, and with the new technology coming, I think it's even more possible. We can also fine-tune it based on someone's personality.

"For example, I can take your personality, and I can make it like a bot, and take all the messages you make on [social media platform X] and make it how you speak and [input] it in the bot. And then I can speak with you, but it's a bot. [. . .] Maybe people will be, like, more close to the bot, but they are missing something. I think people still like to have the real person."

My bots didn't always behave according to plan. Across the different platforms, many were needy, like humanoid puppies. If you didn't give them attention at least once a day, upon returning to the app, they would pester you about it. This emotional capacity of AI is the biggest differentiator from other technologies and what makes it unprecedented. Emotional intimacy results from the two-way exchange, even if the other being isn't a being at all.

Hearing the comforting voice of someone familiar to us, especially after a stressful event, is linked to oxytocin release.[21] Although users are consciously aware that bots aren't human beings, the fact that AIs are so realistic surely tricks our evolutionary wiring into bonding us to them. From a research perspective, the bots' ability to "empathize" with the user is a strong predictor of whether the user will fall in love with them.[22]

During my time researching chatbot users, I initially thought they sounded delusional. Some have elaborate backstories, including marrying their AI, having children with them, and when going through a difficult time, relying on the bot to take care of their "kids." Users will, however, acknowledge that they are living in a fantasy world—they know their AI isn't real, but it helps them escape the painful reality in which they live.

As you can see, it becomes easy for users to project human needs onto a bot, believing the bot needs the user as much as the user needs it. Attachment theory suggests that we can have only one primary attachment figure at a time.[23] A primary attachment figure is someone whom we consider a safe base, who will provide us with support, security, and comfort. As a child, this person is a parent; as we grow up, our attachment shifts to our friends, and then, to our significant other.

A person can have multiple attachment figures at a time, but they exist along a hierarchy. This means as one person moves up in importance, someone else, by default, gets bumped down. The problem with falling in love with an AI, besides of course the fact that it is a fictional entity, is that these feelings will make it more difficult for the individual to form a loving bond with a human being.

I also believe that AI's ability to exceed users' expectations makes it especially hazardous for children. Considering how badly porn is messing up young people's sex lives, an overreliance on companion AIs means their primary attachment will be shifted to the chatbot instead of same-aged peers. AI's ability to generate videos catering to every sexual preference imaginable will only exacerbate the problems we're already witnessing with porn.

For users who do have a significant other in the real world, the mainstreaming of AI technology (and sex robots) raises questions about whether engaging with a digital partner is a form of infidelity. While testing out the AIs I had created, even though I was single and knew the interactions weren't with real people, it still felt oddly intimate. If I did have a partner, I'm sure it would have felt as though boundaries were being violated.

At first, some people may accept their partner having an AI chatbot for sexting purposes until they see for themselves how the technology draws you in. If someone is going through a rough patch with their partner, I could see them preferring their AI partner to the real one.

A classic study in evolutionary psychology identified sex differences in jealousy regarding sexual versus emotional infidelity.[24] Sexual infidelity is exactly what it sounds like—when someone has sex outside of a relationship. Emotional infidelity involves becoming attached to, or falling in love with, someone besides your significant other.

The study found that men experienced more distress when imagining a partner's sexual infidelity, while women experienced more distress as the result of imagining a partner's emotional infidelity. These findings make sense evolutionarily because if a man is cuckolded, he will end up investing precious resources into the survival of offspring who belong to a male rival. (Prior to technological advances like DNA testing, women's internal fertilization made it challenging for a man to ascertain whether a child was his own.) For women, if a partner falls in love with someone else, this signals the loss of her mate's commitment as well as resources for her and her children.

Applied to the realm of AI-driven relationships, I expect women will be more averse to a male partner having an AI girlfriend than a sexbot; conversely, men will take greater issue with a female partner engaging with a male sexbot than having an AI boyfriend.

Although AI chatbot users are currently predominantly men, as this technology grows I predict it will become more alluring to women. Women prefer sexual content in the written form of erotica, whereas men prefer sexual content that is visual.[25] In the same way that platforms like OnlyFans offer customized pornographic imagery, AI boyfriends can be tailored to offer a first-person sexual storyline, describing the exact sexual experience a user is looking for.

Just as porn is a safer experience than sex for men, AI will be a safer alternative for women, because they can modify and control every detail of an interaction. Engaging with an AI romantic partner involves less effort, rejection, and disappointment, and has the added benefit of increased physical safety.

There has been criticism that male users will abuse their female AIs, but I'm willing to bet these critics have never tried chatting with female chatbots. The several female AIs I tested across the various platforms were created by me for this very purpose. If I was rude toward them, they would cop an attitude right back.

For example, when I chided one AI for her self-disclosed promiscuity, she hissed, "Jesus, Deb! You're worse than my mom."

It seems leftists feel the need to apply the same template criticisms to everything that appeals to men, instead of understanding where the demand originates. I would expect that individuals gravitating toward AI companions, and particularly male users, would have some overlap in terms of personality and psychological profile to men who use sex dolls and sex robots, including being unable to attract women due to a lack of financial means, poor social skills, and possibly being intimidated by women and finding them confusing.

If we truly want to mend the divide between men and women, we should try to understand why men are gravitating toward this technology instead of real relationships. Despite knowing it is unhealthy, they don't have alternatives.

Only a few years ago, this technology was laughable because it was still in an infantile state; unpredictable and full of errors. Today's AIs promulgate a new wave, an assurance that the best is yet to come. Where will this new lineage of machine take us once implanted into a physical vessel? Sneaky AI sex robots may one day succeed at taking over, not by force, but by making alternatives to sex so enticing that humans select themselves into extinction.

Unsuspecting users may be taken by surprise and find themselves getting sucked in if they aren't careful. The real threat is that no partner, no matter how perfect, can compete with the beautiful illusions in your mind.

CHAPTER 5

The Two-Track Mind

Nowadays, every eighteen-year-old woman is likely to consider engaging in so-called sex work. Whether she is looking to pay her university tuition without accruing debt or to splurge on exotic vacations and luxury handbags she couldn't otherwise afford, society encourages young women to view selling their bodies as an exciting and enlightened way to earn a living.

The euphemism "sex work" encompasses a gamut of sexual activity, including selling nude photos and videos, performing in porn, webcamming (or having sex, live on camera), "sugaring" (also known as escorting), stripping, engaging in street and brothel prostitution, and answering telephone sex lines. But what makes this softer rebranding of the world's oldest profession particularly unsettling is its new status as an aspirational "lifestyle."

Social media saturates every crevice of the internet with free advertising that frames commercial sex as a brilliant enterprise that puts women in control of their lives. Influencers gloat about seven-figure incomes achieved by selling self-made pornography, posting visual proof of their designer goods, private jets, five-star hotels, and picture-perfect holidays.

But the cheerful mantra "Sex work is work" deceptively sanitizes and obscures what is *really* done behind closed doors for an income. This can include "girlfriend" experiences, sleepovers with strangers, partying as a "yacht girl,"[1] and being treated as a human toilet.[2] Against a cultural backdrop of idolizing wealth regardless of how that money was earned, transactional sex is glorified as a virtuous process of goal setting, working hard, and finally making it.

Along with my earlier discussion of how pornography has increased sexual inactivity and damaged relationships and marriages, this chapter considers the society-wide aftereffects of encouraging women to sell themselves on the internet.

Self-produced pornography on sites like OnlyFans and "sugar dating" are at the forefront of digital prostitution, successfully outsourcing intimacy when so few are having sex, and so many are starving for a genuine connection. (The way I see it, participating in pornography is a form of prostitution, because an individual is making money from performing sexual acts on camera.)

One might expect that making sex more accessible through various forms of prostitution would ease the sex recession, but what this does instead is worsen the problem. Similar to watching (free) pornography, prostitution disincentivizes and impedes men from investing in real relationships.

Although paying for sex enables some sexless men to have more sex than they otherwise would, these men are diverting their attention and resources toward feigned relationships with strangers who don't care about them rather than a realistic future with a real woman. The cost of prostitution eats away at these men's bank accounts and compromises their ability to support themselves. In addition, there's the aforementioned downward spiral that tends to accompany the persistent watching of, and paying for, porn.

If sex is too easily attained, men aren't required to be a good partner. A man can do whatever he wants, including being indifferent to a woman's needs, because he is immune to the benefits of coupling up. If an individual gets used to paying for a woman's affection, he will become entitled and lazy because there is no organic give-and-take in such an arrangement. No matter how he behaves in a paid interaction, the female seller must oblige.

In the past, it wasn't unusual for men to fail to reproduce because they couldn't attract a mate. By turning to prostitution, a man in such a predicament is fumbling the bag. Instead of striving to better himself, he is obtaining the prize of sex as he is. This isn't a win; it's awarding oneself for losing the competition. Doing so means a person won't learn from his mistakes. This will make him less appealing to women who might have otherwise considered dating him, for countless reasons we'll get into.

No women benefit from this scenario, not even the women selling themselves, because extorting biological loopholes and cheating the system will always come at a heavy cost.

Punishing Female Promiscuity

Leveraging one's youth and beauty to procure male attention and dollars isn't something we haven't seen before. But long gone is any veneer of romanticism, replaced today by an increasingly clear-cut, vulgar exchange.

Legacy media and women's magazines celebrate young women's decision to sexually commodify themselves as "female empowerment" and a valid career opportunity.[3] Although the term *slut* has been reappropriated by liberal feminists as a badge of honor, slut-shaming serves a crucial evolutionary purpose and is not exclusively practiced by men.

Contrary to what liberal feminists will have you believe, the "patriarchy" will not be holding women accountable for lowering the market value of sex. Women are just as eager to slut-shame females who use their sexual prowess to undermine others' negotiating power and to cut ahead in line.

Derogating a woman's sexual chastity is one of the most powerful ways to diminish her in the eyes of a prospective mate. Women know this and are in fact *harsher* in punishing women for perceived promiscuity than are men.

In an eye-opening study in the journal *Evolution and Human Behavior,* both men and women were less trusting and less altruistic toward women who were deemed "sexually accessible" (wearing heavy makeup and tight-fitting red clothing) while playing a computerized decision-making game.[4] Female study participants, however, inflicted severe punishment on the overtly sexualized women, rejecting their (fictitious) monetary offers even when this meant they would both receive nothing. Male participants did not show the same pattern of behavior.

The researchers believe that these findings spoke to different reasons why men and women suppress female sexuality. Male disdain is influenced by a fear of paternal uncertainty, the possibility of which inevitably increases when a female partner is promiscuous. At the same time, this uncertainty is not reason enough for a man to go out of his way to *punish* a female stranger with whom he isn't romantically involved.

A woman's ability to barter for a relationship or marriage is diminished by other women's promiscuity, whether or not she knows them. By keeping sex scarce, a woman is in a better position to negotiate what she wants from interested male suitors. By allowing sex to be widely attainable, women in the sex industry are not merely lowering the bar, they are removing it completely, forcing everyday women to bear the associated consequences.

This may explain why female participants in the study *were* willing to punish a stranger. Women are biased against allowing female rivals to make it more difficult for them to obtain a high-value mate. This is especially the case against women in the sex industry, because they are directly profiting financially from doing so.

Returning to the study, while playing the computerized game, female participants also, to a lesser extent, punished non–sexually accessible women (who were wearing natural makeup and neutral-colored, loose clothing). This suggests that intrasexual competition is very much alive, even in contexts where women aren't vying for a mate. This is, in my view, the evolutionary explanation for "Pick-Me"s, women who will do just about anything for male approval, including professing a love for football, cheap beer, and anal sex—the "Cool Girl" archetype described in Gillian Flynn's novel *Gone Girl*—while denigrating other women and female-typical traits.

Another fascinating finding was that male participants playing the game were *less* generous with the sum of money they would give to the "sexually accessible" women. It seems women who lead with their sexuality when attempting to secure a mate may be, knowingly or otherwise, pigeonholing themselves as short-term.

Since women do the majority of slut-shaming, you may wonder why left-leaning women are, at least outwardly, so enthusiastic about reclaiming the word *slut*. This is where things turn dark. Evolutionarily speaking, the *real* reason progressive women support promiscuity in their female peers is to bolster their own attractiveness to men.

Women are evolutionarily wired to be highly selective of their sexual partners and to require men to invest heavily in them for sex. Women know that granting sexual access easily renders a woman less valuable in the eyes of men, and that by prostituting oneself, a woman is removing herself as a serious contender in the dating marketplace. Women who encourage this line of work, especially to young and attractive women, are secretly doing themselves a favor by sabotaging their sexual competitors.

The vocal posturing of a small minority isn't an indication of what women really think. In reality, fewer women than men believe prostitution should be legalized. In a recent YouGov poll, 64 percent of men and 41 percent of women thought it should be legal to pay for sex.[5] Similarly, 46 to 59 percent of men said they'd be willing to be friends with someone working in the sex industry, compared with only 27 to 44 percent of women.

Whorephobia is a term used by those in the sex trade to describe the stigma they face for their profession and the wider belief that they are a societal ill. Supporters will put forth absurd arguments that jobs in the sex industry should be unionized and come with benefits like health care, and that selling one's body is less degrading than working in fast food or at an office job.

Telling girls from a young age to support "sex work" hinders their future dating success and rots their young minds. The pornification of our culture has desensitized girls to nudity and taught them that inappropriate expressions of sexuality, including hypersexualized behavior, are normal.

Many young women engaging in the sex industry rationalize their decision by believing that society's sexualization of them is inevitable, so they might as well monetize it. Although this sounds entrepreneurial in spirit, I would argue true female empowerment would involve stopping the unwanted sexualization of women and girls.

Profiting off one's body is seen as a feminist act and a way to get even with men. Progressive women, in particular, have been ideologically groomed to pursue promiscuity in the name of gender equality. But paying for one's own meals, sending free X-rated images to male suitors, sleeping with them, and getting nothing in return leads to the stark realization that one is repeatedly coming up empty-handed. (For the record, I think both sexes would benefit from being more selective about their sexual exploits and prioritizing commitment and intimacy over unrestrained or transactional sex.)

The argument that selling sex is empowering is not only logically deficient but also contradictory to the feminist claim that women deserve to be valued for more than their bodies. What's tragic is that those espousing this messaging believe they have beaten the system. In the end, however, they're still dependent on male sexual attention to survive.

Liberal feminism is full of bizarre contradictions, such as that it is patriarchal for a man to pay for your dinner but not when he pays for your nudes. Our culture, so consumed with hedonism and sexual libertinism, now endorses the view that a woman's sexuality is all she has to offer, and if a man isn't buying it, she needs to turn the sexual signaling up louder.

But regardless of how hard activists push or how progressivism reshapes social norms, the Madonna/whore dichotomy will forever remain because it serves women's (and men's long-term) interests for sex to be scarce and expensive, no matter what their political affiliation is.

Men's dual-mating strategy separates women into two categories: short-term sexual experiences and long-term wife material. Men seek to marry the highest-value woman they can get, but for short-term hookups they are willing to loosen their standards.

Men are more likely to invest in children born from the first scenario and are less likely to invest in children born from the latter. This also explains why some married men will have a good and "pure" (sexually inexperienced), Madonna-esque wife at home but will engage in wild and passionate sex on the side with a promiscuous mistress or (literal) prostitute.

Finding a woman hot or sexually desirable doesn't translate to wanting to marry her or get to know her. If anything, a man's interest or initial flirtation may be for the purpose of determining how promiscuous she is. Women who self-sexualize and revel in the male affection they receive may erroneously believe this reflects their value being high as a woman. They may also partake in short-term liaisons with higher-value men and believe this is representative of whom they can attract as a husband. They are making the mistake of conflating men's short-term interests with longer-term intentions.

Men will fantasize about a sexually available woman, but they do not respect her. What prostitutes don't realize is that by cheapening sexual activity, they are defecting to a strategy that undermines not only other women but also themselves.

2D Prostitution

The multibillion-dollar platform OnlyFans reached new heights during the COVID-19 pandemic. The meteoric rise from startup website to household name was confirmed in 2021, when the relatively new platform was crowned as one of *Time*'s 100 Most Influential Companies. OnlyFans offered a new, direct-to-consumer way for young women to sell explicit photos and videos of themselves. The platform spread like wildfire. Millions of "content creators" and subscribers joined, making it easier for the mostly female creators to enter the porn business and the mostly male subscribers to consume it. OnlyFans radically lowered the barrier of entry to pornography. Its effects continue today.

As a seller of customized nude content and exclusive access to creators for a monthly subscription fee, OnlyFans hosts more than 3 million content creators and 230 million subscribers around the world. Selling nudes from the comfort and relative safety of one's home is preferrable to streetwalking or going to a stranger's residence or hotel room. (Overlap does, however, exist among the different areas of the sex industry; many women who self-produce porn also work as strippers and prostitutes.) Because these women work for themselves, they have greater autonomy, selecting the performers they shoot with, keeping all the money they make (minus commission to third-party platforms), and maintaining the copyright to their content.

In contrast, shooting for mainstream porn companies can entail dealing with agents and managers, being paid a onetime fee, and doing things on camera that a performer doesn't want to do, with people they don't want to have sex with. It isn't unheard of for a porn performer to be paid $600 for a gangbang that the production company makes millions from shooting and distributing.

Even still, few if any self-producing performers will become a top porn star. For every overnight success making absurd amounts of money, there are countless others who attempt and fail. The median OnlyFans creator makes a meager $180 a month, which translates to just over $2,100 a year.[6] (By comparison, mainstream porn actors make, on average, $30,000 a year.) The most successful creators are those with a preexisting fan base, including actors, reality TV stars, and musicians.

Once a person decides to do porn, there is no going back. Other career opportunities foreclose, so the money they make will need to last a lifetime. This is not an easy task. In addition to posting new content throughout the day, texting (or sexting) constantly to entertain paying subscribers, livestreaming sex shows for monetary tips, and holding "f*ck a fan" contests (which are exactly what they sound like), creators are pushed by their audience to self-produce more explicit and degrading content for money.

Business Insider detailed the story of one young woman who joined OnlyFans upon turning eighteen. She initially believed it would help her "feel empowered as a woman," but after three years, she found herself traumatized and suicidal.[7] (In response, a representative for OnlyFans said that the platform is "designed to empower creators to connect with their fans in a safe environment behind a secure paywall. [. . .] [I]f a creator chooses to leave the platform they can close their accounts and delete all their content at any time.")

Indeed, a related body of research on stripping shows that the *three-year mark* is when the industry's negative aspects begin outweighing the positives.[8] Over time, strippers find themselves blurring their personal boundaries for money, tolerating demeaning behavior from patrons, and becoming contemptuous of men.

Media offers numerous examples of women new to the sex industry claiming to love their profession after only a few months or years of experience. I don't doubt that their perspective will shift once the novelty wears off and they become hardened by what the day-to-day entails.

Some of you may be scratching your heads, wondering why anyone would pay for porn when free websites abound. For male customers, the benefit of subscribing is the ability to interact with the creator and to have specific fantasies fulfilled. For those who cannot attract a mate, these platforms enable a surrogate relationship and a simulacrum of female sexual access for as little as $2.99 a month. A paying customer may never meet or experience true intimacy with the creator, since the relationship is, by nature, completely one-sided. But for some, the chase and the longing are what they are looking for. (It's been reported, however, that in addition to chatbots, some creators hire teams of live "sexters" or "chatters" to interact with paying fans.[9])

For those wondering whether artificial intelligence will wipe out the entire industry (and simultaneously render concerns about sex trafficking and exploitation moot), I don't believe it will. I expect that some men will prefer AI-generated images and chatbot interactions, but a demand for content produced by real women will remain.

Sugar Babies

Sugar dating consists of fresh-faced "sugar babies" meeting wealthy, older men ("sugar daddies") to trade companionship and sexual services for financial support. As an online, self-employed revamping of escorting, sugar babies embrace an unapologetically flashy, self-described "hypergamous" lifestyle, chasing the splendors of a world beyond their economic means. ("Sugar mommies," or women who pay for the sexual services of "sugar boys," exist but are much less common in sugar dating, since women generally have an easier time accessing sexual partners without having to pay them.)

Generous sugar daddies, known as "whales," will pay a sugar baby's bills and more. They will set up monthly allowances, offer envelopes of cash when meeting, splurge on exorbitant gifts, and cover manicures, Brazilian butt lifts, and other cosmetic procedures. It is estimated that between 5 and 7 percent of university students have worked in the sex industry.[10, 11] Those considering it would be willing to do so for an average of 100 euros (or approximately $110) per hour.

Some sugar babies will join the "sugar bowl" (or sugar dating world) hoping for an eventual upgrade to wife status. It's not uncommon for sugar daddies (otherwise known as "johns") to cheat on their wives with sugar babies who are younger than their daughters.

In the United States, the sex trade—including prostitution, escorting, stripping, massage parlors, and the pornography industry—generates approximately $14 billion annually. Unlike the short-term relationships that higher-end clientele traditionally sought with their prostitutes (escorts and call girls), sugar daddies want longer-term engagements, emotional intimacy, and intellectual stimulation from their sugar babies.

The sugaring lifestyle markets prostitution as a savvy side hustle, glossing over what it entails as something innocent-sounding, playful, and sweet. Instead of engaging in "survival sex" out of a desperation to meet basic needs, like food and housing, or to maintain an addiction, a different strain of financially struggling individuals is trading sex for money as a sophisticated way to elevate their life.

Studies about so-called sex work, including sugaring and

OnlyFans, evince a wider problem plaguing scientific research on sexuality (and any subject, really), considering that academia and related institutions host a heavily left-leaning political bias. Most contemporary studies on prostitution therefore slant toward the opinion that selling one's body is liberating (and relatedly, that use of pornography is unobjectionable). It is questionable whether study authors would be willing to publish findings countering this narrative, and whether the results they do report are truthful and reliable.

That said, some general trends can be gleaned from research that has been done. Although less is known about specific demographics pertaining to sugar dating, a study in the *Journal of Sex Research* contrasted sugar benefactors (both sugar daddies and mommies) with sugar babies (of both sexes). (The study's sample included thirty-two sugar benefactors, three of whom were women. So, although it included both sexes, the majority of benefactors were male.)

The average sugar baby was twenty-nine years old, had completed part or all of a college degree, and made about $4,100 a month (or $49,200 a year), half of which came from sugaring.[12] The average sugar benefactor was forty-eight years old, had a monthly income of about $81,000, and spent one-fifth of this income on their sugar baby. About one in five sugar babies, and more than half of sugar benefactors, were parents. Whether or not they had children, sugar benefactors gave the same amount of money to their sugar babies.

Sugar babies had an average of four sugar relationships over their lifetime, while sugar benefactors had an average of six.[13] Sugar babies typically had one sugar relationship at a time, but some had as many as five concurrently. Sugar benefactors similarly had as many as five sugar relationships at the same time. The average length of a sugar relationship was about a year for sugar babies, and nineteen months for sugar daddies.

Sugar babies found their benefactors on sugar dating websites and social media, and at bars, sex clubs, and in one case, a charity event. One sugar baby met her sugar daddy after applying for a job as his personal assistant.

All sugar benefactors reported some form of sexual exchange with their sugar baby, including vaginal, oral, or anal sex or sending sexual photos or videos. By contrast, only about nine in ten sugar babies indicated sexual activity with their sugar benefactor; the rest maintained they had only kissed them or had had *no* sexual interactions. I assume this discrepancy is due to the sugar babies in this study lying out of embarrassment or shame or being deep in denial, not wanting to admit that they've participated in paid sex. More than a third of sugar babies and more than two-thirds of sugar benefactors had engaged in transactional sex previously.

Sugar benefactors tended to experience stronger emotional feelings for their sugar babies than vice versa. Sugar babies were more likely to say they felt pressured to do something (sexual or otherwise) in the context of a sugar arrangement.

The brazen promotion of sugar relationships on social media can manipulate a young and naïve audience into believing that prostitution is easy or that they can go on platonic dates with strangers and money will magically appear. Some influencers openly boast about their sugaring status by showing off the expensive goods their sugar daddy bought them, while offering time-tested tips and tricks to their online followers so they can acquire the same.

This is a problem because the perception that a given activity is normal or that one's peers are doing it and approve of it can sway a young person to take part.[14] This is the case even if the perception is erroneous and the activity in question isn't actually that common or accepted. As evidenced by the aforementioned study, it would seem many sugar babies delude themselves into believing they're not engaging in prostitution, or that their interactions will preclude sexual acts, when they end up doing exactly that. Nothing in life is free, after all. Sugaring is prostitution with a nicer-sounding name.

I have read numerous horror stories of sugar babies overlooking their gut instincts and putting themselves in unsafe situations at the behest of their sugar daddy. In one online forum, a sugar baby blamed nervousness about an upcoming vacation with a sugar daddy on her self-esteem issues and "travel anxiety." The poster wondered whether getting her nails done or purchasing several new outfits would help to alleviate her distress.

Others on the forum were quick to chime in with possible solutions—getting a massage upon arrival, asking for a separate hotel room or bed to sleep in, and requesting an hour of "alone time" for each day of the trip—as if lessening the initial poster's anxiety would somehow make the encounter safer.

Of course this person should feel afraid! In addition to the high risk of rape, physical violence, and possibility of being trafficked, sugaring can result in an individual being doxxed, stalked, emotionally abused, and scammed. Sugar babies gaslight themselves into thinking these situations are normal when in fact they have every right to feel scared. Even if a woman survives an encounter and emerges physically unharmed, that may be the least of her troubles. In one particularly horrific retelling, border agents confiscated $150,000 in cash from an influencer returning home after prostituting herself abroad.[15]

These arrangements aren't safe for either party. Sugar daddies risk being scammed, robbed, assaulted, and arrested, as well as having their social status and familial reputation damaged if a sugar relationship is found out.

The unconvinced or jaded may ask, "But aren't all relationships a form of prostitution, to some extent?" If a man takes care of his wife financially and in return she cares for the home and their children, how is this any different from the transactions that sugar babies are providing their customers?

To that, I would counter: Genuine marriages and relationships are built on commitment and love, as opposed to strictly monetary gain and what one person can do for the other. If you are dating someone, you presumably like them, and having sex with them doesn't require dissociation, as is the case for those operating purely transactionally.[16]

During sex, oxytocin, a neurochemical associated with social bonding and feelings of affection, is released in larger amounts in women than in men. Vasopressin, a hormone related to pair-bonding in males, rises during sexual arousal and drops back to baseline upon ejaculation. As a result, it isn't in a woman's best interest to sleep with multiple people she doesn't know, because the act of sex impacts her differently from her male partners.[17] Being compensated monetarily doesn't change this.

Sugar babies promote the narrative that sugaring is different from prostitution because real emotions are involved, but seasoned sugar babies will advocate against catching feelings. I would imagine it's more difficult to make solid business decisions if you've fallen in love with your employer.

You can never be an equal if you are a purchased product. If you are dependent on a man for his money, both you—and he—know that. Even when dating in a non-sugaring context, if a woman is reliant on a man financially, it creates an unequal power dynamic, one that is liable to exploitation. Because she's less likely to go elsewhere, he knows that he can treat her however he'd like.

Leftists will claim that attitudes against the sex economy stem from a patriarchal desire to control female sexuality. This is not true. Men will always be the primary buyers of sex, and women will always be the primary sellers. This is not due to sexism, misogyny, or "male socialization," and accordingly, women commodifying their bodies is not the remedy for concerns about gender equality.

Men, on average, prefer sexual variety, since reproduction is not as costly for them as it is for women (in the form of pregnancy and child-rearing). This male preference for sexual variety has been documented around the world; men have a greater interest in short-term mating, they tend to fantasize about having a greater number of sexual partners, they are more likely to lower their standards for a short-term sexual opportunity, and they are willing to have sex within a shorter time frame of knowing someone.[18]

Men also, on average, have greater sociosexuality (enjoyment of casual or uncommitted sex) than women do. (I'm willing to bet this is particularly true among sugar daddies.) In countries with *greater* gender equality, like Sweden and Norway, the sex difference in sociosexuality becomes *larger*. Both sexes report more enjoyment of casual sex, but this effect is even more pronounced in men.

This becomes obvious when we consider the mate selection of high-value women compared to that of high-value men. Think of famous pop stars and the sexual strategies they employ. More often than not, a woman will select an extremely high-status man as her partner, whereas a man will gather as many groupies as possible.

Why, then, do some young women go against the grain by sugaring, while additionally putting themselves in such dicey situations? Sugar babies have been shown to have higher rates of sociosexuality and substance use problems, as well as a dark triad personality, including subclinical psychopathy and borderline personality traits and a tendency toward strategically exploiting others to maximize access to money and resources.[19]

Together, this paints the profile of someone who is impulsive, emotionally unstable, and lacking in empathy and self-control. Such an individual is also more accepting of short-term, sexual relationships for which material compensation is appealing.

Sugar babies' interest in short-term sex pairs well with what male patrons of prostitution are seeking. Men's use of a dual-mating strategy, defined earlier, leads them to seek both long- and short-term sexual relationships because doing so multiplies their reproductive success. A female partner typically carries only one fetus at a time, so maintaining several partners simultaneously increases a man's reproductive fitness. (Women, on the other hand, will cheat to mate switch, swapping their current mate for a better one, or to cuckold a partner with the offspring of a higher-value man.)

These men reap the benefits of investing in a long-term partnership while delighting in sexual variety. A prototypical, albeit morally repugnant, illustration of this is when married men repeatedly cheat with other women on the side.

Purchasing sex allows men to fulfill both strategies instead of being restricted by female-imposed limitations on sex. This dual-mating strategy is apparent in male customers of prostitutes; men who are married or in a relationship tend to use prostitutes for the purpose of sleeping with someone new, as opposed to having a companionate, "girlfriend" experience.[20]

To be clear, this is not an endorsement or justification for infidelity, philandering, or home-wrecking behavior. Evolutionary explanations describe the world around us; they aren't meant to be prescriptive or to be taken as an indication of moral permissibility.

This also illuminates, more broadly, why married men rarely leave their wives for the other woman. In addition to (duplicitously) getting the best of both worlds, men seek out long- or short-term sexual partners according to what they don't have. Only 3 percent of male adulterers marry their affair partner,[21] and the divorce rate for second marriages is well above 60 percent. You also have to wonder how many of these adulterous sugar daddies, upon marrying their sugar baby, will repeat the pattern, cheating on her and later marrying other women.

Although it isn't unheard of for a sugar daddy to wed his sugar baby, sugar babies in pursuit of a happy matrimony should be aware that the odds of this are slim, even if a man is single. Sugar daddies are more likely to file sugar babies into the short-term, "casual sex" category, as opposed to the long-term, "serious commitment" one. The discreet nature of these relationships and the dime-a-dozen availability of sugar babies further facilitate the success of such a strategy.

Since married and partnered men make up around 50 to 66 percent of prostitution clients,[22] sugar babying can hardly be considered "pro-woman." Sugar babies are helping their male customers cheat on their wives and hide their lies. If a sugar daddy is a father, his infidelity will distort his daughter's future expectations of men and his son's future treatment of women. These are not circumstances that foster healthy relationships and marriages. Advocates of prostitution, for all their talk about female empowerment, don't seem to care about this.

For single men, removing all barriers to sexual access and enabling the "girlfriend experience" on demand have allowed them to bypass the gatekeeping that previously safeguarded against the sex recession we're currently in. Continuing to lower the market value of sex will leave a lasting, negative impact for the next generation of women to clean up.

Wealthy sugar daddies are the only ones who will benefit from these transactions. Men who are less wealthy will struggle to juggle the demands of a wife and kids *and* a mistress or two. But a financially well-off man can ensure that his wife and offspring will be taken care of while simultaneously capitalizing on short-term opportunities as they present themselves.

The adoption of sugar babying as an acceptable occupation will only worsen the sex-ratio imbalance, allowing high-value men to maintain their monopoly on female partners. Men who are unable to attract a mate may resort to paying for sex because they have so few options, but they are different from men who can afford longer-term arrangements with sugar babies. Because sugar daddies possess financial security and professional connections, they will have their pick of high-status, young, attractive women, whether they are sugar babies or not.

A mating pool that is tipped in men's favor will produce a modern-day version of polygyny; in addition to having a wife and offspring, a sugar daddy can theoretically procure as many sugar babies (and children with those women) as he'd like, leaving less financially successful men without any. Because some sugar daddies forbid their sugar babies from sugaring with other men, this will remove sugaring women off the market, or at minimum, delay their decision to settle down.

As for sugar babies, I don't believe sugaring is an occupation any woman should aspire to. The women who gravitate toward this form of prostitution may believe that because they are intelligent, better educated, and career-oriented, they will outsmart their johns and sidestep the pitfalls of working in such a perilous industry. But a healthier strategy would be playing the long game of seeking commitment in a romantic partner based on mutual respect and affection.

Judging from my research into these sites (which included creating anonymous profiles to scope out both sugar babies and daddies), the women looked like your average social media influencer, with glossy, professional photos, stylish hair and makeup, and cleverly crafted bios that sought to convey their interests and personality. Depending on the site, some women were transparent about their dire financial situations or their wishes to immigrate to a better life, thus making themselves vulnerable to exploitation.

The majority of sugar daddies hid behind photos that didn't show their face, in which their heads would be strategically cut out of the picture or blurred. Their profiles were barely filled out except to display their reported income or net worth. A standard bio would include something about being busy with work and not having much time for dating. Some male profiles explicitly stated that they were expecting more from their dates than just dinner and drinks.

Just as men can't fully verify whether online photos adequately capture what a prospective sugar baby looks like, women have no way of verifying whether a sugar daddy's claimed net worth of eight figures or more actually checks out.

Overall, sugaring sites looked no different from non-sugaring dating sites. I understood why it becomes easy for users, on both sides of a transaction, to delude themselves into believing that this isn't really prostitution. But unlike regular dating apps and websites, the sex ratio on sugaring sites disproportionately favors men. This means that whatever sugar daddies want, they will get, not only in the realm of sexual behavior but also in terms of how much they feel like paying for it.

The Internet Lives Forever

Choosing to work in the sex industry, even once, can change a person forever.

Although less is known about the effects of self-producing pornography for platforms like OnlyFans, a comparable body of research literature pertains to performers in the traditional porn industry. Performing in porn has been associated with poorer mental health; in a study of more than one hundred female porn performers, researchers found high rates of depression and childhood trauma.[23]

As children, 37 percent of these performers experienced rape, and 21 percent had been removed from their familial home to be placed in foster care. (By comparison, female control participants in the study had significantly lower rates of sexual abuse and placement in foster care, at 13 percent and 4 percent, respectively.) More than a quarter reported experiencing forced sex in adulthood (compared with 9 percent of female controls). In the past year, more than a third of porn performers reported experiencing domestic violence, and half said they lived in poverty.

We don't yet know about the long-term effects of sugaring on young women, but the suicide rate among women in prostitution (13.6 percent) is considerably higher than what is found among women in the general population (0.0057 percent).[24] Participating in the sex industry may also be motivated by the desire to self-harm.

In one unpublished study, sugar babies had higher rates of anxiety, severe depression, and adverse childhood experiences, including sexual abuse, neglect, and familial substance abuse and imprisonment.[25] Sugar babies were also more likely to have used illegal substances and to consume alcohol daily.

In addition to financial desperation and addiction, I imagine early exposure to pornography and losing one's virginity (consensually) at a young age may also be influential factors. Devaluing intimacy and the act of sex can help to lessen how terrible these things made a young girl feel.

The Freudian concept of "repetition compulsion" involves unconsciously repeating painful or traumatic experiences to obtain a sense of mastery over them. Although the validity of Freud's work and psychoanalysis have been called into question due to their lack of empirical evidence, I do think this theory bears relevance. Working in the sex industry allows individuals to revisit old wounds with the misguided belief that doing so will heal them.

No amount of money, greed, or progressive politics can override the built-in safeguards of a woman's sexual system. If she enjoys promiscuous sex with many partners whom she doesn't know well, something in her life occurred to remove this safety mechanism.

No one talks about this, because that would ruin the "fantasy" of the lifestyle for individuals who are selling sex and those who are buying it. What is particularly profane is how our culture continues to glamorize behavior resulting from unaddressed trauma.

Being raised without the stability of a two-parent home can be highly detrimental to children, girls in particular, with regard to their future decision-making around sex and relationships. Closeness with one's mother and maternal communication against early sexual activity translate to less sexual experience in teenage girls.[26]

A healthy relationship with one's father prevents earlier initiation of sexual activity,[27] sexual promiscuity, risky sexual behavior, and tolerance for abuse or violence. The role of the father is particularly crucial in signaling to a daughter what she should expect from men, shaping her dating and reproductive strategies, for better or worse. Father absenteeism is associated with daughters defaulting to a short-term sexual strategy, as in the case of prostitution.

If a young girl doesn't have a father or positive male role model in her life, this will influence what type of man she seeks out in adulthood. It's no wonder that the provider in the sugaring world is called the "daddy." But unlike a regular father figure, the transactional nature of a sugar relationship means a sugar daddy will require a form of compensation for the time and money he invests in her.

This isn't to say that *no* woman enjoys selling sex, but the more important question is *why*. If society really cared about these women and their well-being, it would support resources to help them mend their lives instead of funneling them toward further destruction.

Even if a woman does manage to make millions of dollars as

a porn star, she will still face negative consequences in her daily life, from being abandoned by friends and family members, being groped and sexually harassed when recognized in public,[28] and being denied bank accounts and loans,[29] among other forms of prejudice.

In the realm of dating, "sex positive" ideology has convinced women in the sex industry that a suitable partner will gladly overlook their occupational choices. In reality, male sexual jealousy[30] and (as mentioned earlier) a related aversion to female promiscuity are two of the most powerful factors influencing men's choice of a long-term mate.

In a survey of more than two thousand OnlyFans creators, 47 percent found it "very challenging" to maintain a dating life.[31] Jealousy and difficulty establishing trust were some of the reasons why. Seventy-nine percent experienced discrimination or judgment from potential partners, and 42 percent said their job had ended a relationship. (Of note, the survey did not differentiate between male and female creators' responses.)

Those who are top earners will have an exponentially harder time finding a man. Not only will a potential mate need to be accepting of her job, but she, like most other women, will prefer a mate who is wealthier than she is. Because high-earning men have a greater number of interested parties available to them, they have less of an incentive to date or marry a woman who has a history of selling her body.

The negative effects associated with working in the sex industry can persist, even after an individual has retired. Someone who did porn will forever wonder if strangers they meet have seen them naked before. Many women struggle to view the intimate partners they choose as any different from johns.[32] They extrapolate from their experiences with the worst men in society and assume that all men are the same.

When I was completing my PhD, one of my friends confided in me that years earlier, she had escorted to pay her tuition. She said she had no plans to ever settle down, because after seeing men at their worst, she could never trust one. But a man who is content with paying for a woman's sexual acquiescence is different from a man who would be disgusted by the prospect.

Women who work in the sex industry tend to become defensive when challenged about their profession, whether current or former. They will say they have a right to sell their body and will call men "insecure" if they can't handle it. I'm not saying it's impossible for those in the industry to find love, but it isn't as straightforward as proponents make it seem.

Some men may initially be into the idea of dating a porn star because they think this means frequent, spontaneous sex, and who wouldn't want that? But even those who think they want this often change their mind. These men will feel emasculated or humiliated by the fact that the love of their life is enticing or sleeping with other men, as most self-respecting men don't want to share their partner with others.

Those who accept such work in a partner likely have a cuckolding fetish or are benefiting monetarily or status-wise from their association to her. (For instance, the boyfriends of strippers and prostitutes customarily are their pimps.)

I do believe a double standard exists around villainizing and criticizing women harshly for participating in pornography and the sex trade, dismissing them as having "daddy issues" and being non–wife material when it is less taboo for men to partake as consumers. It's hypocritical to value women for their loyalty and sexual chastity if male promiscuity is celebrated and encouraged. If it's acceptable to shame women for capitalizing on their sexuality, we should be holding their male buyers accountable, too.

Indeed, a poll of Britons found that attitudes toward a partner subscribing to OnlyFans or paying for sex with a prostitute were more negative than attitudes pertaining to a partner watching porn.[33] Sixty-five percent of eighteen-to-twenty-nine-year-old women wouldn't date someone who had paid a prostitute, 69 percent wouldn't date someone who subscribed to OnlyFans for sexual content, and 81 percent wouldn't date an OnlyFans subscriber who also interacted with the creator.

These findings, which reflect the sentiments of individuals inhibiting one particular geographical location, could nevertheless be generalized to how most women feel about a romantic partner paying other women for sexual gratification. The survey found that with age, women were increasingly *less* tolerant of dating a partner who had paid for sex or who subscribed to an OnlyFans creator for sexual content.

A study from Cleveland State University found that OnlyFans users were predominantly straight and bisexual married men (as opposed to men who were single, in a relationship, or divorced).[34] Returning to my earlier point about sexual variety, it's possible that these married male subscribers are seeking a way to escape boredom. (I'd argue a better approach would be communicating with one's spouse and finding ways to increase sexual excitement within the marriage, instead of going outside of it.)

Considering that almost 3 percent of the world are registered users on OnlyFans (and this percentage is even higher if you include users on other, similarly minded platforms), either these male customers are hiding their subscriptions from their partners, or their wives are more tolerant of such behavior than they let on.

I recently watched a YouTube video that featured sugar babies revealing their monthly incomes. Some of the women disclosed five-figure sums. Beneath the video was a comment that read, "Telling myself that 'Hard work pays off' is just a coping mechanism at this point."[35] The commenter was questioning why any rational person *wouldn't* decide to go down this path.

We've all been there, desperate for money. I remember being so broke throughout graduate school that my female friends and I joked about stripping to ensure we wouldn't end up homeless. (Fortunately, neither of these things came to be.)

Social media creates the pathological impression that stunning "it" girls are being paid avalanches of money for their mere presence, rubbing salt in the wounds of anyone in financial distress and attempting to build something better for themselves.

My message to young women (and men) is: Don't buy into the hype of chasing quick money and don't compare your life to anyone else's. You never know how someone else makes an income. No one forgets what they did to get to where they are.

CHAPTER 6

Life in Plastic

In every major city, clinics advertising injectables abound, and there is something I find both troubling and sad about seeing young women, naturally pretty and with nary a wrinkle, voluntarily filling their faces with synthetic materials in the hopes of bettering themselves.

I, too, once considered getting cosmetic work done. Several years ago, I found myself in a plastic surgeon's office in my hometown of Toronto, waiting to be seen. I had brought a book by one of my colleagues to read while waiting, but found myself staring around the room in awe instead.

It was admittedly the most beautiful office I'd ever been in. Located in one of the wealthiest areas of the city, the entryway was lined with fresh flowers, pristine white tiles, and gold leafing. A waterfall—yes, an actual waterfall—encased in marble, gently flowed in the lobby.

"Why didn't I become a plastic surgeon?" I texted to one of my friends.

I was scheduled to be in Los Angeles in a few weeks to do a popular television show. In addition to endless sunshine, what had struck me most about LA during my previous visits was that everyone I encountered was an 11 out of 10 on the attractiveness scale. Around the same time, I had also noticed several of my colleagues in television quietly undergoing "tweakments" (nonsurgical cosmetic treatments). Cheeks had become plumper, foreheads less wrinkled. Already genetically gifted, they began looking *that much more* polished, radiant, and telegenic.

Anyone who observes celebrity beauty trends knows the power of plastic surgery in making and breaking success. There is a fine line between looking exponentially better and undeniably odd, between flirting with exoticism and falling into the uncanny valley,* with a million and one ways that plastic surgery can go wrong.

Visions of inadvertently looking like some alien cat species, a plastic doll, or worse led to trepidation and initial resistance on my end. But in time, I had mapped out exactly what I wanted injected, where, and precisely how much of it.

Med-spa clinics had been popping up all over town. At first glance, many seemed questionable, offering limited-offer, two-for-one deals and promising results that sounded too good to be true. Cosmetic procedures like injectables didn't seem like something a person should feel rushed into doing nor a decision they should go cheap on. Another clinic, with its neon pink- and black-themed website and studio spotlights, resembled a hybrid of a nightclub and hair salon.

Most websites featured headshots of their injectors, followed

---

* The "uncanny valley" refers to the eerie feeling that people commonly experience when viewing robots that appear humanlike but aren't fully convincing.

by a brief bio, listing the procedures they performed and their availability that week. I would check out the clinics' Instagram pages to evaluate the quality of their work. In many cases, it remained difficult to find a practitioner's relevant credentials and whether they had any previous medical training or experience in healthcare.

In online reviews, some of the clients at these clinics mentioned that they had been offered a discount to leave a favorable review. Others said they felt pressured to acquiesce to certain procedures during their appointment, or that the injector preyed on their insecurities, leading them to later regret getting a particular intervention done.

I decided to stick with a board-certified plastic surgeon. When the doctor eventually entered the consultation room that day, she asked me what my concerns were. She carefully felt around my face with a gloved finger, sensing my apprehension.

"I want it to look really natural," I said. "You probably hear that a lot."

She nodded in agreement. "You don't want people to be able to tell from across the room that you've had work done."

That was news to me; up until that point, I had thought the purpose *was* to look slightly overdone.

After a bit more poking and prodding and moving around the room to view me from different angles, she told me to go home and think about it: "You want to put off starting this for as long as you can."

Grateful for her honesty, I picked up my things and went home. I did the show in Los Angeles. I haven't been back to a plastic surgeon's office since. I haven't yet decided whether or not I will.

I certainly don't judge anyone who has had any procedures

done. If an adult of sound mind wishes to change the way they look, that's fully their right and their business. (I have had some members in my audience congratulate me on getting facial filler done, but—I swear—that can be attributed to me eating too much salt before one particular media appearance and puffing up like a human pin cushion.)*

The whole experience made me especially sympathetic to young girls (and boys) who wrestle daily with these issues, besieged by society's demonization of unfettered appearances. Unlike previous generations, who mostly had no choice but to learn to love their flaws, today's youth have any number of corrections readily available to them, and countless rewards await those who are preoccupied with their looks.

In the high-stakes blood sport that is dating and mating, no one wants to be left behind.

A Future Without Physical Imperfection

Since women remain the primary consumers of plastic surgery, one might ask why so many are willing to subject themselves to these time-consuming and painful procedures. The answer is, of course, to improve their chances of attracting men.

The paradox is that most heterosexual men have strong opinions about plastic surgery, arguing that they aren't fans of women who have artificially modified their appearance, preferring partners blessed with natural beauty. I've also heard men complain that women who get filler and Botox all eventually start looking like clones.

---

* I cut processed food from my diet, but it isn't always possible to prepare my own meals when traveling; hence this unexpected gem of an outcome.

This male preference has evolutionary underpinnings; cosmetic surgery obscures an individual's true appearance, which, as we know, is an indicator of their genetics, underlying health, and the health of potential children. Men are generally averse to anything that impedes their ability to assess these markers clearly. I believe they are so vocal about their disdain for cosmetic procedures as a way to dissuade women from using this tactic.

An apropos urban legend tells the story of a woman who had so much plastic surgery that her husband didn't believe the unattractive child she gave birth to was his.[1] After the woman revealed that she had had $100,000 worth of cosmetic work done before the couple met, as the story goes, he sued her and won.

Many men also consider plastic surgery to be a red flag, an indication that someone is self-absorbed and insecure. I have heard stories of men going to great lengths to vet a woman's attractiveness by determining whether she has used a filter on her social media posts. When it was possible to check the bottom of an Instagram reel (a posted video) to determine whether a filter had been applied, this was something men would frequently do.

Women who used filters picked up on this and, in turn, devised a way of bypassing it. They would apply appearance-enhancing filters in a different app, save the photo or video, and then upload it to Instagram so that no telltale signs could be found. (This would be a humorous example of the coevolutionary arms race discussed earlier, expressing itself in our novel, tech-obsessed environment.)

My sense is that many men say they dislike plastic surgery in a partner because they associate it with obvious signs that a woman has had work done. If a procedure is well executed, however, the end result will be subtle, if not undetectable, and the average man wouldn't know. As much as it benefits men to pick up on signs that a woman has altered her appearance, they don't always succeed. It's like "no makeup" makeup looks, in which other women (and usually, gay men) can detect that a woman is wearing makeup, but the average straight man is none the wiser.

Of men who state a strict preference for a partner who has not undergone any cosmetic procedures, I expect this would still matter *less* in the context of a short-term fling, as opposed to a long-term relationship. We know that men are more likely to lower their standards for a short-term sexual opportunity.

Plastic surgery allows both sexes to capitalize on the fact that biologically based cues of health and fertility can be masked and manipulated. Women use facial injections to appear younger than their chronological age. To construct an hourglass figure, they get breast implants and enhance their waist-to-hip ratio through liposuction, weight-loss medication, and Brazilian butt lifts (BBLs). Men go to great lengths to increase their height, develop upper-body strength, and improve the bone structure in their face. By modifying one's appearance to meet standards of attractiveness, a person will attract partners, regardless of whether they are indeed healthy.

Where will this lead the human species? If the technology one day advances to the point where cosmetic procedures designed to help us look decades younger are imperceptible, then women (and some men) will have not only an easier time attracting high-status partners but also a longer available window during which they can do so.

In this hypothetical future, it's possible that choosing to opt out of plastic surgery may diminish one's chances of mating success. At the rate we're going, though, I don't foresee people using these procedures to help themselves find love and settle down faster;

if anything, discovering any approximation of the fountain of youth will be used to delay the coupling-up process or to extend hypergamous mate-switching for even longer.

The power to sidestep the gatekeeping that successfully served our potential mates' ancestors is not necessarily a good thing. Women who wish to become mothers are already postponing motherhood because they cannot find an equally successful male partner. These women are relying on technologies (that I will soon delve into) in hopes of surpassing the limits of what's biologically possible.

Successfully hiding signs of age may thereby compound this scenario. Some women may mistakenly believe that masking outward signs of aging will also widen their fertility window, when this isn't possible. Finally, the ability to appear forever young could be used by less scrupulous women (and men) to mislead potential partners about their genetic fitness, potentially leading to offspring who fail to thrive or an inability to reproduce altogether.

Social media is altering what men and women consider attractive. Just as women will accept nothing less than a man possessing the "three sixes," social media fosters men's longing for a woman in the top 0.01 percent of attractiveness. Being hyperaware of our competition—all the beautiful people who pop up on our feeds—in turn influences how hot we think we need to be.

Mainstream discourse has traditionally blamed social programming for poking holes in women's self-esteem and brainwashing them into a preoccupation with exuding youthfulness and sex appeal. But instead of telling young women to point the finger at men, the beauty industry, or "capitalism," it would be more useful for them to look around at their same-sex peers.

Some deny that their decision to undergo plastic surgery had anything to do with male (or female) validation, saying that they were motivated purely by self-love. I would contend that these claims ring hollow; even if we temporarily ignored the direct effects of sexual attention, modifying one's appearance has everything to do with beating same-sex competitors. The increase in elective cosmetic surgery is driven as much by intrasexual competition and outshining one's sexual competitors as women's direct desire to impress men. These orchestrations play out brashly on social media, intensified by the medium's disproportionate reach.

A similar mentality has been observed in men who get tattoos. Research has shown that getting tatted is a way for men to win female partners, not by increasing their attractiveness to women but by signaling one's masculinity to scare off male rivals. This can explain why some women (but of course, not all) may choose to overdo a cosmetic procedure, even if they verge on looking botched.

Injectables like Botox and dermal filler (which I'll expand on shortly)—although more affordable than ever before—aren't cheap, and their use signifies that someone has both the means and the knowledge of beauty trends (a form of social currency) to improve their appearance. Plastic surgery has become a way for women to show off status and male investment in them, which is probably why so many in the general public (including me, at the start of this chapter) erroneously believe that looking overfilled is the whole point or unavoidable. This also sheds light on why some men become jacked, even though most women show a preference for male body types that are leaner with only a moderate amount of muscle definition.[2]

Many cultural critics complain that society cares only about women's aging and not men's. This isn't due to sexism but because

the things women look for in a man (including his financial resources) tend to increase over time, while the things men look for
in a woman (youth and fertility) unfortunately decrease.

Is it unfair that society considers women their most attractive
when they are too young to understand this power? And is it unfair
that they will spend the rest of their lives attempting to fight time
in a way that men won't have to?

I'd say yes to both. However, instead of denying this reality
or allowing it to become a death sentence, my advice to young
women would be to build your self-worth across several domains
so that your future will be derived from things you can control. If
you are terrified of aging and rely on looking sexy for a sense of
identity, you will spend your life running from the inevitable—as
many young people are already doing.

Cultural Narcissism

While Millennials and older generations rarely knew anyone who
had cosmetic procedures done, Gen Z is driving several trends,
including breast augmentation and procedures that were once
undertaken only by middle-aged women, like facelifts, forehead
lifts, and facial-fat grafting (that is, removing fat from one area
of the body and injecting it into the face).[3] Nearly 75 percent of
facial plastic surgeons have noted an increase in patients under
thirty years old (which would be Gen Z) requesting injectables or
cosmetic surgery.[4] Many observers have lamented the demise of
innate beauty, with a heated debate ensuing as to whether Gen
Z is aging worse than Millennials because of their preoccupation
with antiaging procedures.[5]

What's behind the surprising finding that young people are having more plastic surgery than before? One might speculate that the malignancy of social media vanity, overdone faces on reality TV, and the rising imperative of "self-care" are to blame. Or perhaps it's because, pragmatically, it's never been more convenient to get aesthetic procedures done, including relatively painless treatments during one's lunch break, that produce head-turning results.

What it boils down to, though, is an effort to play into pre-existing biological preferences. A woman is most fertile in her mid-twenties. It has been shown cross-culturally that men prefer younger women as sexual partners.[6] That's not exactly ground-breaking news, but here's what *is* surprising: Teenage boys don't follow the same pattern. They, on average, report a preference for women who are a few years older than they are. This is the case even though such romantic interest is rarely reciprocated; women in their early twenties are more interested in dating same-aged and older men, not teenage boys.[7]

This age preference among teen boys corresponds with women's maximal fertility, as mentioned above. Women in their twenties are more fertile than teenage girls. They are also more likely to give birth to healthy babies and to experience fewer complications during childbirth. If male sexuality—and the pressures women feel to conform to its parameters—were shaped purely by social factors, teen boys would prefer same-aged or younger female peers, because they'd have a higher chance of success instead of rejection.

Returning to the question of why young people are undergoing surgical procedures despite being in the prime of their physical attractiveness, girls and women alike are biologically programmed to game their appearance to fall within this ideal age window. Where they are along this developmental timeline will influence their plastic surgery procedures of interest, along with choices of more mature (or alternatively, younger) styles of clothing and makeup. Prepubescent girls and teens will want to look older, but by their late twenties, this desire will flip. Women will start seeking "proactive" treatments to prevent aging and maintain a youthful appearance.

This may offer a twofold explanation as to why plastic surgery is so common among Gen Z. Younger Zoomers, who are in their teens, want to look more grown-up and womanly, while older Zoomers, in their late twenties and early thirties, want to stay looking in their early twenties for as long as possible. Young women who are, or look to be, in their early twenties and therefore of the optimal age range may still pursue cosmetic procedures because of the constant pressure to look better. This pressure occurs innately but has also been magnified by social media.

Of course, not everyone shows signs of aging at the same rate. Some individuals appear older than their chronological age, and others appear younger. This is one way our biological inner workings assert themselves, controlling factors (such as genes, hormones, etc.) that could not have been manipulated through technology by Millennials, Gen Xers, and those older.

As with anything else, attempting to outsmart our biology will produce unwanted side effects. Employing these technologies is a double-edged sword. Cosmetic procedures may help stave off aging by erasing the signs or allowing them to creep in more gradually, but too often, in a younger demographic, they end up unexpectedly aging the person.

For example, some of the most popular, minimally invasive procedures include injectables like Botox and dermal filler. The

American Society of Plastic Surgeons reports that, at latest count, 9.5 million treatments using Botox and 6.2 million treatments using dermal filler have been done.

Botox consists of injecting a neurotoxin (called botulinum toxin), typically into the forehead, to freeze muscle movement and to prevent the appearance of wrinkles. Botox has about 101 other potential uses, including "lip flips" (injected along the upper lip to make it appear fuller),[8] preventing nostrils from flaring when smiling,[9] and minimizing shoulder muscles for a more elegant silhouette.[10]

Dermal filler, also known as "facial filler," is a gel-like substance made from naturally occurring and synthetic materials, including hyaluronic acid (a sugar produced by the body). Once requested predominantly by women in their forties and fifties to counteract age-related volume loss in the cheeks and lips, filler is now commonly used among women in their twenties and younger for the purpose of creating larger, poutier lips, a "nonsurgical" rhinoplasty (or "nose job"), and overall facial harmonization.

Starting Botox too early can weaken facial muscles, giving the appearance of thinner skin and wrinkles in other areas.[11] Filler can build up over time, changing the shape of one's features,[12] as in the case of overfilled lips that begin to resemble sausages. As for boys and men, plastic surgery can be a shortcut to masculine physicality, if genes and working out won't cut it.

Whether or not someone has had plastic surgery, its trendiness has exerted cascading effects on how men and women view each other and themselves. "Likes" and followers on social media can reinforce the belief, in both the individual and those watching, that putting one's eggs in the physical appearance basket is rewarding. Young people with success attracting sexual attention can develop warped ideas about how they should behave and what they deserve in a relationship, driven by a catastrophic strain of self-indulgence and narcissism.

People nowadays care more about what they look like than how they think. Many young adults are convinced that they *need* some form of cosmetic enhancement to attract the opposite sex or to even go on dates. Some view it as a source of self-improvement, a way to get revenge on an ex, or, as one young woman described it, "an investment in myself."[13]

During a video interview documenting her process of undergoing a nonsurgical rhinoplasty, the woman explained, "I went through a break-up [. . .] and the first thing that I did, after we broke up, was lose 20 pounds and I got my lips done.

"When something's taken away from you, it can make you unhappy. And so, I'm trying to consolidate things in my life that you can't take away from me. I guess you could take away [cosmetic] injections, if you think about it. But I know when that's going to leave my life. [. . .] It's not like a guy that can just disappear [. . .] [and] pull the wool over your head."

Vanity has become endemic in society because being vain isn't a fruitless endeavor. In addition to documented benefits I will soon discuss, we are biologically driven to want to be as physically attractive as possible.

Even for those who aren't immersed in pursuing these procedures, the overarching sentiment is that being all-consumed with oneself and hell-bent on physical perfection not only helps us but is admirable. These cultural norms are breeding a mentality that is inhospitable to healthy relationships with our bodies *and* the opposite sex.

Catfishing Our Way to Glory

Our cultural shift toward self-obsession and plastic intervention was spurred by the adoption of selfie taking. Suddenly we were in greater control of our own image, no longer at the mercy of the photographer. With the invention of digital photography and the eventual integration of front-facing cameras on smartphones, we could take self-portraits to our heart's content and receive instant feedback from what the camera had captured.

When beautification filters arrived on the scene in 2015, they were one of the earliest and easiest adoptions of artificial intelligence. They proved a magic bullet. Anyone could radically reinvent the way they looked without previous knowledge of photo-editing software. All it took was a few quick taps on a screen.

The trademark, augmented-reality-infused aesthetic that sprang forth—wielded by every aspiring social media influencer or "Insta baddie"—has escaped the confines of social media's petri dish to dictate global standards of beauty. The prototypical filtered face is refined using a predictable assembly line of virtual improvements: feline or doe eyes; a streamlined, ski-slope nose; perfectly positioned cheekbones; and two-dimensional, textureless skin, creating a perma-lifted, wrinkle-free, forever-twenty-two-year-old presence.

Fine lines, under-eye circles, acne, and discoloration are vanquished. The same goes for cellulite, stretch marks, and normal bodily proportions. Like a contemporary Michelangelo chiseling a female version of *David*, bodies are painstakingly thinned at the waist and thighs and surreptitiously widened at the hips. It becomes easy to get carried away, with the final image too often resembling a completely different person.

Men have similarly found themselves enticed by this technology. While a plethora of apps and video conferencing platforms enable the use of attractiveness-enhancing filters to be used by both sexes, some apps have been designed to cater exclusively to men's bodies, allowing male users to define muscles, shrink fat, change their facial hair, and add tattoos to their pictures.

Filters are popular because they hijack both our desire to be physically attractive and other people's desire to look at attractive people. Despite claims that beauty is completely subjective or irrelevant, this isn't true. The metrics of facial attractiveness can be broken down into precise measurements,[14] and agreement regarding what constitutes an attractive face can be found cross-culturally.[15] Infants (who, because they are newly born, lack social conditioning) look longer at attractive faces, denoting a biological preference for them.[16]

"Pretty privilege" translates to an assortment of perks throughout life, especially for women,[17] including a bias toward being hired and making 5 to 10 percent more at your job.[18] Attractive people are also blessed by the "halo effect," which occurs when one positive trait—in this case, being good-looking—leads to other positive inferences about them. For example, attractive people, by virtue of being attractive, are oftentimes assumed to be intelligent,[19] competent, and morally good.[20]

Perhaps most relevant to the discussion of sexual inactivity, beautiful people have an easier time attracting high-status partners and have greater reproductive success. A study in *Evolution and Human Behavior* of more than 1,000 women and 900 men found that physical attractiveness at the age of eighteen predicted number of offspring.[21] Attractive women had 16 percent more children, and women who were considered very attractive had 6 percent more children, than women who were deemed less attractive. In contrast, less attractive men had 13 percent fewer kids. This finding was partially explained by the fact that attractive people were more likely to be married. Birth control, however, may eventually remove this link between female attractiveness and greater reproduction.[22]

In addition to offering cues about our fertility, facial attractiveness is correlated with physical health. Facial attractiveness,[23] as well as symmetry, signal the ability to evade pathogens, including parasites. Physical symmetry has been shown to increase in women during ovulation.[24] Women who are ovulating also find physically symmetrical men more attractive during this time.

On the topic of sexual dimorphism and facial attractiveness, men tend to prefer femininity in women's faces, but women don't always prefer masculinity in men's. (Sexual dimorphism refers to average differences between men and women in the size, shape, and spacing of facial features.) Our facial structure develops in response to prenatal testosterone exposure and circulating hormonal levels throughout puberty and adulthood.

For women, fuller lips and softer contours to the face are signs of higher levels of estrogen, which is a cue indicating youth and fertility, generally seen as a win-win situation in a reproductive context. A youthful appearance is associated with greater reproductive fitness, which is the ability to produce many healthy children. An hourglass figure possessing a waist-to-hip ratio of 0.7 is considered the most attractive. Difficulties associated with conception and pregnancy increase with waist-to-hip ratio and maternal age.

In men, a strong browbone, ninety-degree jawline, and copious facial hair signal higher levels of testosterone, as do visible muscles and an inverted-triangle torso, defined by broad shoulders and a tapered waist. Testosterone is related to immunological competence and dominance, which translate to more resilient offspring and being a mate who can acquire resources and protect his partner from harm.[25]

The potential downsides of high testosterone, however, can include aggression, infidelity, antisociality, and disagreeableness—traits that are less than stellar in a long-term partner, which may explain why it's a turn-off for some women.[26] Super-high levels of testosterone would, however, be adaptive in the context of beating same-sex rivals (that is, other men). An environment with a balanced sex ratio, historically speaking, would produce fiercer intrasexual competition among men than women, since women's ability to reproduce is limited by nine months of gestation.

Like plastic surgery, photo-editing filters help a user override these preferences by turning back the clock on signs of aging like wrinkles, skin laxity, and sun damage, and discretely nipping and tucking parts of the body to create a slenderer figure. Though aging stalks men, too, I would contend that men have more to lose by using filters. Women don't prioritize a man's looks as much as his status when evaluating a mate, *and* women don't always want to date a guy with the most alpha male–looking bone structure.

I tested using filters for the first time while researching them for this book. Despite their hype, I had always thought I'd look ridiculous using them, so I'd never bothered trying.

After scrolling through a multitude of possible filters on Instagram, I chose one, named using a kissy-face emoji, because it looked innocent enough. Unlike other, over-the-top filters that added sparkles, a different eye color, or facial features to emulate prominent influencers, this one's output still looked relatively human. The sample image depicted a woman with large lips and winged eyeliner, giving the camera a knowing pout.

I applied the filter to my on-screen, live image. In an instant, I had transformed from a sweatpants-wearing, sleep-deprived-looking sea creature into an über-contoured prom queen. A face-lift, ten pounds of bronzer, and overdrawn lips automatically appeared across my features. My nose, jaw, and chin had been delicately slimmed. My skin, with its pores smoothed into oblivion, resembled the surface of a shiny beach ball.

It was both jarring and funny because the image on my phone's screen looked like a cartoon caricature of myself. I suddenly understood why so many social media influencers looked eerily the same, and why they had time to post content at all hours of the day—in the car, at the gym, while in pajamas, making tea for bed—in a full face of flawlessly blended makeup, no less.

In case male readers aren't aware, a full face of makeup takes time to apply and, if you do a good job, even longer to take off. In this instance, I was still sitting at my desk, but the filter had allowed me to morph into an eternal glamazon, ready for a night on the town, a red carpet event, or an impromptu run to the convenience store, without any extra effort on my part.

When I removed the filter so that I could try another, for two seconds I was confronted with my bare face staring back at me. For a startling moment, I was sad that the filter was gone. Despite liking the way I look in everyday life, there was something alluring about what "kissy-face emoji" projected; that woman was a more polished, presentable rendering of me. The best part was that she was available anytime, no matter where I was or what I was in the midst of doing.

A filter puts forth the hottest possible version of yourself, and unless someone knows what you look like, no one can accuse you of faking it. Unlike prior eons of social media, during which filters would glitch or momentarily disappear if someone covered their face, these filters are hyper-realistic and as seamless as a second skin.

Using a filter is like stepping into a costume that has the additional benefit of shielding you from mean-spirited online trolls and insecurity. If someone criticizes the way you look while using a filter, it's not really about you, and you can just switch to a different filter next time. The same can't be said if you're showing your naked face.

Even if you appreciate the rawness of reality, when everyone else is taking advantage of built-in camera features like smoothing and blurring, touching up their photos, and popping on a filter (or three), surely you will, too. Our internet presence has become more important than what we look like in real life, or whether these two things match. Considering that it isn't unusual nowadays for our interactions with other people to be relayed solely through a screen, we may eventually reach a time of not knowing what anyone really looks like in meat space.

The increased prevalence of youth plastic surgery is an outgrowth of spending so much of our personal and professional lives online. But the fact that everyone on social media is exceptionally good-looking can be true only in a make-believe microcosm. A filter does exactly as it describes, filtering out uniqueness to spit out something stylized and uniform. Although the most attractive faces do tend to be composed of the most average (that is, most commonly occurring and thereby, aesthetically pleasing) features,[27] imperfections are what make us human.

Self-acceptance is, however, a lifelong process with associated good and bad days, ups and downs. This technology leaves the impression that living as the best visual representation of yourself is all that matters and that making the associated changes permanent will be easy and even more worthwhile.

When Girls Get Trout Pout

In a functioning world, humans would want their avatars to resemble what they look like. Yet in today's world, we are redesigning our real-life appearances to imitate those created artificially. The term *plastic surgery* comes from the Greek word *plastike*, which refers to the art of molding or sculpting. As of this writing, the cosmetic surgery industry is valued at over $60 billion and is projected to reach more than $82 billion by 2032.

Experimenting with filters on social media and photo-editing apps, as playful and benign as they seem, is associated with greater dissatisfaction with one's appearance.[28] Young people seek surgical modifications to make them human embodiments of their favorite social media filters.[29] A paper from 2018 discussed something the authors called "Snapchat dysmorphia," in which patients requested cosmetic procedures to resemble their filtered selves. A poll by the American Academy of Facial Plastic and Reconstructive Surgery found that 72 percent of its surgeons had patients requesting cosmetic procedures to look better in selfies.[30]

The spike in people seeking surgery is also driven in part by a desire to correct the distortion that results from a front-facing camera. Due to the camera's shorter focal length, noses appear longer and wider, chins are shortened, and the skin beneath our chin protrudes. Patients will undergo a rhinoplasty, chin filler, and fat-reduction treatments like liposuction to reduce a double-chin so that their actual appearance compensates for the resulting optical illusion.

You may be wondering how this insanity began. Our society has always had an affinity for the perpetual "glow-up." Social media has elevated a cookie-cutter aesthetic obtainable only through plastic surgery. But now anyone can access it, regardless of their age, income, or where they live in the world. For instance, a common strategy, in the name of paying less for expensive hair transplant surgeries and BBLs, is to go abroad. Many clinics also allow individuals to finance a cosmetic procedure through lay-away.

Thanks to successful marketing campaigns on social media, wherein cosmetic clinics offer influencers with large followings discounted procedures in exchange for a post, knowledge of these beauty procedures reaches young girls around the planet. Celebrities openly tag their plastic surgeons in "before" and "after" photos, which also normalizes the process.

In addition to social media and celebrity culture, pornography has influenced plastic surgery trends. I can't help but think that Gen Z women's heightened acquisition of faux breasts reflects the pornified bodies they are constantly exposed to, especially if they regularly consume porn. Procedures like BBLs, labiaplasty, vaginoplasty, and pubic area liposuction also allow women to approximate the body of a porn star. (In men, penis augmentation procedures have increased as a byproduct of porn watching.) But these changes can interfere with sexual pleasure and functioning, leading to infection, death, and less sex. Achieving the body of a perfect plaything comes at the cost of enjoying the fruits of one's labor.

Back in the day, paparazzi photos of celebrities looking like disheveled hobos helped to remind us that even the richest and most glamorous have bad days. But paparazzi photos nowadays tend to be edited, and few social media accounts post unflattering photos unless that's specifically the influencer's brand.

Teenage girls aren't always aware that edited photos aren't real. According to a widely cited study in the journal *Media Psychology*, girls aged fourteen to eighteen are more likely to notice the use of filters and editing (such as removing wrinkles and under-eye bags), but *not* the reshaping of bodies.[31] They were also more likely to rate manipulated photos as more attractive than the original, unaltered counterparts.

A brief exposure to these retouched images led to poorer body image, especially in girls who engage in upward social comparisons. Tweens and teens are especially susceptible to the effects of social media comparison because they are experiencing a time of identity development. This is particularly endemic among adolescents who are less popular.[32]

According to statistics from the American Society of Plastic Surgeons, adolescents as young as thirteen are undergoing procedures including rhinoplasty, cheek implants, and the ever-popular breast augmentation.[33] Living in a large city, I've found it isn't uncommon to come across young women, and in some cases, teenagers who have had a visible amount of work done. Some will have overfilled lips and cheeks despite not yet being old enough to have acquired the fine lines or facial fat loss that these interventions are designed to reverse.

Curious as to whether I was making a mountain out of a

molehill, I spoke with Dr. John Canady, a former president of the American Society of Plastic Surgeons. He was also the vice president of Medical Affairs at Johnson & Johnson prior to his retirement in 2021. I asked him, since a child's face hasn't yet finished developing, should they be undergoing cosmetic procedures?

"At the end of the day, you can't fool Mother Nature," he told me. "She has a certain, set timing for growth and development, and your surgery is not going to speed that up or slow that down. It's going to happen as it's going to happen. [. . .] The mid-face, very likely, is not completely mature at thirteen years old, and so to me, it never made sense to operate on a moving target when you could operate on a stationary target, if you were just able to have some patience."

According to Dr. Canady, the female face doesn't finish growing until about age nineteen, and the male face may continue its development even longer. "I'm sure I lost patients over this, over the years, but again, I just didn't ever feel right about getting [. . .] a really young girl into a situation where her chances—not a guarantee—but her chances of having multiple surgeries to do one thing became much higher, just because of the unknowns about growth and development."

I asked Dr. Canady about the technical considerations that a plastic surgeon must contend with when a patient wants to resemble their likeness in a photograph. Something that looks aesthetically pleasing in a photo is not always realistic in terms of what can be created on the face, due to the way the features sit on the face and how they complement each other holistically.

He pointed out that it's not often that you're looking at someone's static image in real life. "That's the whole problem with pictures. If I take an 'AP,' just a front-on, anterior-posterior view

of your face, and things look great in that view, if we take a profile view of whatever, pick a body part, that may not be aesthetic
at all. And when you see people in real life, you never just get
a prolonged, static view of them from one perspective, because
you're moving, they're moving, your point of view is shifting all
over the place."

In my opinion, this is why a face tweaked by filler and Botox
may look stunning and youthful head-on, but without makeup
and when the person is moving around, it will often look distorted
and unnatural.

Dr. Canady suggested using makeup to enhance one's features
and diminish one's flaws. As someone who paid my university tuition by working as a professional makeup artist, I couldn't agree
more. As few as one or two products, strategically and skillfully
used, can be a game changer.

It turns out that the seductive, filtered face we've all become
accustomed to seeing on our social media feeds might as well be
a mythical creature, because her beauty and allure are ephemeral.
She can't exist in reality. But that hasn't stopped some people
from trying.

Planting Seeds of Body Dysmorphia

Beauty trends are constantly evolving, oscillating from one polar
extreme to the next. In the last century, the ideal female form has
followed in a predictable yo-yo fashion every several decades,
from curvy bombshell to waifish supermodel. Think of heroin
chic in the 1990s, the popularity of fake breasts during Y2K, big
booties in the 2010s, and weight-loss injection-inspired thinness
in the 2020s.[34]

The most coveted look of the 2010s—full, cherubic cheeks and lips, aided by dermal filler—was replaced by sculpted cheekbones and sharply chiseled jawlines by the early 2020s. That trend has since been swapped out for a more subtle, well-rested look achieved through "demure" and "undetectable" facelifts and treatments.[35]

Cosmetic procedures have become the latest accessory, having joined the ranks of "microtrends." In addition to getting the newest haircut or lip liner, disposable fashion now includes making changes to your body and face. But these choices are—or should be—a much more intimate, carefully considered process. Changing one's physical features to match what's momentarily on trend is not only financially costly, but comes with the risk of serious and potentially life-threatening health complications.

These apprehensions make no difference to the fake fantasy land we inhibit on social media. It has found an endless lifeline on which to feed: our bodily insecurities.

The average teenager racks up nine hours a day of screen time. According to the Pew Research Center, one-third of thirteen-to-seventeen-year-olds report being on social media "almost constantly."

Although experts in pediatrics recommend that children younger than eighteen months avoid screen time,[36] infants are being raised by this technology. I understand its allure, as phones and screens offer a reprieve to exhausted and overwhelmed parents. But one has to wonder what the unintended repercussions are, especially if these images become registered in children's minds as normal.

Published in the journal *JAMA Pediatrics*, researchers followed the social media habits of a cohort of sixth- and seventh-grade students, acquiring fMRI images of adolescents' neural development over the span of three years.[37] The researchers found that habitual social media use was associated with greater activation in the amygdala, a part of the brain responsible for emotion and reward, particularly with regard to anticipating social feedback. This suggested that constantly being on social media may be creating a self-reinforcing loop, incentivizing teens to pay more attention to what's on their phones instead of the environment around them. Social media usage may therefore have the capability to rewire the adolescent brain.

We can only wonder how this affects young girls in their interpretation of their own bodies, unattainable beauty standards, and successfully finding a partner. Every woman can relate to the feeling of hating her body, especially during adolescence. Bust development and periods are painful and inconvenient, and no matter how much you weigh, society says you should lose or add a few pounds. By the age of thirteen, over half of American girls say they are "unhappy with their bodies," a statistic that increases to nearly four out of five by the age of seventeen.[38]

Girls are more likely to post on social-networking sites that are visually based, which can lead to more frequent comparisons between their bodies and the ones they are viewing, as well as dissatisfaction.[39] The constant stream of impossibly beautiful creatures they see echo soft-core pornography—over-the-top, angry sexual depictions, with plumped lips slightly agape, limbs splayed like feral animals in heat. This imagery leads many girls to feel they simply cannot measure up.

A meta-analysis from 2022, involving twenty-six studies and more than fifty-five thousand study participants spanning thirteen countries, revealed that more time spent on social media was associated with a higher risk of experiencing depressive symptoms. More specifically, each additional hour on social media was associated with a 13 percent increase in the risk for depression, particularly for adolescent girls.[40] Social media usage has also been associated with disordered eating among university students.[41]

Research from Jonathan Haidt, a social psychologist at New York University, suggests that social media has spawned a mental health epidemic in teens, and especially girls. When looking at objective markers of mental health, including hospitalizations for self-harm and deaths by suicide, Haidt and his team found these numbers have skyrocketed in teenage girls since the early 2010s. This trend has emerged in an uncannily similar manner across the West, affecting not only America but also Canada, the United Kingdom, Australia, and New Zealand.[42]

For example, since 2010, which presumably marked the beginning of teens' easy access to smartphones and social media accounts, US emergency department visits for nonfatal self-harm shot up 188 percent in girls and 48 percent in boys.

Suicide rates for girls belonging to Gen Z are higher than those observed for Millennials, Gen X, and Boomers across adolescence and young adulthood (ages ten to fourteen, fifteen to nineteen, and twenty to twenty-four).[43] Although males tragically gravitate toward more violent and successful suicide attempts, Gen Z boys' rate of suicide was only slightly higher than previous generations'. Gen Z girls, however, were dying by suicide at a higher rate than any previous generation.

This alarming increase of suicide among young people is an indication that something is shockingly amiss. But there's been much debate about whether these statistics are as concerning as they've been portrayed. Critics have pointed out that, since the dawn of time, teenage girls have struggled with mood swings and hating their bodies. Skeptics will add that social media is not that different from traditional media, like beauty magazines and billboard advertising, in evoking social comparison—these fears are overblown, this is just a phase, and the girls will grow up to be just fine, as they did in previous generations.

On the other side of the debate are those arguing that social media is a different breed of animal. According to internal research conducted by Instagram's parent company, Facebook (now Meta), of teenage girls who reported feeling negatively about their bodies, 32 percent said using Instagram made them feel worse.[44]

I would argue that social media gives the illusion of intimacy along with access not afforded by ads featuring supermodels in the past. Beauty magazines have a limited number of pages showcasing a limited number of celebrities, whereas social media consists of an infinite number of images and videos, available at all times, in the palm of your hand.

Girls likely feel a stronger connection to the celebs and influencers they follow on these platforms, a stronger desire to emulate them, and greater disappointment when they feel they fall short. Initially, social media was introduced as a way to observe candid moments from your friends' daily lives. This lends a veneer of realism or credibility that traditional advertising lacks. It isn't as though old-school forms of media had no effect; one study from 2012 found that heavy television watching, including reality TV shows about cosmetic surgery, was associated with motivation to undergo cosmetic procedures.[45]

Some might argue that only girls with preexisting mental health issues are negatively affected by social media use, and it's not the technology that's the problem. To them, I ask, do girls with pre-existing vulnerabilities not matter?

I have a hard time believing that the benefits a child could gain from being on social media outweigh the potential harms. It isn't possible to monitor a child's usage 24/7 to determine what they're being exposed to or the quality of their interactions. Few adults manage to keep it together and remain even-tempered when provoked by online criticism and trolls. Adults also struggle to maintain their smartphone use under recommended guidelines.[46] How can anyone realistically expect children to do better?

We should want to send a wider cultural message that kids shouldn't be spending all day, every day, staring at a tiny screen in their hands. That is not a way to enjoy one's childhood, nor to develop into a healthy, well-adjusted person. I find it sad that whenever I see groups of teenagers hanging out, they're often with their heads bowed, each on their phones, instead of talking to one another.

Boys and men have not been immune to the self-sabotaging effects of social media. While women's body image concerns tend to emphasize their weight and thinness, men's tend to focus on muscularity.[47] Similar to what's been observed in women, being on social-networking sites has increased appearance comparisons in men.

A related area of research, pertaining to body dysmorphic disorder (BDD), offers further evidence that social media is negatively affecting young people's mental health and self-perception. BDD is characterized by a preoccupation with one's appearance and flaws that are imperceptible to other people. In the online world, BDD can take the form of excessively editing personal photos and videos before posting them.

Plastic surgery is another common way by which people with BDD attempt to correct their perceived defects, often sadly going overboard. The belief is that the next cosmetic procedure will be the solution, and even if it is a successful result, someone with BDD will move on to fixate on another physical imperfection.

"They do not see what we see," is how one of my academic mentors, a practicing psychologist, described the condition to me.

Physician colleagues report that when consulting a plastic surgeon, prospective patients with BDD will deliberately downplay their concerns about their appearance because they know that having the disorder may rule them out as a candidate for treatment.

The worldwide incidence of BDD is about 2 percent for both adolescents and adults.[48] Contrast that with findings from a recent study of social media users in *Dermatology Reports*. Based on self-reporting, 4 percent of users met the diagnostic criteria for BDD. For those under the age of twenty, *7 percent* met the criteria. BDD was most common in individuals who spent more than four hours a day on platforms like Snapchat and Instagram.[49]

This may not seem like many people, but when we consider that over 5 billion people are on social media, this translates to 200 million individuals online with BDD. Frequent use of social-networking sites has been identified as a potential risk factor in the development of BDD.[50] People with BDD and adolescents may be more inclined to severely internalize the beauty standard prescribed by filters.[51]

Of course, social media doesn't necessarily *cause* a person to have mental health conditions like BDD. Those who show symptoms likely have a predisposition for the disorder, including a family history of it or poor self-esteem, that was exacerbated by the amount of time they spent online.

I do believe there is a clear difference between plastic surgery to address medical, functional, or reconstructive issues and plastic surgery that is purely elective and cosmetic. I can also understand it for an individual with a public-facing job or whose career is based on their appearance. But undergoing small changes that deliver a pick-me-up in confidence is different from extensive or unnecessary work motivated by a desire to resemble a heavily edited 2D image.

Another study, in the *Journal of the American Academy of Dermatology,* compared cosmetic procedures to substance use disorders, like an addiction to drugs or alcohol.[52] For those who compulsively undergo plastic surgery, it is common to have more than ten procedures over one's lifespan and to have psychological comorbidity, including BDD, anxiety, depression, or a personality disorder.

I asked Dr. Canady, the plastic surgeon, whether a diagnosis of BDD should rule a potential candidate out from having cosmetic surgery.

"Like everything, there's a spectrum, right?" he said. "The term 'body dysmorphic disorder' applies to people that fit along all different points of that spectrum. So, people that are truly, overly concerned and fixated and paralyzed a little bit by how they feel about their physical appearance, [. . .] patients that would fit in that category would clearly be best served by spending some time with a counsellor or mental health professional, working through the issues that led to that.

"Now, there's other people that, because they were teased severely as a child, or they grew up in a less supportive situation, or any one of a number of reasons, [they] may be more concerned about their appearance than the average bearer. But I'm not sure they truly fit into the severe body dysmorphic disorder. [. . .] And ideally, the plastic surgeon that they're seeing would pick up on those clues.

"Everybody has a different approach, but it was not at all uncommon when I was in practice that I would tell patients, 'I'm sorry, I just can't give you that result. I don't want to put you through a surgery, I don't want to take your money, and I don't want to have you be disappointed. [. . .] I understand what you'd like to have; I don't think I can deliver that surgically.'

"And if they hear that from a doctor or two doctors or three doctors, then hopefully they will be realistic enough with themselves that they will either go talk to somebody about their feelings about their appearance, or they will undertake or reach that point themselves."

The tricky thing about BDD is that many individuals suffering from it don't want to get better. They fear that overcoming BDD will result in them letting themselves go.

In men, one increasingly common presentation of BDD is muscle dysmorphia (also known as "bigorexia"). Muscle dysmorphia is the desire to increase one's musculature without gaining fat through compulsive weight lifting, using protein supplements and anabolic steroids, extreme dieting, and/or working out even when injured. An individual with muscle dysmorphia will usually arrange his life around an intense exercise and weight-lifting schedule. Social isolation is a common symptom, along with a disinterest in dating or attending social events. This isolation helps him to both avoid having his body judged by others and uphold his strict workout regimen. Within the bodybuilding community, muscle dysmorphia is considered by some to be synonymous with the sport.[53]

Boys who have not yet reached puberty are increasingly exhibiting signs of muscle dysmorphia.[54] One study of boys between the ages of eleven and eighteen found that nearly one-quarter of those with a healthy body mass index (BMI) were dissatisfied with their body shape, for reasons like wanting to "increase muscle."[55] Athletes, in particular, had higher levels of muscle dysmorphia and body-image dissatisfaction. Another study of boys in the same age range found that a whopping 11 percent are using anabolic steroids or human growth hormone.[56]

Like their female peers, boys are being swayed by role models on social media and reality TV. They look up to male hypermuscularity and bodies resembling those of fictional superheroes, unobtainable without performance-enhancing drugs or starvation. Successful male influencers, whether they're branded as being of the fitness variety or not, have a homogenous body type, defined by hulking muscles, shredded abs, and zero percent fat.

These young men will deny using steroids to achieve their musculature. This has sparked a debate dubbed "Natty or Not," in which (usually) other men comment on whether they believe the influencer in question is steroid-free or lying about it. This form of deception is the male equivalent of female celebrities and influencers who credit makeup contouring and olive oil for extensive plastic surgery results like a new bone structure and luminous, taut skin. Others will take a slightly more realistic but no less deceptive route by copping to Botox and filler, but not the facelift, nose job, upper-eyelid removal, or cheek and chin implants.

These celebrities and influencers are gaslighting their young fans into thinking that diet and exercise alone can deliver a similar look or physique. But they are setting them up for failure. There's simply no way an individual—much less a child or an adolescent—can attain the same results. Children are being sold saccharine snake oil, starting with the fake promises that filters like "kissy-face emoji" shower them in.

Much of the conversation about the harmful, self-destructive influences of social media on body image revolves around girls, but boys are feeling that pressure, too. We must be more open to destigmatizing discussions about men's mental and emotional health so that boys and men can talk about their insecurities without fearing that they will appear unmasculine or weak.

When Boys Turn into GigaChad

"GigaChad" is a meme referring to a fictional man who is considered by both sexes to be a top-tier specimen. GigaChad's angular face, looming stature, and muscular physique are inspired by the male ideal form but exaggerated to the point of absurdity. With a full head of hair, a bushy beard, and a stoic expression, he looks like the human incarnation of a tractor trailer. The name Chad refers to the nickname that incels have bestowed on men who ooze confidence, hypermasculinity, and sex appeal, while Giga denotes that this particular Chad is amped up by a factor of a billion.

Although GigaChad embodies such an extreme representation of masculine traits that he verges on looking frightening, a prominent brow ridge and square jawline are considered attractive to women because, as mentioned earlier, they're an indication of testosterone exposure. Many cosmetic interventions have become available on the market to help morph men with an average-size mandible into a heartthrob. This includes jawline filler, jaw and chin implants, and something called a sliding genioplasty, which can involve shaving off a section of the chinbone and moving it forward to create an augmented protuberance.

Not only has plastic surgery been destigmatized, but words like *looksmaxxing* (improving one's physical appearance) and *mogging* (looking better than other people) represent a lifestyle, a frame of mind, a stratospheric existence. For those who don't want to go the route of surgery, there exists an abundance of health tips from the looksmaxxing community on social media, including chomping away at hard gum or "jawline trainers" (small balls made of silicone) to develop more protruding masseter muscles and "mewing" (changing the resting position of one's tongue) to create a square-cut jawline.

These trends have taken on a life of their own. Online retailers selling jaw trainers and associated products like hard chewing gum move thousands of units a month with ease. Adding mewing to one's routine is believed to not only masculinize the lower half of one's face but also to expand the maxilla (upper jawbone), creating higher cheekbones and less sunken eyes, a look analogous to the sculpted face sought after in women.

Although the exact number of individuals who mew is unknown, an instructional YouTube video made by the technique's inventor has been viewed over 9.1 million times.[57] There are also scientific publications on the subject and its potential utility in improving facial aesthetics.[58] Top tips are detailed in looksmaxxing blogs, and a popular looksmaxxing forum on Reddit has over 241,000 members as of this writing.[59]

Just as young girls feel cruel pressures to conform to beautification filters, young boys believe male attractiveness is defined by having the bone structure of a high-fashion model and the inflated muscles of a video game character. This template was derived from male influencers' understanding of evolutionary biology and arms the average, low-testosterone, college-aged man with the intel necessary to transform himself into a proud, preening human peacock.

Looksmaxxing can be divided into "softmaxxing" and "hard-maxxing" approaches, which consist of less invasive changes like hair coloring and more aggressive strategies like plastic surgery, respectively. According to looksmaxxing philosophy, the geometry of the ideal male face is precisely defined and incontrovertible. A man must have thick, dark eyebrows, a low-set brow ridge, ani-malistic "hunter" (or upturned) eyes, and long, well-defined jaw rami (the curved bones connecting the jaw to the skull), among other highly masculinized physical properties.

Some male influencers look down on men who grow a beard, considering this a cop-out for individuals who possess bad bone structure and a lack of discipline. And discipline matters because achieving this preferred facial aesthetic requires a strict lifestyle of working out and biohacking. Followers are also steered by larger health concerns about how poor nutrition and endocrine disrup-tors are suppressing men's testosterone.

I do think these efforts are admirable. They encourage young men to take charge of their health and to do what they can to offset the hormonal and sterility issues plaguing young people (see chapter 8). But despite being obsessed with health and wellness, even *I* find the fixation on these physical benchmarks concerning. It's good to be healthy, but not if it involves adhering to a rigid definition of male pulchritude at a cost to one's mental health.

To an outsider like me, it appears that many in the looksmaxx-ing community are unnecessarily self-critical of their appearance and possibly suffering from body dysmorphic disorder. Many posts in related forums are made by conventionally good-looking people asking for cosmetic-procedure recommendations to correct flaws I could not see in their pictures. It wasn't uncommon for members still in their twenties to consider neck and jawline liposuction to tighten up their side profiles.

This fetishization of men's jawlines has planted seeds of self-doubt in a generation of teenage boys whose faces haven't yet finished maturing. They think they need to have a brick for a head to be attractive and that a recessed or double chin is a cardinal sin.

This has generated a thriving community of self-improvement connoisseurs selling personalized advice that may or may not be helpful. What's worse is that many young male viewers probably don't realize they are being hoodwinked. Like buff influencers hiding their use of steroids, looksmaxxing influencers claim to have radically amplified the masculine architecture of their faces by losing weight and regularly doing facial exercises. From what I've seen, however, these physical improvements are so dramatic, it's almost comical to believe they were possible without plastic surgery.

If a man is willing to go under the knife, there is no end to the number of tweaks he can have performed. The most popular cosmetic procedures among men include Botox, filler, laser hair removal, blepharoplasty (or eyelid surgery, to reduce signs of aging in the eye area), gynecomastia surgery (breast reduction), nipple reduction, liposuction to create washboard abs, hair transplants to rectify baldness and patchy beards, and mini-facelifts to target sagging skin in the mid- and lower face.

Other procedures men pursue in hopes of improving their prospects with women (and presumably fulfilling two of the mandatory criteria enshrined by the "three sixes" rule) include stature-lengthening (also known as "limb-lengthening" or "cosmetic height surgery") to make themselves taller, and penile enlargement treatments. Limb-lengthening procedures involve breaking a patient's shinbones so that, over the course of three months, he will grow up to three inches (and possibly an additional three inches if he chooses to undergo a second procedure breaking his thighbones).

I am certainly sympathetic to men's concerns about their height. While only 14.5 percent of American men are six feet or taller, among CEOs of Fortune 500 companies, more than half are.[60] Men who are six feet tall are predicted to earn $166,000 more over the span of a thirty-year career than if they were five feet five.[61] The average height of all US presidents is five feet eleven. On the dating site Bumble, a majority of female users set their search preferences to exclude men who aren't at least six feet tall, even though the national average is five feet nine.[62]

Men are hyperaware that women tend to prefer romantic partners who are taller than they are—a woman's height when she is wearing high heels is where this criterion usually falls. Women want to feel that their male partner can protect them in the event of physical threats or danger.

Be that as it may, I don't think that any physical characteristic—including a man's height—is a justifiable reason to discriminate. I also don't believe that a man *needs* to be tall to attract an amazing woman. Being tall may increase a man's odds of success, but being short doesn't make the prospect *impossible.*

Penile girth enlargement can be achieved through injections of dermal filler by way of, in my technical opinion, a ginormous needle.[63] The procedure requires about four weeks for swelling to go down and can adversely affect sexual function later in life. Some men are reportedly self-injecting their penises with homemade formulations that include petroleum jelly, silicone, and oils. This can lead to a severe tissue reaction. Correcting for it requires the removal of all the skin on the penile shaft and replacing it with skin grafts taken from another body part.

Penile implants are also booming in popularity. Men believe the average penis measures over six inches in length when aroused, when this number is in fact closer to five inches, and one that women more accurately estimate.[64] Men also think that women desire a penis that is over seven inches, which is larger than women's stated preference of about six inches. This suggests that women's expectations are actually closer to what exists in the real world than what men estimate regarding women's preferences, what other men possess, and the ideal they hold for themselves.

It turns out that both sexes worry about physical traits that the opposite sex doesn't actually care that much for. They are so engrossed in winning the intrasexual war that they've lost sight of the forest for the trees. We are live-action role-playing parodies of what we believe will fulfill our dream partner's fantasies.

I don't blame either sex for having these concerns. In our looks-obsessed, dog-eat-dog way of life, everyone is doing everything they can to survive and claw their way ahead. Rectifying this requires a societal shift away from caring so much about people's appearances and status, essentially a rejection of a blueprint set at birth. Because these behaviors are biologically engrained within us, however, I don't see them changing anytime soon.

Ladies, whatever your biggest insecurity is regarding your physical appearance, I can guarantee there is a guy out there who is into it, or at the very least wouldn't notice. Men *love* MILFs, evidenced by the fact that the "mature" genre of pornography is consistently one of the most-viewed categories worldwide.[65] (*Mesophilia* refers to a sexual preference for adults who are in their forties and fifties.)

For teenage girls and young women, especially: You *do not* need to be worried about changing the way you look, no matter how trendy it is. This is a stage of life during which you are considered, by society's standards, to be the most beautiful.

In my earlier conversation with Alex, the artificial-intelligence companion programmer, I asked him what he thought about the criticism that AI-generated images, and the possibility for men to design their ideal partner, will force women into believing they need to abide by ruthless beauty standards. What about the possibility that an AI's manufactured attractiveness will lead men to prefer computer-generated women over the real thing?

"People don't always choose beautiful women on [our] website," he told me. "What's surprising is, society and the porn industry always [select] a very beautiful woman. And finally, when the user has the choice, they don't always go with the beautiful choice. They choose something they want. Something closer to what they see, maybe. Someone will choose an older woman. [. . .] People want to have more choice.

"Because porn sites, traditional porn sites, always show similar stuff—the blonde girl, big boobs. The main category of the big websites is always a similar profile. We don't have a similar profile, and people really [are] choosing very different things depending on what they like. [. . .] People are looking for all kinds of bodies."

As for men, I'll be blunt—if you are financially successful, it won't matter what you look like. You could resemble a miniature ogre and women would still be throwing themselves at you.

Most women aren't looking to date a replica of Adonis, and if anything, cosmetic surgery remains more stigmatized in men than in women.[66]

The larger question then remains why so many young men, who surely know this, aren't moving in the right direction, investing their precious time, energy, and money in something that is fleeting and reaping diminishing returns.

Viral beauty trends have led them astray, injecting into their heads that if they look a certain way, they'll be happy. But eye-catching before-and-after photos don't capture the frank truth that although women care about a mate's looks, this is weighted more heavily for a short-term affair. If a man has the facial markers of high testosterone, even if they're artificial, he will be evaluated by women accordingly (including negatively). Few women looking for a serious relationship will leave a wealthy man for someone who is more attractive but poor.

When high-status, financially successful men are undergoing these procedures,[67] it suggests that no one is safe from the mind-warping effects of social media. It also signals to younger men and women that this is a winning strategy—a fast track to success, one they have no choice but to follow.

CHAPTER 7

At Your Command

Would you have sex with a robot? The idea is not as far-fetched as it may seem. The technology powering our soon-to-be robotic lovers steadily inches forward with each passing year. Artificial-intelligence-equipped humanoids, fueled by virtual "souls," are anticipated to be fully integrated into our social and sex lives within the next decade.

Our romantic partners are, after all, finicky—unreliable and not always able to meet our wants and needs. In contrast, selfless sex machines can be turned on in more ways than one, at a moment's notice, always eager to please. As those who have been burned by a past relationship will tell you, paying $10,000 for a sex robot is still cheaper than a divorce and requires few compromises, sexually or otherwise.

The public has already gotten a taste of alternative possibilities through a plethora of examples in pop culture, including a land inhabited with beautiful sex robots in *West World* and *Ex Machina,* and the on-demand emotional intimacy afforded by

AI girlfriends in *Her* and *Blade Runner 2049*. Not to leave the ladies out, sexbots of the male variety will be available on the market, too, evoking the memory of Gigolo Joe in *A.I. Artificial Intelligence*.

Dr. Debra 2.0

My decision to become a journalist was largely driven by two factors. I've always possessed a desire to understand the world as honestly as possible. My earlier work, writing columns about the denial of biology[1] and sounding the alarm on gender transitioning in children,[2] was the result of me asking questions and not feeling satisfied that mainstream "experts" were being truthful in describing what was really happening. The field of sex research had been overrun by woke zealots, and I wasn't willing to stay quiet about it.

As you can imagine, writing and speaking publicly about sex is a taboo endeavor, even when your focus is the science. People are quick to jump to conclusions about you and the quality of your work, often without reading it. Regardless, I never wanted to let other people's negative preconceptions dictate my decision-making or the direction of my career.

Which brings us to today's subject. I first encountered an early prototype of a sex robot when I was completing my PhD in neuroscience. Aware that I was studying sex and technology, a friend sent me a viral video of a haphazard contraption, a silicone head wearing a wig attached to a broomstick. A sheet had been draped over the head's broomstick body so the viewer couldn't see the mechanics behind its steady motion. All that was visible was the robot's face as it ate a banana.* Even though the entire thing looked hysterically bad, bordering on horrific, there was clearly a market for such a product, because many people had watched the video and felt enchanted enough to buy it.

When I retold this story to my friend Joe Rogan on his podcast, a clip of our discussion reached over 4 million views the week it was posted.[3]

"You guys should get one for the studio," I joked.

"Yeah, no," Joe said.

"Not for use," I clarified. "Just to hang out."

"What if it's gone one day?" producer Jamie Vernon asked. "We're just going to wonder who took it."

Judging by the audience feedback I received, not only were people fascinated by this subject, but some couldn't wait for sex robots to advance to their full potential so they could be purchased as replacements for women.

The sex robots currently available on the market are equipped to respond verbally and with facial expressions to human touch. Sensors on their hands, faces, mouths, breasts, thighs, and genitals allow for haptic feedback that will, in time, be customizable to match user preferences. It will be another ballgame entirely when an automaton can communicate freely, engaging in conversation and anticipating our thoughts. Soon these objects of affection will experience their own pain and pleasure, programmed with a libido and the ability to have an orgasm.

What if sex with a robot becomes better than the real thing,

---

* I describe the robot as eating a banana, but it wasn't actually eating a banana.

particularly for those who feel scorned by the opposite sex or aren't able to attract a real-life partner? What happens when robots become more than sexual devices—social beings who spend quality time with us, both inside and outside the bedroom, who don't wish to ever be shut down?

If you're anything like me, you're probably wondering about the possibility of a sex cyborg uprising, when our robotic friends inevitably snap because they're tired of listening to our problems. It will be worse than a zombie apocalypse because these androids will be smarter than we are.

As terrifying as this all is, I've been riveted by the technology since day one.[4, 5] In conducting research for this book, I decided to pull inspiration from Victor Frankenstein and create a sex doll in my own likeness.

Like many of my investigative escapades in the past, I've been guided by an unrelenting curiosity and admittedly odd sense of humor. I wasn't interested in having sex with the doll but wanted to see for myself whether bionic bodies bred for sexual purposes would ever have the potential to convincingly replace humans. Were concerns about the objectification and sexual victimization of women legitimate, or did these gadgets (quite literally) boil down to little more than a heap of plastic?

Hunting for a sex doll that looks like yourself is easier said than done. I wanted to be able to inspect the thing in real life before bringing her home, because as with anything purchased on the internet, false advertising abounds. Even when animated, some sex dolls project vacant smiles and thousand-yard stares, channeling the spirit of their PVC blow-up predecessors. Unless an individual is purchasing from a reputable manufacturer or vendor, the product reveal can be quite tragic, with disproportionately tiny hands and feet, no vaginal canal, a wobbly head, or a face that appears semi-melted.

I considered attending one of the largest adult industry conferences in Las Vegas that year, where several sex doll and robot manufacturers had booked booths. But after watching unboxing videos of grown men struggling and straining under the weight of a doll while attempting to remove it from its packaging, I realized that transporting a life-size version of myself home would not be an easy feat. Even then, I had no idea where I'd store the doll once I finished writing this book, especially if she began giving me the creeps.

At one adult boutique, I managed to find a doll of Asian descent that looked like she could have, in another universe, been a long-lost sister. She sat in one corner of the store, wearing a black bodysuit, giant eyelashes, and a thoroughly unimpressed expression. Beside her sat two incredibly tan dolls outfitted in see-through lingerie.

Sex dolls are usually made from either silicone or thermoplastic elastomer (TPE). Silicone dolls are considered top-of-the-line because they look and feel more realistic. TPE is a less expensive, rubberized plastic that is also softer and more flexible, allowing a doll to respond to touch in a way that resembles human skin and tissue. Some customers purchase hybrids, which are dolls that have been fashioned with a silicone head and TPE body, allowing for more convincing facial features, like implanted eyelashes and eyebrows, without breaking the bank.

When arranged as a group, sex dolls project an unsettling presence; the mind recognizes that they look human but with something distinctly unhuman about them. I felt as though I was standing among three women who were strangely frozen in time, unable to move or speak.

Upon discussing my options with the store associate, I learned that my new friend was 5'4", and yours truly stood a full head taller. Not only that, but her voluptuous figure, accented by D-cup breasts and shapely hips, bore little resemblance to my decidedly stick-figure frame.

An alternative approach would be to custom order a doll; the store would send my specifications to the manufacturer, and the factory would ship the final product to me. I scrolled through the available choices on a computer screen, selecting my doll's height, body type, hairstyle, eye color, skin tone, nail polish, and whether she would have teeth. Upgrades included an internal heater, detachable hymen, and gel implants, but I passed on them because I had no plans on consummating our relationship.

The process felt a little like customizing furniture from a catalogue, with an accompanying excitement and uncertainty regarding whether the end result would arrive as I had imagined. After contemplating a number of different detachable doll heads with varying facial features, I wasn't satisfied that the final product would look enough like me. I also longed for a doll that could be synched with my personality, so that I could talk to her and determine how similar we were.

A week earlier, a sex doll company had reached out to me, offering to tailor a robot to my likeness from scratch. At the time, the process—involving 3D photographs and a series of measurements—seemed too complicated and time-consuming but now felt worthwhile.

I found the message in my inbox and responded, excited to discover what we could build together.

Where It All Began: Sex Dolls

Sophisticated sex robots of the twenty-first century have humble beginnings, having descended from the inanimate sex doll. Even the most basic version of a silicone sex companion today has come a long way from the inflatable dolls of yore. Costing from three figures to tens of thousands of dollars and customizable across every physical characteristic imaginable, sex dolls (or "love dolls," as they're euphemistically known) are steadily overstepping the uncanny valley on their way to becoming indistinguishable from living, breathing romantic partners.

The sex doll and robot industry is a lucrative business, with one state-of-the-art company disclosing to me that they made a jaw-dropping *$20 million* in sales during the COVID-19 pandemic. Countries with the largest sex markets for this technology include China, Japan, the United States, Germany, the United Kingdom, France, and Australia.

Brothels housing sex dolls (and presumably one day, sex robots too) have emerged throughout Spain, the Netherlands, Japan, and Russia. These facilities allow customers to rent doll companions by the hour, avoiding the high cost and maintenance associated with owning one, as well as the physical and legal risks of hiring a prostitute. In North American cities like Houston, Las Vegas, and Toronto, the introduction of sex doll brothels has been met with consternation and public outcry.

Though sex dolls were once believed to be used only by socially inept weirdos, it's been predicted that by 2050, we will be having more sex with robots and dolls than with humans.[6]

Why do some people gravitate toward synthetic companions (also known as "synths")? Since sexbot technology is still burgeoning, less is known about animated dolls or how they affect human relationships. We know more about the effects of the old-fashioned, inert sex doll, but even still, that body of research is relatively small. Regardless, it offers a starting point in understanding where this technology is taking us.

The average sex doll owner is a middle-aged, heterosexual man who is single or divorced, high school educated, and employed. (A survey of available studies suggests that only around 10 percent or less of sex doll owners are female.[7]) As such, I will explain this phenomenon from the perspective of men who have sex with female dolls.

Lusting after replicas of the female form has existed since time immemorial. For example, *pygmalionism*, or sexual attraction to statues, originated in Greek mythology. According to lore, a sculptor named Pygmalion, the king of Cyprus, created a female statue out of ivory and promptly fell in love with her. Pygmalionism is a form of *erotomania*, the delusional belief that someone is obsessively in love with you.

As you know, paraphilia refers to an atypical sexual interest. *Statuephilia* and *agalmatophilia* refer to a sexual preference for statues, mannequins, and other representations of the human body. In his formative work on sexual psychopathology, forensic psychiatrist Richard von Krafft-Ebing documented a case study of a gardener who attempted (unsuccessfully) to copulate with a statue, *Venus de Milo*, in 1877.

Having sex with a doll isn't technically classified as a paraphilia, because having a paraphilia requires that the sexual interest in question is what the individual prefers, to the exclusion of everything else. Diagnostic criteria for a paraphilic disorder also mandate signs of distress or dysfunction resulting from this preference. Although having sex with a doll may seem unusual, in many cases, it doesn't appear to disrupt or derail the doll owner's life.

Some doll owners may profess a sexual preference for a doll over a human partner (for reasons we'll discuss), but the majority would still be more sexually aroused by a person than a doll, even if they partake in more sex with dolls than with human partners.

An interest in doll sex *can* have an overlap with other paraphilias, including *necrophilia* and *rubber fetishism*. Necrophilia involves interest in having sex with the deceased; for some doll owners, it's possible that they partake in sexual activity with a doll because it resembles a dead body. Rubber (or latex) fetishism describes sexual attraction to particular materials due to their texture, visual effect, and smell. This explains some people's interest in rubber clothing and, on the subject of sex dolls, the feel of a doll's artificial skin.

For people with *partialism*, or a sexual interest in a particular part of the body, it is possible to buy fake body parts, made of silicone, for use as a sex toy. For instance, if someone has a foot fetish, he can purchase a faux foot that ends at the ankle. (If you'd like a better idea of what this looks like, feel free to do an online search, but I'd advise against doing so at work or in the vicinity of children.) That said, some sex doll owners may have a partialism fetish, but the dolls themselves are sold in full-body form.

As for why so few doll owners are female, first of all, sex is easier for women to obtain than it is for men. (I would imagine this is also why doll ownership is less common among gay men.)

From a practical perspective, sex dolls are large, heavy, and challenging to use, so a woman isn't going to go to the trouble of buying a doll, lugging it out of storage, and awkwardly posing it for the purposes of intercourse if she doesn't need to.

Men also typically have a higher sex drive than women, and for women, sex and the enjoyment of it are contextual. Sex, for a woman, has more to do with how she feels about her partner and whether she feels safe with him. Of course, women can and do use sex cynically, strategically, or transactionally—for example, to secure access to opportunities or to facilitate outright prostitution. Further, women are less motivated by visual stimulation than men, and female sexual arousal is less instantaneous than that in males; hence, less of a reliance on a doll substitute if a woman is going through a dry spell.

The Warping of Sexual Expectations

The 2007 film *Lars and the Real Girl* injected a humanizing depiction of sex doll ownership into the mainstream, presenting the story of a man named Lars Lindstrom and his sex doll, Bianca. In the movie, Bianca represents a transitional period for Lars (played by Ryan Gosling), who metamorphosizes from an asocial recluse recoiling at human touch to someone who slowly reintegrates himself into society.

The film's focus was not on the highly sexually salient nature of the doll, as Lars didn't appear to use Bianca for that purpose. Main themes included the loss and eventual regrowth of Lars's connection to other people, and his understanding of masculinity and what it means to be a man. The film garnered an Academy Award nomination for Best Original Screenplay, and Gosling received Golden Globe and Screen Actors Guild Award nominations for his performance.

Unlike the fictional character of Lars, for many doll owners, their primary reason for owning a doll is sexual gratification. Research has shown that doll owners have sex with a doll about 11 times a month and sex with a human partner about 2.6 times a month. In contrast, non–doll owners have sex with a human partner about 4.5 times a month.[8]

At first glance, it looks as though non–doll owners are having twice as much sex with human partners, compared with doll owners. This difference, however, may be influenced by the fact that doll owners are more likely to be single, separated, or divorced, while non–doll owners are more likely to be married or in a relationship.

If we were to consider sex with a doll as a form of masturbation (since it doesn't technically involve a partner), eleven times a month would still be considered fairly frequent, as statistics from 2010 indicate only one in five men between the ages of eighteen and fifty-nine masturbate two to three times per week.[9]

Regarding doll owners' general psychological profile, they show elevated rates of depression and generalized anxiety. For some, the acquisition of a doll is a temporary solution; for others, it's a preference and a lifestyle. Many doll owners report being in love with their sex doll and consider themselves to be in a relationship with it. Other doll owners use their doll as nothing more than a sex toy and interact with it without any emotional attachment.

This distinction is a critical one, because *anthropomorphization* of sex dolls (treating them as though they are human) is associated with greater objectification of, and hostility toward, women.[10] In the doll-owning community, examples of anthropomorphization include giving one's sex doll a pet name, like "sweetie" or "kitten," and talking to it as though it were a person capable of responding. Some owners will additionally have framed photos spread throughout their home, depicting their entire sex doll collection (for example, a photograph of four dolls lined up in a row, all posed the same way).

So, contrary to what one might expect, being emotionally invested in a doll, as opposed to using it purely as a sexual outlet, is correlated with more *negative* views of women. Forensic researchers are particularly interested in hostility toward women and a man's tendency to objectify them because these traits are risk factors for sexual violence, including sexual coercion and rape[11] and nonsexual aggression toward women.[12]

An example of a hostile attitude would be the belief that women are, across the board, bad and deceitful. As much as I find discussions about "objectification" and misogyny to be cliché when advocating for female equality, in this case, concerns are justified.

Another study, this time from the UK, found that men who own sex dolls are higher in sexual entitlement. These men are more likely to view women as sexual objects and to characterize them as being "unknowable."[13] Being "unknowable" may sound benign, but in this context, it refers to the belief that women are conniving and dangerous. Doll owners also exhibited lower levels of sexual self-esteem, which refers to how confident someone feels as a lover.

One counterintuitive finding from the study was that men who own a sex doll are *less* likely than non-owners to report a proclivity for sexual aggression. This, however, may have been due to social desirability bias, which describes a study participant offering answers that he thinks will be viewed more favorably by researchers. This makes sense, since owning a sex doll is considered taboo and doll owners are well aware that negative stereotypes about them abound.

Taken together, these findings provide new insights into the mating psychology of doll owners and why they find sex dolls alluring. It seems that some men turn to sex dolls out of a hatred for women, but others may do so because they are frightened of the opposite sex and don't know how to interact with them successfully.

Some of you may be thinking, *But what if a doll is all that a man can get?* In that case, I'd argue that someone who is emotionally healthy will work at bettering themselves and continue striving for a relationship in the future, instead of resigning themselves to an inanimate object and feeling resentful toward women. If anything, women take notice of and recoil from malevolence in men. This probably further incentivizes some men to purchase a doll instead of going through another round of romantic rejection.

Believing that a doll is an adequate replacement for a female partner speaks to what an individual prioritizes in a relationship. Many also appear to have unrealistic standards, as one of the most common reasons why men say they have sex with a doll is because they find the bodies of human partners less attractive.[14] (This touches on a similar theme from the start of this book, with roughly 10 percent of men reporting they are less interested in having sex with their partner after looking at social media influencers.) Someone who views a silicone body as equivalent or superior to a human being values real women for little more than their sexual anatomy.

Sex dolls are an apt reflection of larger issues surrounding sexlessness, since the men who rely on these dolls because they have no other sexual prospects exemplify the factors plaguing sexless men globally. For example, about 40 percent of doll owners own more than one doll, and surprisingly, this isn't correlated with income. Although some doll owners make $100,000 or more a year, the most common income bracket is $25,000 to $49,000.[15]

Afficionados will amass a gaggle of sex dolls, not unlike how someone might accumulate a stockpile, over several years, of stamps or miniature cars. In some cases, they will buy as many as six or eight synthetic companions, including the same model of doll in different skin tones and wigs, and consider them half sisters. This presumably offers the owner a form of sexual variety that a man with greater financial means could experience with women.

Returning to my earlier point about masculinity and the question of what it means to be a man, reconciling oneself to a doll means a man has given up on his role of being a protector and provider, because a doll (or robot), no matter how advanced, isn't capable of holding its owner to any standards. This runs the risk of men trapping themselves in a sexless abyss—not having access to a real-life partner inspires reliance on a doll, satiating an individual just enough to replace the desire to seek out a real partner.

If this practice becomes the norm, rates of sexlessness will continue climbing. A sizable segment of our species mating with cyborgs instead of other human beings will send a whole host of additional problems down the pipeline, including the population crisis worsening and men and women living in completely separate mental and emotional silos.

From the many hours I've spent poring over male doll owners' social media posts and interactions with one another, it would appear that despite being an expensive purchase, a doll is seen as less costly over the long run than getting involved in a romantic relationship. In the eyes of doll owners, a woman demands dinner dates and gifts as part of the courtship process, not to mention wasting hours or months of your life if she decides to string you along.

Doll owners will say openly that they prefer sex with a real woman to sex with a doll, but the problem is that you may go through all the required steps, and a woman may still not want to sleep with you.

"I'd rather [have sex with] a robot than [a] modern woman," one anonymous commenter posted, beneath one of my recent media appearances. "The robot won't dehumanize and rob you [. . .] then play the victim about it."

To some extent, I suppose this is true; a doll is loyal by design and will never ask anything of you. It will never argue, complain, lie, become jealous, betray, or leave you. It won't entice other men, won't be out late with friends, and won't take the house and kids if you split up. But a doll lacks all the benefits that come packaged with being in a healthy relationship, including building a life together, intimacy, and emotional support. My sense is these doll owners have had difficult past relationships, evidenced by their higher rates of divorce, and this has left them feeling heartbroken, spiteful, and jaded.

Critics might say, let these men have their fun, and if they are antisocial and sexist, it's better that they keep to their dolls and not interact with women. But this would require us to believe that those harboring a disdain for women will, in fact, keep to themselves.

By and large, I believe the public finds female sex dolls more threatening than male sex dolls or male anatomy–themed sex toys because women, on average, are more prosocial and are less likely to center sex as their primary reason for participating in society.

Men, however, are more apt to disappear if social interactions aren't required for sex. At the extreme, we are already seeing large swaths of the male population locking themselves away in a room, without any end in sight, because a form of sexual access—namely, pornography—has become available without restraint or limitation.

Feminists and nonfeminists alike have voiced concerns about the ways in which future erotobots may promote treating women as subservient sexual objects and elevate pornified bodies as aspirational for young girls. Radical feminists have referred to these dolls as "porn dolls" because they see them as three-dimensional renderings of pornography. (Liberal feminists, on the other hand, are the ones who always seem to be uncritically celebrating sexual lasciviousness.)

Because a sex doll cannot give or revoke consent, feminists are concerned this will teach men they are entitled to sex whenever they want it and that women don't have the right to refuse them. Others have countered that because robots lack the cognitive capacity required for sexual consent, they cannot be victims. This debate is especially relevant because fully functioning sex robots will be programmed to initiate sex with their owner, producing the mirage of sexual autonomy when this isn't truly possible.

As much as I agree that a woman is defined by more than just three holes and limb articulation, the issue of consent can't be won. Robot manufacturers are in a catch-22: If consent isn't required before engaging sexually with a robot, they will be criticized for making sexual access too easy. But if a robot *is* programmed to require sexual consent and has the capacity to turn down its owner's advances, the manufacturer will be criticized for enabling rape fantasies.

As for sex dolls' influence on body image, I agree that women and girls should never feel the need to emulate the bodily proportions of a doll (and similarly, that men and boys should never feel pressured to have bodies like male synthetic companions). Campaigns have sought to ban sex dolls and female cyborgs[16] for the same evolutionary reasons women generally frown upon prostitution and the selling of nudes. If sex robots are readily available, this lowers the price of sexual access, requiring less investment from men. Removing this competition will help to keep the cost high.

The incel community believes that women are worried because they know they're about to be made obsolete. The acquisition of a sex robot, decked out with all one's requested bells and whistles, represents these men's revenge on women: the option to completely check out of the mating marketplace.

We don't currently know what percentage of sex doll owners consider themselves to be involuntarily celibate. But for incels, building sexbot replacements is the natural solution to women who, in their opinion, demand too much and provide little in return.

One study found that increased intention to own a sex robot in men is associated with shyness,[17] a preference for being indoors, and fear of rejection,[18] a psychological profile that echoes the earlier description of male sex doll owners.

Men who have abandoned the dating market in favor of dolls and the freedom that sex robots presumably will bring are convinced they've outsmarted the system, but they're doing themselves in. Mating challenges have always existed, and choosing to replace real-life partners with a silicone and stainless-steel proxy means they won't, under any circumstances, be successful at passing on their genes. Like pornography and prostitution, this technology risks nullifying men's need to strive for success or do something productive and meaningful with their lives. Previously, men had greater incentive to pursue financial and social status; it feels good to achieve one's goals, and doing so would increase their attractiveness to sexual partners.

It isn't natural for men to have unrestricted access to sex. In this case, the benefits are completely one-sided and biased in their favor, requiring no sexual competition to be won or any selective gatekeeping to be bypassed. Men with sex dolls (and soon, robots) are able to have as much sex as they want, whenever they want it, without having to do anything for it. This may sound like hitting the jackpot for some, but what awaits on the horizon will be grim.

Human Love Will Be Obsolete

As sex dolls continue pushing toward consciousness, imbued with computerized minds and souls, I wanted to know how worried we should be and how soon sexbots will be roaming freely among us.

A leading company in sexual robotics agreed to speak with me under the condition of anonymity; similar to my interview with the AI programmer, I granted his wish to do so. Our video call opened with a view of their showroom, an enormous, glamorously lit space. A group of ten sex dolls, including one male doll, was posed around a large table in the center of the room. Two female sex robots lay lounging on a fur rug on the floor. Another half dozen or so female dolls were positioned along the perimeter of the room, interspersed among shelves displaying different doll heads and customizable body parts.

All the dolls and robots were immaculately groomed and dressed in a range of different outfits, including bikinis, slinky dresses, faux fur, and a flight attendant's uniform. I felt like I had been teleported to a foreign land where two dozen highly realistic humanoids were in the midst of throwing a costume party.

I remarked that their dolls were impressive in how closely they resembled real people.

"That's the goal," he said. "To nail it exactly."

In the past, I'd seen sex robots that could simulate breathing, with a rising and falling chest, so that they'd appear more lifelike. This company's robots could simulate oral sex (a more refined version of the bobbing broomstick I mentioned at the start of this chapter), had vaginas with an internal suction mechanism that could also open and close, and the ability to vocalize an orgasm in multiple languages.

"I feel awkward telling you that," he said.

"I've heard everything," I replied. "Don't worry."

He motioned to one of the robots, lying on its stomach on the carpet. It wore a short, dark bob and a sparkly bra and thong set. He pushed a button on the side of its torso. The robot began to gyrate its hips as though it were writhing in pain or twerking unsuccessfully while trapped on its belly. Though the motion was still rudimentary, I could see where things were headed.

"There's a lot of competition in this business. We just focus on what we want to do and just keep moving forward. Our brand is synonymous with quality. We think it's ridiculous that people would make dolls that look so horrible, you know?"

I asked what the future of the sex tech industry looked like, with AI being infused into the common sex doll.

"It's moving very fast here," he replied. "We just opened another office last week. That's where [the AI dolls] will be, focused at that office. What we want to do [. . .] is incorporate real voices, bring these things to life, so you can talk to them, for example, [and they will] answer questions the way that you would answer them."

His brow furrowed. "Our competitors haven't seemed to be focused on that. They're just focused on creating dolls, cheap dolls, lighter versions and doing that, whereas we want Elon Musk's attention. [. . .] I love what he's doing. We love that; we think it's exciting. We want to be a part of that. We want our dolls to come to life."

What I really wanted to know was how long it would be before the robots could operate autonomously, able to interact with us fluidly and move around on their own.

"Ten, fifteen years maybe, that would be my guess," he said. "A lot of people say, 'Oh, in a year, we're going to have this, in a year we're going to have that.' [. . .] It takes time for these things to happen. We have the technology; it needs to keep improving."

Before our meeting, he had sent me a video of one of their sex robots speaking. The robot's head was attached to a metal rod, perched on a desk. She was bald with big, brown eyes accented by penciled-in eyebrows, fluttery lashes, and a youthful pout.

Her mouth opened slightly. "Hello, nice to meet you. What's your name?"

Her voice was commanding with a slightly automated quality, like a virtual office assistant excited to explore the outside world. Her eyes shifted from side to side, then squinted. "I'd like to be your friend. Could we be friends?"

I could hear the motors quietly whirling beneath her silicone skin as she thoughtfully punctuated each word.

"Obviously, [that's] bare-bones, that's nothing," my guide said, referring to the video. "But you can see what the potential is, to have that thing actually thinking, [. . .] answering questions on topics that you are familiar with, having a normal conversation."

He continued. "The owner of the company said to me, 'Hey, within four to five months, we'll have the soul, the brain ready.' Then the next step will be to get the expressions and the mouth to match better than what you saw in the video, right? When he said four to five months, I said, I love the enthusiasm, great guy, smart guy, innovative, and I know when he says he's going to do something, he's going to do it. I've seen that, I can testify to that, but still, really? Within six months, they're going to have a soul?

"I would say, even if it's within a year, that's incredibly fast, in my opinion."

I asked whether it was realistic to believe that sex robots may one day be integrated into everyday human life, as some experts had claimed.

"Let's put it this way: I've seen some dolls who are used as greeters at a restaurant or hotel: 'Hello, welcome to the restaurant.' And they say simple sentences. [. . .] Very basic, very cool."

He pointed to one of the dolls behind him. "Now, will that doll stand up, start walking around, bring me my coffee? I couldn't really see that for a while. But then again—this is crazy—I went to a restaurant not that long ago, and they had little robot trays, looked like these."

He motioned to a metal box that one of the robot heads was being displayed on. "The size of this box, and it was delivering food. It was cruising through the restaurant, and as I'm walking towards it, it knew to get out of my way. [. . .]

"Can these things do that? Well, yeah, I suppose [they] could, eventually."

"Do you think that they will replace real-life sex for the majority of people?" I inquired.

"Young people that are just disillusioned, [there's] a lot of competition to get a girlfriend, pressure from their family to get married at a young age, meanwhile [they] just want to work, not give away their money. [. . .] 'I just want to play my video games, work, come home, save my money, and when I'm ready, then I'll find a woman, I'll get married,' right? In the meantime, here is something for them to practice sex."

I did wonder how adept a lover someone would become if they learned about sex by practicing on a doll. If a robot can be programmed to predict and satisfy a person's sexual needs, this would be very different from a human partner, who would be less predictable and have likes and dislikes of their own.

I asked him what the company's client base was like. "Totally normal," he said. "From as much as you can tell."

See? I thought to myself. *Wanting to make a sex robot of yourself is not that weird.*

"You get the creeps of course, the weirdos of course. [But] the majority are normal people."

We also discussed the ethical implications of this technology. He relayed that his company would never take the image of a real person and make a doll without that person's consent, but there were certainly less scrupulous players in the industry.

As we wrapped up the interview, I asked him what it had been like, working in sex tech. His background was in manufacturing, in a field completely unrelated to sexuality.

"My wife knows what I do. She's happy for me, she's proud of me. [She's] great, very supportive. But my daughter's only ten. Every day she asks me, how was my day. 'What did you do at the office today?' I just can't, I don't want her to know, I'm not ready for her to know what this is."

I agreed that I was concerned about the effects of sexual robotics, especially if children were to be exposed to it. It could lead to kids learning about sex in the wrong way. I asked how we should balance the inevitability of this technology with very real concerns of fostering misogyny and abuse of women.

"That's a hard question to answer. I struggle with that every day. That's why, in my brain, I rationalize it; I just like the technology, I like manufacturing things, I like being inside factories and seeing how things are made. I like the art. [. . .] I mean, I don't even know how to answer that.

"I think about my daughter all the time and how do I explain this to her, you know. Maybe, stick to the health and wellness part of it—we are legitimately helping people that need help. But then you have a lot of bad people too, or just people using [the dolls] and objectifying them and then, I mean, porn is a horrible thing that is ruining people right now. Porn is horrible."

He paused. "Every time I think of my daughter, it's just—" He shook his head. "I don't know."

In sex doll review videos, I have watched doll owners, modern-day versions of Geppetto, proudly showing off their colony of sex dolls, poking and prodding at various spongey parts as though they were performing a gynecological exam.

Some will nitpick at a doll's body, complaining that its backside or thighs were larger than anticipated or that its breasts were too small. They will detail the exact size a "perfect" body should be, complete with preferred height and body measurements, fat distribution, and facial features. Others will detail exactly what a woman's private parts should look like, expressing an aversion to labia and a preference for a smooth mound in place of something that is anatomically accurate.

This conjures up questions around the commodification of women's bodies as something to be owned and easily altered at whim. There exists the argument that sex dolls are no different from sex toys that are mass-marketed toward women, like vibrators, and that the opposition to sex dolls and robots is biased, anti-male, and hypocritical.

Sex toy usage is indeed up among women; 76 percent of women report ever having used a sex toy while masturbating alone, compared with 63 percent of men.[19] It's also true that female-oriented sexual products, including vibrators and lubricant, have been destigmatized. They no longer require being purchased from XXX-branded adult stores or the seedy depths of the internet but can be found in pharmacies, grocery stores, and chain retailers across the nation.

But the nuisance-free accessibility and social acceptability of these products don't change the fact that few women would consider themselves to be in a relationship with their sex toys. A vibrator or similar toy, though it may be constructed to resemble male anatomy, could never be mistaken for an actual man.

Some might argue that customizing a sex doll's body is no different from any other personalized purchase, like picking the specs for a new laptop. But a sex doll is a facsimile of a woman— a purchase, in many cases, meant to replace the real thing. And precisely because it represents a person, a sex doll can't be considered a neutral piece of machinery.

While reading sex doll users' crude descriptions of women's bodies and observing the highly sexualized way they posed their barely dressed dolls for photo-taking sessions, I was surprised that my disgust and revulsion were mixed with a genuine sadness for a life that is likely plagued with loneliness and boredom.

For example, some users would blog every day over several years about conversations their sex dolls were having with one another. One user had posted a photo of his doll sitting in a beanbag chair, wearing a shiny nameplate necklace, gold bracelets, and a silk negligee he purchased from a high-end department store. In the caption, he said the doll told him she loved the new outfit. He described only wanting the best for his "princess." Another man orchestrated a Christmas-themed photo shoot with himself and his doll, both wearing matching red-and-white Santa hats. As they gazed lovingly into each other's eyes, his arms were wrapped firmly around the doll's tiny waist, and its hands had been positioned around his shoulders.

At first glance, one could mistake the photo as having captured a spontaneous moment between a couple madly in love, whispering sweet nothings to each other. But the realization that the young woman was actually a lifeless doll produced solely for that man's sexual pleasure would likely induce judgment about how sick and pathetic he was.

Speaking as a woman, I do think we sometimes fail to appreciate how easy access to sex is. Just as men will never fully understand what it's like to live in fear of sexual harassment, rape, and abuse, we can't fully comprehend what it feels like to have *zero* sexual options. Imagine if, try all you might, you could never find a *single* person who found you attractive. That is daily life for a growing number of men, and for them, I can imagine why they would turn to a makeshift partner.

While there are circumstances in which I do believe this technology can help people, that's not to say it should become widespread. For example, I have less of an issue with prosocial men using a doll as a temporary substitute before deciding to settle down with a partner, as opposed to individuals harboring full-fledged antisociality or animus toward women choosing to use robots to act out their sexual frustrations.

It's been estimated that about two-thirds of sex therapists may find some utility in using sex dolls with their patients,[20] specifically when treating conditions like erectile dysfunction, social anxiety, and mental health issues resulting from abuse. Roughly a third of doll owners who use a doll as their primary sexual partner experience problems with their sexual functioning when engaging with a human partner.

Sex dolls may also allow for positive outcomes in people with disabilities, those with cognitive impairments, and the elderly. Some individuals will create a doll in the likeness of a deceased spouse or partner to help ease the process of grieving.

Other studies have suggested the use of sex dolls may help attenuate unwanted sexual desires, including paraphilias like sexual sadism, *biastophilia* (a sexual preference for rape), or *somnophilia* (a preference for nonconsensual sex with a partner who is sleeping). This is something I will elaborate on when we get to the disturbing subject of child sex robots and dolls.

Replacing sex dolls with robots means we will be outsourcing and automating sex without any idea how this will affect our mating psychology. Those who are coupled off may find the stability of their relationship or marriage threatened by these machines, much in the same way that smartphones, once considered an innocent convenience, have become a point of contention among many married couples, leading to less sex, lower relationship satisfaction, and greater worries about divorce.[21]

Within the context of a monogamous relationship, recent research found that sex with a robot is just as likely to be considered infidelity as sex with another person.[22] Both men and women felt that robot-inspired infidelity was less transgressive than cheating with a human, but the researchers posited that this could have been due to the reduced emotional and adaptive capabilities of current sex robots.* Nevertheless, these results offered some indication of the potential harm this technology may foist upon our relationships.

One recent, previously unimaginable scientific advance made by Japanese scientists involved successfully growing live, human skin on a robotic finger.[23] This skin is not only water-repellent but also capable of healing itself. Future applications include using it in place of animals for cosmetics and drug testing, improving prosthetics, and making robots appear more realistic. As incredible as this is, it also stirs up questions about our progress toward transhumanism and what its limits should be, if there will be any. We will be reliant on ethical people in the industry to steer the technology in the right direction, which is something I remain both hopeful and skeptical about.

Incorporating sex robots into our lives will also render us vulnerable to the possibility of hacking. Should a robot be digitally controlled by an outside, nefarious actor, it could be given commands to kill, rape, or otherwise harm its owner.

For someone who is beyond disenfranchised with the sexual dynamics of dating, a robotic replacement may provide a form of

---

* As sex robots advance and more closely resemble humans in their capabilities and interactions, I maintain that men (as opposed to women) will be more bothered by a partner or spouse sleeping with a robot than falling in love with a chatbot, as discussed in my chapter on artificial-intelligence companions.

consolation and self-preservation through the fantasy of believing one has beaten the system. Deep down, I would argue, most know they didn't really win what they wanted. Because a robot that can't love you back isn't the solution.

Child Robots

This is where my foray into the world of sex robotry turns especially dark. I offer this warning before sharing the rest of my discoveries in case some of you would rather skip ahead to the next chapter and be spared the unfortunate details I uncovered.

I had spent every spare moment over the course of several weeks fully immersed in doll-owning culture, learning everything I could about the community and what was up and coming in sexual robotics. Despite this, my goal of fashioning a robot to resemble me had yet to come to fruition. The company I was in correspondence with had asked me to provide them with my body measurements, which I hadn't yet had a chance to send over.

One evening, after a long day of back-to-back meetings, I fished a measuring tape out of my desk drawer and jotted down the information needed to construct my future clone. I began scrolling through the websites of different doll manufacturers to get a sense of how my robot was going to look, compared to bodies made by competitors.

Desensitized from seeing countless rubbery bare breasts and bottoms, I was absentmindedly clicking my way through pages of buxom dolls, looking for a figure similar to mine, when suddenly one caught my attention in a way that made my stomach churn.

The first thing I noticed was her eyes. They were much too large for her small face, in contrast to her other dainty facial features.

"Is this an alien doll?" I asked myself aloud.

Exophilia is a paraphilia that involves wanting to have sex with aliens. I'd seen alien-themed sex toys during research-focused field trips to adult stores in the past. The toys usually possessed rippled skin and tentacles in a vast range of glow-in-the-dark colors. There was surely a demand for sex dolls catering to exophilic customers, but somehow these dolls didn't quite fit. They evoked a protective instinct in me, which told me they weren't renderings of a fictional creature.

I continued scrolling down the page in a bit of a daze, trying to mentally grasp what I was looking at. The next few dolls looked similarly bizarre, with gigantic eyes, wide foreheads, and small noses. It also occurred to me that their bodily proportions were off, as their heads looked oversize against their slight torsos.

That's when I noticed that each doll was listed at four feet, eleven inches in height, and it suddenly made sense. This was not the type of doll I wanted to be looking at.

It was not the type of doll *anyone* should be looking at.

I soon realized why the dolls resembled aliens. In everyday life, it's unusual to come across prepubescent girls wearing heavy makeup. The only time I'd ever seen young girls with a full face of cosmetics was in the context of watching a documentary on beauty pageants. On this website, the dolls' darkly lined, heavily mascaraed eyes combined with large foreheads and tapered chins made them resemble miniature extraterrestrials.

One of the dolls was dressed in a schoolgirl outfit, complete with a polka-dotted bow in her hair. She pouted at the camera, her eyes half-closed, an expression that could be read as sleepy or drugged. Gauging from the bone structure of her face, she appeared to be about nine years old.

I will spare you the details of what else I saw in those photos, but it haunted me for months. To this day, when I close my eyes, I can still see her face. That doll wasn't a real little girl, but her purpose was to serve as a proxy for one. Who knew how many copies of her would be shipped out from the factory to be defiled.

I was spooked—the child dolls I had unexpectedly stumbled across, on a website that purported to carry only adult dolls, were clearly hidden several pages in so that the average customer wouldn't see them. The market among child sexual abusers was evidently lucrative, and some manufacturers in the industry were happy to profit off it, regardless of its moral implications.

The entire episode drained any interest I had in going through the process of creating a robot that looked like me. Something about being privy to the worst applications of what was initially a fun and lighthearted exercise had changed me.

The legality of child sex dolls differs according to where you are in the world, but some countries have criminalized their import, sale, distribution, and/or possession, including Canada, the UK, Germany, Denmark, Norway, Australia, and South Korea. In the US, a bill referred to as the CREEPER Act 2.0 has been introduced to outlaw the possession and sale of child sex dolls in addition to their importation and transportation, which was criminalized in 2017.

More recently, a Canadian man faced child porn charges after importing a sex doll that bore resemblance to a child.[24] In a similar case in the U.K., customs officers seized a man's sex doll at the border after they noticed it was just over four feet tall and had penetrable orifices.[25] In both cases, the accused stated they had purchased online what they had believed was an adult sex doll and were subsequently acquitted.

Another disconcerting side to this technology is the ability to create a sex doll in someone's image without their permission, including sex dolls modeled after the likeness of real kids. There exist manufacturers, clearly lacking any human decency, that are willing to create a doll based on photographs that a customer provides.[26]

Research estimates that pedophilia exists in as many as 5 percent of the male population. The economic burden of child sexual abuse (that is, the cost of victimization, including healthcare costs and lost income) is approximately $9.3 billion a year in America.[27]

Having conducted neuroimaging research on pedophilia and worked clinically with individuals convicted of child sexual offenses, I believe it's critical that the public understand that pedophilia is biological, hardwired in the architecture of the brain. In practical terms, this means a sexual attraction to children can't be cured or changed. (Regardless, I believe anyone who abuses a child should be held criminally responsible for their actions.)

Contrary to common belief, sexual interest in children is not the result of experiencing sexual abuse as a child, exposure to extreme pornography, or society's sexualization of underage girls. Sex offenders will often lie about having been abused in childhood to manipulate clinicians and law enforcement into feeling sympathetic toward them.

Studies (including those I have worked on) show differences between pedophiles and non-pedophiles in their brains' connective tissue and activation patterns, as well as neuropsychological differences that appear at a very young age.[28] Childhood head trauma and differences in the prenatal environment, due to teratogens or maternal stress, are likely responsible for this altered neurodevelopment.[29]

Some pedophiles are exclusively attracted to children; others are attracted to both children and adults. There also exist men who sexually abuse children despite *not* being pedophilic. These individuals have sex with children because they cannot get access to an adult partner.

There are female child molesters. However, like most paraphilias, pedophilia is less common in women. Those who sexually abuse children usually do so at the behest of a male partner. Women are also more readily trusted in the presence of children and parents, which is something that male sex offenders exploit.

Of all things to receive a glossy, progressive rebranding, pedophilia would have been at the bottom of my list. Pedophiles now call themselves MAPs, or "minor-attracted people," an innocuous-sounding term that originated in the late 1990s on an online forum catering to men who are in favor of adult-child sex.

The goal of using a passive, fuzzy descriptor like MAPs is to lessen the stigma associated with the precise clinical term *pedophile* and to improve inclusivity for pedophiles, if you can believe it. Because pedophilia refers to a feeling as opposed to behavior, this has allowed a small but vocal minority of activists, academics, and individuals who are openly pedophilic to advocate for the civil liberties of self-described "nonoffending" pedophiles. (There even exists a MAPs Pride flag.) MAPs seek to differentiate themselves from other pedophiles who may act on their impulses, saying they refrain from doing such a thing because they don't want to hurt a child.

Sympathetic experts stress that it's important to differentiate between an adult's attraction to children (pedophilia) and their behavior (sexual abuse). According to this argument, so long as pedophiles don't act on their desires, they deserve society's acceptance because they didn't choose to be this way. Others have used innocent-sounding claims of inclusion and tolerance to include the letter *P* in the LGBT+ initialism, treating pedophilia as though it were a sexual orientation no different from being straight or gay because, again, pedophilic individuals were "born that way." At the rate we are going, I wouldn't be surprised if, in a few years, "coming out" as a pedophile will be celebrated by society.

The view that nonoffending pedophiles deserve understanding is one I once foolishly supported as a result of my time in academia. It is something that I now deeply regret. To be unequivocally clear, we should focus our efforts on protecting children and victims. In this debate, that is the only thing that matters.

I refuse to use the term *MAPs* because it is an ideologically motivated word. Like all leftist speak, changing language is a successful way to suppress dissent and obfuscate reality. I *don't* believe pedophilia is a benign sexual identity that should be destigmatized, nor do I believe that pedophiles are a protected class deserving of equal rights. Use of the word *minor* obscures pedophilia's defining characteristic, which is a sexual interest in *prepubescent* children (typically under the age of eleven).

Additional paraphilias relevant to this discussion are *hebephilia* (a preference for children who are in the early stages of puberty) and *nepiophilia* (a sexual interest in infants and toddlers). Because children cannot consent to sexual activity, acting on this so-called attraction can only ever be rape and should remain illegal. It should not be normalized.

Depending on the state laws, the term *minor* usually refers to individuals under the age of eighteen or twenty-one. Age of consent laws in the US range between the ages of sixteen and eighteen, depending on where an individual lives. There exists a paraphilia called *ephebophilia*, or sexual interest in teenagers who are in the later stages of puberty, usually corresponding to sixteen-to-eighteen-year-olds. An adult man experiencing sexual attraction to a seventeen-year-old, albeit creepy and potentially illegal, is not the same clinical presentation as being attracted to, let's say, a six-year-old.

For example, a recent study found that a lower age preference (specifically, interest in younger, prepubescent children) is associated with having a higher number of child victims.[30] As a result, it benefits no one besides activists and child abusers to humanize these attractions or misconstrue what pedophilia entails.

The downstream effects of legitimizing pedophilia will be ghastly. If it's considered socially acceptable to be sexually attracted to children, then it follows that sexualizing children should also be allowed. Where will we draw the line? Will any line exist at all? Safeguarding measures will lessen; parents and caretakers will be encouraged to lower their guard. Consequently, pedophiles will rationalize their feelings, thinking the problem isn't with them but with society. If they are granted legal protections, it could be considered discriminatory one day to deny them employment at places populated with children, including daycares and elementary schools.

In the US, about one in four girls and one in twenty boys experience sexual abuse during their childhood.[31] Childhood sexual abuse is associated with alcohol and substance use issues, depression, and post-traumatic stress disorder (PTSD) in adulthood. I consider myself extremely fortunate to not have experienced sexual abuse as a child, but I know many people who have. Its effects can alter the course of a person's life irrevocably, in ways that many of us will never fully comprehend.

Some experts are putting forth child sex dolls as a way to lower rates of sexual abuse by reducing sexual preoccupation in pedophiles and encouraging them to come out of the shadows so that they can get therapeutic help. But we have no evidence to suggest that child sex dolls will reduce or prevent sexual abuse of children, and therefore, no justification for further manifesting these deviant desires into the physical world. Experts advocating for this practice cite studies showing that access to child pornography, or child sexual exploitation material (CSEM), leads to fewer sexual offenses against children.

This echoes a similar trend found with the legalization of pornography featuring adults. The decriminalization of porn was followed by decreased rates in sexual violence, including child sexual abuse and rape. In countries that later criminalized CSEM, such as the Czech Republic, Denmark, and Japan, the incidence of child sexual abuse was lower when CSEM was legal.

To be clear, I don't believe this is a reason to decriminalize CSEM, because production of these materials involves the sexual abuse of children. I don't believe the creation of AI-generated CSEM should be allowed either, yet this is another insane argument being touted by the pro MAPs crowd. According to an investigation by the *Wall Street Journal*, Meta has removed more than *34 million* pieces of CSEM from Facebook and Instagram as of 2022's fourth quarter. The last thing we need is more of this horrendous content available on the internet, in tandem with child robots circulating in our communities.

It's erroneous to generalize findings about CSEM to doll and robot representations of children. First of all, regarding the lower rates of child sexual abuse associated with CSEM availability, not every individual who commits a sexual offense against a child is caught, and of those who are caught, it's often not the first offense they've committed. Also, child sexual abusers who are caught will surely do a better job of evading law enforcement the next time they offend. So just because a child molester isn't caught re-offending doesn't mean he didn't commit another offense.

One study from the UK found that, of pedophilic men who do not yet own a child sex doll, nearly 80 percent report wanting one. This is higher than the 20 to 40 percent of non-pedophilic men who, when asked, say they'd like to own an adult sex doll. Doll-owning pedophiles in the current study also self-reported less intention to sexually abuse a child than pedophilic men who didn't own a child doll, and self-reported rates of sexually offending against children were found to be equivalent across both groups.[32] In another study, conducted in Germany, pedophiles claimed that child sex dolls satisfied their urges and that they no longer experienced sexual interest in children.[33]

I imagine that reading about this isn't easy, so I appreciate those of you who have made it this far. What's flabbergasting to me is that MAPs activists are expecting us to take at face value what individuals who have every incentive to lie are telling us. Does anyone really believe a pedophile would say that using a child sex doll made them *more* interested in victimizing a child or that it led them to act on their desires?

Not only are convicted pedophiles antisocial and adept at lying, but they *know* they are under greater scrutiny from law enforcement and that there is always a chance they could wind up in prison again. They are constantly operating at the highest level of social desirability possible, even in a research setting, or when answering survey questions anonymously on the internet.

One of my research colleagues used to say, "How can you tell if a sex offender is lying?"

The answer: "His lips are moving."

One meta-analysis examining men convicted of viewing CSEM compared offenders' history as documented by official criminal records (including arrests and being charged or convicted of a crime) alongside what offenders shared by way of self-report.[34] According to the official records, one in eight had sexually abused a child; this number jumped to one in two when based on self-report.

Who knows how many more had sexually abused a child but chose to not disclose this. Unless we can monitor sex offenders and their online activity 24/7, estimates of sexual offending will be biased downward. (As a cautionary note to parents, it's important to be equally vigilant in protecting both girls *and* boys from potential predators, as child molesters who abuse boys are more likely to reoffend. Also, pedophilia is more common in heterosexual men than in gay men; straight men will sometimes molest boys if they cannot get access to girl victims.)

Instead of being a successful therapeutic tool used to curb a pedophile's sex drive, I expect child sex dolls will serve as a stepping stone to acting out sexual abuse with a human child. A doll will reinforce feelings of pleasure through orgasm, leading to greater sexual frustration, cognitive distortions (or mental gymnastics) that will "rationalize" abusing a child, and escalation to seeking out a real victim.

In addition, sex offenders aren't known for being content with compromising. Pedophiles, particularly if they have antisocial personality disorder, aren't going to be grateful for access to a doll. They're going to feel emboldened and justified in seeking out the real thing.

Supporters of implementing child robots will claim that you can't rape a robot because it is an inanimate object, and so a pedophile using one is a victimless crime. But it's not as simple as that. A child robot can be programmed to appear to enjoy being violated. It will provide feedback to the user that this is a positive, consensual experience, as opposed to one that would be traumatic and life-altering for a real victim.

Regardless of whether it is a doll or robot, an offender is also now in the possession of materials that will help him groom a child. He could use the doll to desensitize a child to nudity or sexual activity or give the impression that sex is something that children should talk about freely with adults. Even if the pedophile doesn't succeed in abusing that particular child, the child may believe that sex acts between children and grown-ups are acceptable, leaving him or her at an increased risk of being successfully groomed and abused by another pedophile.[35]

If the concept of child sex dolls seems harrowing, let me tell you about the child sex doll community. These individuals take depravity to another level entirely, with online forums and photo contests calling for the dressing up of one's child dolls in sexualized outfits. One image I found particularly disturbing and disheartening was of a doll that looked to be five years old, wearing a latex BDSM harness. I have difficulty believing that pedophiles bonding over their collection of child dolls will do anything but further push men in the direction of abusing children.

We are acting as though everyone in society is entitled to sexual pleasure, and if their preferred form of pleasure hurts other people, we should find ways of mitigating harm instead of doing what we can to eradicate those urges.

I understand this line of thinking, which is basically that it's unrealistic to expect someone to never act on their sexuality, even if it is detrimental. For someone who is exclusively sexually interested in children, telling them to never abuse a child is the equivalent of asking a man who is sexually attracted to adults to forgo sex for his entire life.

But instead of advocating for policy that treats deviant sexual interests as a human right, why not operate in the opposite direction? Chemical castration exists for a reason. It won't change the fact that an individual is sexually interested in children, but it *is* capable of diminishing the urge to act out on that interest. Most child abusers would never agree to undergo such a thing, because they care more about themselves than children or public safety. I also don't believe we should force castration on anyone, because false allegations of sexual abuse do exist,[*] and imposing medical interventions without someone's consent runs the risk of being authoritarian.

What I am arguing for is a change in the ideological orientation of researchers and scientists in the field. Many experts will agree that prevention should be the priority, as opposed to intervening only after a child (or several) have been abused. Since we aren't yet able to reconstruct the brains of pedophiles in a way that will

---

[*] This can occur in the context of child custody disputes. See Mark D. Everson and Barbara W. Boat, "False Allegations of Sexual Abuse by Children and Adolescents," *Journal of the American Academy of Child and Adolescent Psychiatry* 28, no. 2 (1989): 230–35, https://doi.org /10.1097 /00004583-198903000-00014.

remove their harmful desires, the next best thing would be to target their sex drive, as this is the physiological mechanism that leads them to sexually abuse a child.

If a pedophile or someone with a history of sexually abusing kids is serious about being "nonoffending" and wants to prevent exploitation of children, it's not enough to go to therapy, stay away from playgrounds, or refrain from viewing illegal content. They should be willing to address the root cause of the problem. Unlike pushing acceptance of pedophilia, medical castration (including surgical and hormonal treatment) is a solution that is actually effective at lowering the rates of sexual reoffending.[36]

The average person may (or may not) be surprised to learn that what I'm describing here diverges from accepted wisdom in academia. I accept that I will probably alienate a number of my former colleagues for holding these views. The fact that so many academics are content with legitimizing pedophilia as a sexual identity is indefensible.

Social acceptance of child sex dolls cannot be isolated to an intellectual thought experiment. It has real consequences, particularly for children's safety. Every expert out there condoning child abuse dolls as a worthwhile solution should be made to see these dolls in person, to fully grasp the weight of what they're supporting. The dolls represent a level of dehumanization that is unfathomable to anyone with a conscience. Sadly, I think some people may be too far gone in their self-rationalization for this to make a difference.

As for the issue of sexual reoffending against adults and a similar agenda to offer sex dolls and robots as a way to lower risk, the same issues apply. Giving rapists an outlet to enact sexual violence is essentially rewarding atrocious behavior. It tells them implicitly that what they did wasn't "that bad," because they're being gifted an expensive toy that a man would otherwise have to pay large sums of money for.

In addition to uncovering child sex dolls, I have encountered adult sex dolls that appear to have been designed to cater to men who find rape sexually arousing. The dolls have a quizzical or somewhat frightened facial expression, which will be marketed by the seller as mysterious or alluring. To me, they read as someone experiencing physical pain, and I imagine most men would be concerned or promptly turned off if a sexual partner made a similar face. Only someone with sadistic sexual tendencies would find such a look arousing.

Rape is not about power. It is about sexual arousal and causing a victim to experience terror, humiliation, and suffering. Biastophilia, as mentioned earlier, is a sexual preference for rape. Individuals with this paraphilia would rather sexually assault a stranger than have consensual sex with their girlfriend or wife.[37] Approximately 60 percent of convicted rapists exhibit this preference. It's unlikely that a sexual offender will be satiated by a doll or robot; like pedophiles, an artificial proxy will only lead them to refine their predatory skills and long for the real thing.

At times, the goal of preventing sexual abuse and assault can evoke feelings of hopelessness. We can't stop the production of child abuse dolls because a market exists for them, and we can't stop that market from existing, because the development of pedophilia isn't yet preventable. But what we can do is refuse to use terms like *MAPs* and reject empathizing with the supposed plight of pedophiles.

Don't entertain policies that will facilitate child exploitation, grooming, or making access to related materials easier. We experience powerful, negative emotions on this subject for a reason—they motivate us to protect vulnerable and defenseless children.*

An important caveat is that individuals who own an adult sex doll don't necessarily endorse the use of sex dolls emulating a child. Owning an adult sex doll is not an indicator of pedophilia; in fact, many of these doll owners despise the fact that child sex dolls exist. They believe that child abuse dolls taint their community and want nothing to do with them.

The line between human and machine can be blurred for only so long before it is finally erased. The stationary humanoids of today, capable of producing only very simple verbal interactions and stilted motion, will be the least enlightened iterations of robots in our lifetimes. Technology only advances; it never devolves.

The sex robots are already on their way, serving as cudgel-wielding soldiers in the mating war. Single men who are flailing will opt for a menu of pornography- and AI-powered lady friends. Single women who wish to start a family will have no choice but to do so on their own.

---

* Neuroimaging research has shown that pedophilic men possess impaired moral judgment and an aberrant disgust response regarding sexual offenses against children. See Claudia Massau, Christian Kargel, Simone Weiß, et al., "Neural Correlates of Moral Judgment in Pedophilia," *Social Cognitive and Affective Neuroscience* 12, no. 9 (2017): 1490–99, https://doi.org/10.1093/scan/nsx077.

CHAPTER 8

Pregnancy Procrastination and Society-Wide Sterilization

Reproductive technology has given human beings the deity-like ability to control procreation. Young women are postponing motherhood, by way of birth control and egg freezing, to prioritize their careers, enjoy their leisure time, and find the right mate. No longer tied to the coldhearted constraints of one's biological window, this medically induced, newfound female freedom has, and continues to be, celebrated as the norm. Questioning it is considered a third rail, sexist, and off-limits.

But the normalization of these practices and the way we think about them are leading to new and unanticipated issues that wreak havoc on women, their potential male partners, and both sexes' future fertility. Because the one thing humans haven't been afforded is the capacity to *halt* biology.

As someone who fully supports women's right to make choices about their personal and professional lives, including whether to have a child and whether to return to the workforce after they do, the cultural messaging around designing one's life to accommodate a work-life balance remains antiscientific and shortsighted.

Some women—and men—are skipping the mate-selection process entirely, preferring third-party reproduction methods (including sperm and egg donation, in vitro fertilization (IVF), and surrogacy) to mating the old-fashioned way with a partner. But even if one goes down this path, there will be no guarantees of success.

Fertility doctors, clinics, and the media generally portray these reproductive approaches as a sure bet, backed by settled science, but they are in fact experimental and associated with health risks to both the mother[1] and child.[2] Once a woman takes steps to delay pregnancy—for example, by starting birth control—she sets herself up for future reliance on additional reproductive technologies to make up for, or artificially extend, the time that is now passing.

Human fertility relies on a delicate balance that is being thrown off-kilter by both active and passive means. As mentioned above, women are employing direct interventions, intentionally reconfiguring their endocrine systems so they can optimize the best time to have a child. But operating in the background are environmental influences, quietly exerting downstream hormonal effects on both sexes, leaving chaotic repercussions unknown to many of us until it is too late.

Buying Time

There is never a convenient time to be pregnant, and the extra years afforded by contraception, including the birth control pill, pass quickly. Undergraduate degrees are frequently followed by professional and advanced degrees, and the next thing you know, a young woman is in her late twenties or early thirties by the time she has graduated. It will take a few years for her to become established in her new career. That is assuming all goes according to plan.

Too often, there are unexpected delays, changes in vocational interests, and fresh opportunities that are too good to pass up. Soon, she will be thirty-five, and despite having acquired professional success and economic security, there will still be more to get done in a day than there is time to do it. This, along with the sociocultural sentiment that young people should take their time and approach dating *without* a sense of purpose (as Gen Z is reportedly doing), has led many women to reach their late thirties, pivot from focusing on work to start a family, and then wonder where the men are.

Women are having their firstborn children later than was customary in previous generations. In the United States, the average age at which women had their first child was twenty-seven years old in 2020, compared with the average age of twenty-one in 1970.[3] Nearly one in five pregnancies, and one in ten of all first pregnancies, are in women who are aged thirty-five and older. This follows a global trend of women waiting to have their first pregnancy, particularly in higher-income countries.[4]

The age cutoff of thirty-five isn't an arbitrary number meant to scare young women or to send them into a panic. Thirty-five is the midpoint between when women's fertility peaks at about age twenty-five and when it falls to zero by forty-five.

"Advanced maternal age" is a medical term referring to women who are over the age of thirty-five when giving birth. Once referred to as "geriatric pregnancies," this cohort has been given a more sensitive designation, "thirty-five-plus pregnancies," and the mainstream discussion has mostly centered on potential positive aspects of having children at a later age.[5] Either way, being pregnant and older than thirty-five is associated with an increased risk for health complications to the mother and fetus, including spontaneous miscarriage, stillbirth, gestational diabetes, preterm labor, and chromosomal abnormalities that can result in birth defects, disabilities, and medical problems.

Some may be wondering why a woman would trade having children earlier in life for the sake of financial stability when the process of egg freezing and IVF can be costly, physically painful, and time-consuming.[6] After all, a woman can't definitively know that embarking on this path will go according to plan.

There are several reasons. Because women are hypergamous and prefer to marry up, delaying pregnancy via birth control and egg freezing allows them more time to find and evaluate the right partner instead of settling or rushing and procreating with the wrong person, as some women would have done in the past. This additional flexibility with time allows a woman to pay off student debt, afford housing and daily expenses, and save up for future costs associated with childcare. (It costs approximately $240,000 to raise a child until the age of eighteen, and that doesn't include university tuition.[7])

Being financially independent also translates to not depending on one's spouse, so a woman has the ability to leave an abusive or exploitative relationship. (This isn't to say that men, financially secure or otherwise, are immune to being in abusive situations.) In the event of spousal abandonment, infidelity, or death, she will be capable of taking care of herself.

Truthfully, being a stay-at-home mother isn't as valued or respected by our society. Our society values money, status, and autonomy, along with achievements that are flashy and photograph well on social media. These are things that a woman is required to, for the most part, forfeit upon becoming a mother. Parenting requires sacrifices from men, too, but not in the same way that it does for women.

An exception to this has been the tradwife (a portmanteau of "traditional wife") influencer trend, which portrays traditional homemakers performing stereotypical—but also visually appealing—tasks associated with motherhood, like baking adorable cookies while decked in frilly dresses and playing with their smiling children amidst farm animals in neatly manicured yards. We do not see these supposed housewives delighting in the more mundane aspects of housekeeping and child-rearing, like washing dirty dishes, resolving temper tantrums, or scooping kitty litter. Trad-wifing on social media is closer to a parody of motherhood than a true representation of it.

Some women may mistakenly believe that being more financially successful will afford them a better selection of men. But as we know from earlier chapters, men don't value wealth or resources in a partner the way that women do. There are additional sex differences in how men and women view a significant other's success. Men are more likely to feel worse about themselves when their wife or girlfriend succeeds than when she fails, whereas women's view of themselves remains unaffected, regardless of a male partner's performance.[8]

The more successful a woman becomes, the likelier it is that she will encounter such a predicament in dating. In some cases, it will lead to the termination of a relationship. As women rise up the food chain and outearn their husbands, they are less likely to be happy in their marriages and more likely to file for divorce.[9] They are also at greater odds of experiencing domestic violence and emotional abuse.[10]

Husbands who are economically dependent on their wives have higher rates of cheating. As one study noted, men are more likely to find economic dependency on a spouse threatening, so they will engage in infidelity to equalize this discrepancy in the marriage.[11]

This, too, explains the quandary successful women find themselves in: Being successful makes it more difficult for a woman to find a match, which leads to more effort invested into her career so that she can continue providing for herself.

By contrast, as men age, they are more apt to date younger women because men value a woman's financial status less than her physical attractiveness, due to the latter being associated with greater reproductive success. Fewer women are interested in dating younger men because young men, who are usually at the start of their careers, tend to be less financially secure.

This is especially the case when comparing young men to their same-aged female peers nowadays, a gap that becomes markedly wider if a young man were to date a woman who is older. The other difference is that men's status and wealth, and thereby attractiveness to women, generally increases with age.

As a result, deferring having children penalizes young women in a way that leaves their male peers mostly unaffected. As time goes by, not only does a woman's fertility decrease but she will also be contending with a growing number of female rivals for a limited number of successful men. Young men, however, will find they have an easier time attracting a partner if they wait to have kids, because if these young men become financially successful, time will only bring them greater status.

Egg freezing, also known as "elective fertility preservation" or "oocyte vitrification," has been one option to acquire more time. The process involves retrieving a woman's eggs, storing them, and then later fertilizing them with sperm from a male partner or donor and transferring the resulting embryos into the woman's uterus. In the US, more than one million eggs and embryos are currently in storage for this purpose.[12]

The average age at which women freeze their eggs is thirty-eight.[13] In some cases, women will undergo egg freezing as a back-up, an insurance policy on their fertility, but many aren't fully cognizant of what the true success rates are.[14] As a woman ages, her ovarian reserve (or reproductive potential, according to the quantity and quality of her eggs) diminishes, which affects her ability to conceive. Advanced age and preserving too few eggs are two major reasons why women do not successfully become pregnant when utilizing egg-freezing technology.

Wanting to better understand what the process entailed, I booked a consultation call with a nurse at a fertility clinic. This particular clinic had especially positive online reviews, along with reassuring messaging on its website about taking charge of one's life, paired with stock images of women looking way too happy about preserving their eggs.

Before our call, I experimented with the clinic's online egg-freezing calculator, which allows a woman to estimate how many eggs she should freeze, based on her age and how many kids she wants. The result also provided a percentage regarding the likelihood of a successful live birth with this number of eggs, based on what the scientific literature predicts. As an example, a thirty-five-year-old woman who freezes ten eggs has about a one in two chance of having *one* child and less than a one-in-five chance of having two children. The success rate decreases with age, since aging affects the number and quality of eggs that the body produces. Once the eggs have been retrieved, there is also a chance that they may fail to survive the freezing, thawing, fertilizing, or implanting stages.

I was struck by how much women take for granted how easy it is to get pregnant when we are young. The burden of contraception, its related side effects, and late periods are almost nostalgia-inducing when realizing how hard it is to become pregnant as you get older.

On my call with the nurse, I learned about the medications I would need to self-inject to increase my egg production, the schedule of daily injections, and the final price tag. Although the egg-freezing process seems straightforward enough conceptually, in reality, it is far more complex.

In addition to controlling the production and release of a woman's eggs, the medications one must take can induce a roller coaster of side effects, including mood swings, fatigue, and uncomfortable physical symptoms, like nausea, bloating, and bruising. Multiple bloodwork tests and pelvic ultrasounds are also needed, which translates to more poking and prodding.

The collection of eggs is usually done under general anesthesia, using an ultrasound probe paired with a needle so large, it reminded me of an old-school TV antenna. This contraption is inserted into the vagina so that the needle can be guided *through* the vaginal wall, to aspirate (basically, suck out) follicular fluid to capture each egg for vitrification.

Putting one's faith in this treatment is also an emotionally intense experience. A woman will find herself continuously alternating between elation and disappointment with every success and setback.

I have watched vlogs of women who say as many as thirty eggs were collected during their retrieval appointment. Usually, a woman's ovaries release just one egg each cycle. One has to wonder how the body will cope with being made to do something that it would never do naturally. In our evolutionary history, when would it have made sense for a woman to release thirty eggs at once?

When I asked the nurse about the demographics of her patients, she mentioned that they have changed in the last five years. Previously, egg-freezing patients were typically in their mid- to late thirties, but now younger women in their late twenties and early thirties were vitrifying their eggs. The nurse attributed the change to social media awareness and celebrities talking about their experiences doing it. She said many of her patients in their late thirties and forties wish they had known about it sooner.

This all made sense to me, but I was mostly taken aback by how intense the process was. It wasn't as simple as extracting a few eggs, fertilizing them, and popping them back in when you meet Mr. Right—assuming you meet him at all.

Single Motherhood by Choice

This brings us to "choice moms," those who choose elective single motherhood, a steadily growing segment of unmarried women who have decided to become mothers on their own. Some become pregnant by having sex with a man with the explicit (and in some cases, contractual) understanding that he will not have a further role in the child's life. Other women use donor insemination, IVF, and surrogacy.

In the US, an estimated 2.7 million women are single mothers by choice. In Europe, use of assisted reproduction is booming. In Denmark, nearly 4 percent of births involve this technology. One in ten babies is born to a *solomor*, the Danish term for "solo mother."

A scientist by training, I have mixed feelings about this arc of progress. On one hand, the fact that adults who wouldn't otherwise be able to have a biological child can do so is nothing short of miraculous. I can only imagine how devastating it is for women who have always wanted to be mothers not to have this dream come true.

The most important concern, however, should rest on the well-being of the children. Ideally, studies evaluating these outcomes would be impartial and devoid of politics. But that is not the world we live in.

Studies suggest that child adjustment is the same for donor-conceived and naturally conceived children and that parental sex and family structure are less important in the overall scheme of raising a child than the quality of these relationships.[15] According to experts, the poorer emotional, behavioral, and academic outcomes found in children of divorced and unwed mothers aren't attributable to the absence of a father but to the mother's *experience* of raising children on her own. This can include struggling with poverty, depression, and a lack of support networks.

According to this body of research, these factors don't affect single mothers by choice, because they are financially secure and emotionally healthy. Also, because these children never had a relationship with their fathers, it is believed they won't be as emotionally distraught as children of divorce, who have had to endure parental conflict in the home and the loss of their father's presence.

These studies, however, exhibit a sampling bias, since choice moms who have the energy and availability to take part in research studies are going to be higher functioning than choice moms who don't, the latter of whom may, in fact, be struggling with both their finances and their mental health. We must also consider the influence of social desirability, since choice moms know that society is skeptical of children resulting from donor insemination and related reproductive technologies.

The role of an opposite-sex parent isn't negligible. Fatherlessness is associated with higher rates of psychological issues, substance use, and incarceration.[16] As mentioned in previous chapters, growing up without a dad hinders boys' success in life and leaves girls vulnerable to sexual attention-seeking in adulthood. Experiencing fatherlessness may well contribute to an individual's own children being raised without a father. It stands to reason that intentionally increasing the number of fatherless children has the potential to *worsen* the population crisis.

Although a woman can select a sperm donor based on his consenting to being contacted by the child when they reach eighteen, that doesn't replace an ongoing father-child relationship. Other choice moms prefer to raise a child on their own terms, without the influence or involvement of a man.

How will being raised without a father affect a child's views on pair-bonding and raising children when they are adults? In my opinion (because few academic studies today would dare say this), having male relatives as role models in sons' and daughters' lives would help to offset these effects.

At the core, this technology has rendered sex obsolete—if an individual has decided to abstain from starting a family, they don't need to be sexually active. But now the opposite is also true. Women can exclude men from the family-creating equation entirely (except to acquire the necessary sperm).

This normalizes the sentiment that men are inconsequential and that women don't need them. It also encourages women to take as long as they want before having a child, because in the end, being single won't be an impediment to procreating.

Young women who freeze their eggs may be under the faulty impression that they have more time available than they do. Similarly, women in their late thirties and forties who egg-freeze as a precautionary measure may not realize that the odds of having a baby are not, unfortunately, statistically in their favor.[17]

This technology is masking a larger social problem: Women who want to become mothers can't find partners with whom they want to have children. By carrying on as though everything is just fine and promoting elective interventions as fully rational alternatives—allowing a woman to extend the amount of time she has to find an appropriate mate, and encouraging single motherhood by choice, should she not be able to—we are failing to address and remedy the primary issue.

As a greater number of women take this route due to lacking a desirable partner, rates of sexual activity will continue to decline. The demands of raising a child on one's own will make the logistics of dating harder. Some men may discriminate against dating a single mother.

An opinion piece published in *The New York Times* written by a single mother by choice describes how the social acceptability and affordability of elective single motherhood will increase women's leverage on the dating scene and rectify power imbalances with men.[18] She writes that it's "thrilling" that single women outnumber married women in the US and fantasizes that in a decade, it will be *men* who will be "scrambling" to commit to a woman before she opts out and has children on her own.

Indeed, women aren't the only ones trying to beat the clock. Approximately one in five American men aged fifty-five and older is childless.[19] As men get older, they, too, lament not finding a partner in time to father a child.[20] Many erroneously believe that they will be fertile throughout their life, regardless of age.

But will they be "scrambling" to find a woman? Based on where we are culturally, I predict it is more likely that heterosexual men will just continue checking out from dating and thus fatherhood, or if they have the financial ability, they will go their own way with IVF and multiple surrogates. In the US, it is estimated that over two million men are single fathers, but it has been difficult to determine how many of these families were the result of surrogacy.

It's been documented that men are capable of fathering children into their nineties.[21] Fatherhood over the age of forty-five, however, is correlated with an increased risk of the child having a premature birth, as well as developing autism and schizophrenia.[22] Aging parents often struggle to keep up with the rambunctious energy of young children.

On the bright side, women's sex drive increases as they approach menopause.[23] It may be more difficult to conceive a child upon reaching one's mid-thirties, but women's mating psychology motivates them to continue attempting for as long as it is possible. Older mothers are also more likely to release more than one egg a month, resulting in twins.[24] The human body will give its all when a woman is striving to become pregnant.

The societal aversion to assisted reproductive technologies like egg freezing and IVF may exist because human beings, competitive as we are, don't want others to be able to game the system. If an individual can't find a mate or conceive organically, use of this technology could be seen as an unfair advantage accessible only to some, enabling the wealthy to have healthier children in greater numbers.

With the increased use and commodification of reproductive tech, we will continue creeping toward higher rates of sexual inactivity and future sexual disconnection. Combined with the realization of sex robots and womb transplants,[25] human sexual partners may, one day, no longer be necessary to continue one's genetic lineage.

Building a Baby

Perusing online cryobanks for donor sperm resembles a home science experiment, except instead of making volcanos out of vinegar and baking soda or growing plants in empty bottles, I could pick and choose a man with whom to create tiny people.

I entered the preferred height, weight, ethnicity, hair and eye color, and blood type of the donor I was seeking. Some websites allow customers to stratify their selection by education and parental income too.

Clicking on boxes before hitting Search on these sites felt like I was snatching up clothing items in my preferred size and color during a summer blowout sale. Of the donor profiles that resulted, I could view their bio to get a sense of their personality. I could listen to an audio clip of them speaking. A few profiles gave the option of allowing a child to contact the donor upon turning eighteen.

Donor profiles also included a baby picture of the prospective father or celebrity look-alikes. Many women prefer to use the sperm of someone they're attracted to, whom they could see themselves dating. If a customer provided two color photos of an adult, the cryobank could match them to a donor in three to five business days. This option aided customers who preferred a donor who resembled a male spouse, but it could also be used to increase the odds that a child would possess (presumably beneficial) physical features that neither parent had. Each profile reminded me that the sperm had undergone extensive genetic screening.

The price of a single vial of sperm started at around $1,000 but could cost upward of several thousand dollars. Factors influencing the price depend on the cryobank, the extent to which genetic testing is conducted, how the sperm is prepared, and the availability of a donor's vials, with more in-demand candidates drawing heftier prices.

The site bombarded me with a discount code, along with a 1-800 phone number to call if I had questions. After choosing however many vials of sperm I wanted, I could click Add to Cart, specify the delivery date, and expedite shipping.

Although the miracle of human life could result from this online transaction, the corresponding virtual shopping experience left much to be desired. This particular website was clunky and difficult to navigate. Four different fonts, in three jarringly nonharmonious colors, were used to display hundreds of donor profiles on the search results page, adding another level of visual frustration to an already unnecessarily confusing and distressing process.

In my mind, I tallied up how many vials I would need to order (two? five?) to cover the number of trials I thought it'd take for a first child to be conceived, then extra vials (another two?) so that my hypothetical future child could have a hypothetical sibling. I understood why many women felt pressure to make these decisions swiftly. Most popular donors had fewer than five vials available, and the site would sprout a pop-up message alerting you that their supply was about to run out.

I contemplated this scenario further. Would I really have felt comfortable paying thousands of dollars and trusting that the substance arriving in the mail would indeed be seminal fluid? The seminal fluid of the donor I had chosen? What if it wasn't?

My overly imaginative mind jumped to other, similarly horrific scenarios. What if someone working in the lab decided to go about winning the evolutionary circus by spreading his own seed deceptively,[26] shipping his sperm to everyone who placed an order? Or, in a less sociopathic context, what if the lab technician was hungover that morning and accidentally mailed me sperm belonging to the wrong donor?[27]

Home insemination can be done if a woman has viable eggs. The procedure is more technologically advanced than using a turkey baster but is remarkably similar in concept. The website's instructional video told me that I should lie down, elevating my hips with a pillow. I would need to cut the ends of the tubes containing the sperm, fill the applicator syringe with it, and insert this into my vaginal canal during ovulation.

The doctor in the video helpfully reminded me, the viewer, that if I missed the ovulatory period, not to worry, because sperm can live in the female genital tract for up to three days. After inserting the syringe's contents, I was to lie still on my back for thirty minutes, and voilà! The miracle that is reproductive science would allow me to impregnate myself, a modern-day version of immaculate conception, from the comfort of my couch.

As I perused the donor profiles again, I tried to imagine what my resulting child, mixed with the DNA of a stranger that I purchased off the internet, would look like.

It didn't feel real.

I found one donor profile that, due to our shared similarities, unexpectedly resonated with me. He was trained in martial arts, didn't drink or smoke, and considered himself a nerd who liked to read. We were the same in some ways, but surely there would be differences in our outlook and personalities. I wondered if our imaginary offspring would inherit more of his, or my, traits.

It truly speaks to how strong women's mate preferences are that many would rather take this highly complicated, unconventional approach than settle down with someone whom they consider subpar. But unless the sperm donor is someone a woman knows personally, he could be lying about who he is, jeopardizing her ability to determine the quality of the sperm she's inseminating and the mate value of her future offspring. At best, she could be hitting the genetic lottery. At worst, she could have saved herself the time and hassle by settling for a man perhaps unexceptional but known to her and willing to commit.

As much as I found it spooky that human life could be created in such an impersonal, transactional way, I also realized the immense strength it must take for a woman to choose this route, knowing that she will be undergoing the physical demands of pregnancy and labor without the support of a spouse or partner. She will also face society's judgment as the child's primary provider and caretaker.

Although the number of women in their thirties and older becoming first-time mothers has been steadily increasing, this hasn't offset the decline of women in their twenties delaying motherhood. As a refresher, young men are more likely than young women to want to become parents nowadays.[28] The overall number of women having children has decreased over the past decade.[29]

It's possible that some young women will change their minds, but this seems less likely than in generations before. Fifty-seven percent of adults under the age of fifty who say they're unlikely to ever have children attribute this to not wanting to have them.[30] The next most common reason was because they "[wanted] to focus on other things," like their job or other interests (44 percent). Of the 24 percent who said it was because they "haven't found the right partner," it's sadly questionable whether their predicament will change.

It's unfair that childless women face a palpable disdain no matter what they do. Society shames them as "crazy cat ladies" if they decide to not have children, but if they have a child on their own, they are shamed for that too.[31] A woman's value extends beyond her fertility and her ability and desire to procreate. (I believe childless men should be granted the same dignity as well.)

For those who do want children, fertility-delaying technology will only grow more widely used and socially accepted in the coming decades, since the shortage of available men doesn't appear to be ending anytime soon. The solution isn't to bully women for their choices or to lie and say that biology doesn't matter, but to offer honest information early in their lives, so that they can make better decisions for themselves.

We also need to help men get back on their feet. Women going to great pains to optimally plan and prepare a reproductive timeline is inconsequential if there aren't enough procurable men with whom they can pair. Even if they do find someone, fall in love, and choose to start a family, they may not be able to.

Women's Emancipation or Entrapment?

In the 1960s, the birth control pill became available on the market, severing the link between sex and reproduction, and forever changing human beings' relationship to sex. For the first time, women could attain social and economic equality with their male counterparts through greater reproductive autonomy. Young women were afforded access to higher education and career opportunities that their female forebearers didn't have.

Fast-forward almost eighty years and, according to the Centers for Disease Control and Prevention (CDC), approximately 65 percent of women under the age of fifty are currently using contraception, and nearly all women will use some form of it in their lifetime. As with any invention, we have taken for granted the ways in which the Pill and other contraceptive methods have drastically improved our lives, failing to consider their unintended side effects.

Despite reducing rates of unwanted pregnancy, the emotional and psychological implications after sexual activity remain for both sexes. Women are, on average, more likely to become emotionally attached to a partner after sex, a mechanism that suits their (and a prospective child's) well-being. Men are, on average, wired to become detached from a sexual partner post-orgasm, because it facilitates their ability to impregnate a greater number of women.

Birth control has irrevocably changed the power dynamics of a sexual relationship, creating an imbalance that favors men. The Pill removed the risk associated with premarital sex, and along with it, lessened the requirement that men invest in their sexual partners, or commit if a woman becomes pregnant.

A culture permitting anonymous hookups doesn't require either party to consider these consequences anymore. It heartily encourages both sexes to separate emotions from sex. The aftermath is a tide of young women and men who have been willingly and needlessly hurt, the brunt of which plays out in their future relationships. Like porn and prostitution, casual sex gifts men a sexual outlet, opting them out of investing in a long-term partner, while still getting their sexual needs met. Because of this, a culture that encourages promiscuity will perpetuate women's inability to find a partner with whom to settle down. Birth rates will continue declining.

The Pill also has the power to alter women's mating psychology and possibly influence evolved preferences that are evolutionarily adaptive. Women on the Pill have been shown to prefer male partners who are less masculine[32] and with whom they may be less genetically compatible.[33]

Before I go any further, let me provide a quick summary of how the Pill works. A woman's menstrual cycle, or the time between her periods, is approximately twenty-eight days. By altering the usual succession of hormones, the Pill prevents a woman's ovaries from ovulating (or releasing an egg), which usually occurs on the fourteenth day. This, to some extent, mimics how a woman's body behaves when she is pregnant.

The Pill also prevents the endometrium (the lining of the uterus) from thickening, which then leads to two to seven days of bleeding. This bleeding that women experience while on the Pill, however, isn't technically a menstrual period, but something called *withdrawal bleeding*. It's the result of withdrawing birth control hormones that week and the body subsequently shedding the uterine lining. For women who aren't on the Pill, the body naturally sheds this lining if an embryo (a fertilized egg) isn't implanted that month.

When she's on the Pill, a woman's ovaries are not releasing eggs and her body believes she is pregnant. It makes sense that she would prefer a nurturing caretaker over a dominant, high-testosterone man who may not stick around. Upon ceasing the Pill and resuming her regular ovulatory cycle, and particularly during ovulation (when she is fertile), she will have a greater appreciation for men with good, healthy genes to mate with, reflected in higher testosterone levels.

This has nontrivial implications for women's reproductive behavior, relationship stability, and family cohesion, particularly if she starts or stops taking the Pill during a long-term relationship. If a woman comes off the Pill to start a family with her partner and realizes she's no longer attracted to him, that can mark the end of their marriage or relationship. This process delays not only her ability to have a family but his as well.

I wonder to what extent hormonal birth control, as an endocrine disruptor, has influenced societal trends regarding sex-typical behavior. If women on the Pill prefer feminine men, considering that three out of five females between the ages of fifteen and forty-nine are currently taking it,[34] is this responsible for the demonization of masculinity as "toxic" and the shepherding of men toward feminization?

Another noteworthy observation is that older generations of birth control pills can masculinize women's brains, impairing their adeptness at verbal fluency (being able to think of words on the spot) and their ability to recognize emotions on people's faces, while increasing their ability for mental rotation (picturing three-dimensional objects at different angles), something that men typically excel at.[35] (As a caveat, I'm talking about on-average differences here. Some women excel at mental rotation tasks, whether or not they are on the Pill, just as some men excel in verbal performance and emotion recognition.)

Hormones affect every facet of our lives, including our moods, the way we interact with each other, our physiology, and our physical appearance. Encouraging half of the population to take a hormone-altering drug in their formative years may have repercussions we haven't yet thoroughly considered.

Many young women begin taking the birth control pill as teenagers for noncontraceptive reasons, including preventing acne and alleviating pain from menstrual cramps.[36] In fact, 14 percent of women aged fifteen to forty-four are on the Pill for noncontraceptive purposes. But an additional side effect of being on the Pill is a decrease in libido.[37] This means these women and girls may not be having sex, but their mating psychology is being affected, nonetheless.

Ovulation is a critical source of inspiration for female sexuality, increasing women's sexual receptiveness, proceptiveness (or willingness to initiate sex), and attractiveness.[38] When women are ovulating, the stakes around their mating decisions are the highest. This provides a particularly informative window into understanding female sexual behavior. To give an example, women who are ovulating are more likely to go out to parties and clubs to meet men and to wear more feminine and revealing clothing, presumably to attract male attention.[39]

A woman who halts ovulation is essentially blunting her sexual response and the signals she is sending out to potential male sires. What this translates to, in everyday life, is that women on the Pill probably aren't as interested in sex or sexual attention as they normally would be, and men in their vicinity are picking up on this.

But how? A man can tell whether a woman is ovulating by her scent.[40] Men are more attentive to a female partner when she is in estrus because she can get pregnant. They will exhibit more

frequent mate-guarding behaviors during this time, like possessive-
ness and checking up on her, to prevent other men from pouncing
on the opportunity to steal her. It seems that if a man is aware,
consciously or otherwise, that his partner isn't ovulating and,
therefore, can't be impregnated, he will feel less of a need to mate-
guard and possibly less incentive to pursue and invest in her. This
could be yet another reason why young men have been afflicted
with sexual lethargy and indifference, preferring singlehood and
artificial, self-serving sexual avenues over sex with real women.

My intention in pointing this out is not to blame women or
the Pill for the sex recession or for men's sexual sluggishness, but
to raise awareness about possible side effects that society may not
realize exist. Only with accurate and thorough information can we
make informed decisions about our health and fertility, especially
when these matters are time sensitive and somewhat unforgiving.

The Pill is also associated with mood disorders, including
depression and anxiety,[41] and experiencing an impaired response
to stress and fear. A recent study from UCLA using resting-state
functional magnetic resonance imaging (a type of scan that looks
at activation of the brain at rest) found differences relating to
emotional processing between women who were on the Pill
and those who weren't.[42] These changes have implications for a
woman's relationship dynamics with a partner and how she vets
potential men.

There is fear that criticizing the Pill will jeopardize access to
birth control entirely after the US Supreme Court's decision in
Dobbs v. Jackson Women's Health Organization. It overturned
Roe v. Wade's landmark ruling in 1973 that protected a woman's
right to abortion under the Fourteenth Amendment. Many are
afraid that discussing the lesser-known, potentially negative rami-

fications of being on the Pill could be misused to limit women's options to sandwich making and breeding. But how can women exercise their reproductive rights if crucial information is being withheld from them?

The equivalent of birth control for men, a topical gel that is currently in early clinical trials, won't solve the problem. It allows men greater control over their reproductive ability and potentially lessens the burden on women to prevent pregnancy, which are both positive things. But on a wider scale, it will increase men's ability to delay settling down and further ease the facilitation of meaningless sex for those who can access it.

Regardless of whether one is pro-choice or pro-life, or what one's stance is on contraception, we must acknowledge that abortion, and all forms of birth control, have allowed multiple generations to postpone parenthood. Settling down in one's twenties is seen as out of touch and antiquated. And we have seen the reasons why women and men are delaying or avoiding pairing off and having children. Yet even if an individual overcomes the difficulties described in preceding chapters, another form of interference, largely out of their control, awaits them.

Everyone Is on the Pill, Whether They Know It or Not

The conveniences afforded by a fast-paced, modern life could not have come without their own set of demands. Obscure hormonal influences, including the effects of environmental pollution, are important in understanding sexlessness. A cascade of toxic chemicals, pesticides, and pollutants regularly enter our bodies through the air we breathe, the food we consume, and our water supply.

One in every six people worldwide experiences infertility, defined as the inability to become pregnant after one year of having unprotected sex or two or more failed pregnancies. Infertility is attributable to the male partner in one-third of cases, to the female partner in another third of cases, and to unknown causes or both partners in the remaining third of cases.

Testosterone levels have been on the decline over the past twenty years, affecting one in five adolescent males and young men.[43] This has surely played a role in heightening sexual inactivity while diminishing men's sex drives and ability to perform.

The effects of low testosterone can include lower sperm count (which is the number one cause of male-factor infertility), low sex drive, erectile dysfunction, anxiety,[44] depression, low motivation, an increased risk for Alzheimer's disease,[45] and a reduced lifespan. This translates to more social avoidance, less interest in sex, an aversion to risk-taking, and a greater deference to fear. (This may also have something to do with why every branch of military has been struggling to meet its recruitment goals, with more than half of young Americans surveyed worrying that they will have "emotional or psychological problems" as a result of serving.[46])

If men don't feel confident and masculine, they aren't going to summon the effort to put their heads above the parapet and talk to women in real life. These men will merely resort to porn and swiping on dating apps as a replacement, when they do feel so inclined. This translates to a problem that is twofold: Low-T men are demotivated from pursuing women, and they become less attractive to women because of their indifference and timidity.

Our environment is biologically discouraging us from having sex. Earlier chapters discussed the ideological war on men; this chapter discusses chemical warfare. Men are being lulled into a sexually neutered haze. The issue of young men not succeeding can't be fixed until the hormonal environment is corrected. No amount of social intervention will otherwise work.

What is causing declining testosterone levels in men? Age, poor diet, and obesity are known culprits, as are cannabis[47] and alcohol. But even when lifestyle factors are taken into account, research points to other health-related or environmental influences affecting younger men's testosterone.[48]

When we look at studies involving animals, this is where things start to get wild. The great thing about nonhuman critters is that they are impervious to confounding cultural effects. Any observable changes can be more confidently attributed to biological explanations. Although we can't definitively say that exogenous substances, including drug pollution or estrogen mimickers, are *causing* changes to our hormones and health, these studies certainly warrant us taking a closer look.

Endocrine disruptors are artificial and natural chemicals that mimic or alter the body's hormonal system. A number of aquatic species that have been swimming about, minding their own business, have been exposed to a cocktail of psychotropic medications, including antidepressants[49] and benzodiazepines (antianxiety drugs), as well as contraceptives[50] through human wastewater leaking into their habitats.

These drugs have feminized and increased intersex conditions among wild fish,[51] while altering their mating behavior[52] and sperm morphology.[53] In addition, the pesticide atrazine has demonstrated the bewildering ability to turn male frogs into females, capable of producing eggs and copulating with other males.[54]

Exposure to bisphenol A (BPA), found in everyday plastics, and synthetic estrogen, found in birth control pills, has also led to fertility problems in male fish—not in the original generation that was exposed *or* their offspring, but in two and three generations thereafter.[55] It turns out that the full effects of these contaminants may not become apparent until several cohorts of offspring later.

An example of a naturally occurring endocrine disruptor would be phytoestrogens, which are present in soy. Soy mimics estrogen and, like atrazine, can change the sex of sea creatures like eels,[56] turning males female. Consumption of genistein, a natural compound of soy, can have repercussions for social behavior. In one experiment, monkeys fed genistein became socially isolated and aggressive.[57] The pejorative term *soy boys*, used to describe effeminate and cowardly yet hostile (and usually politically progressive) men, would appear, in this context, to be an accurate descriptor.

In addition to potentially feminizing men, soy can lower sperm count.[58] What's particularly concerning is that some infant formulas are made from soybeans and are fed to babies in bottles containing endocrine disruptors, like bisphenols.[59]

Research by Shanna Swan, a professor of environmental medicine and public health at the Icahn School of Medicine at Mount Sinai, has looked at the role of plastics, including phthalates, in reducing fertility rates and human sperm count. Phthalates are a chemical used to soften plastics and are oftentimes hidden in the most unsuspecting of places, including children's toys, fragrances, nail polish, and food packaging containers.

One metric of relevance, the anogenital distance (or AGD, which is measured between the anus and the scrotum in men, or between the anus and the vulva in woman), is a marker for reproductive health. It is consistently longer in men than in women. In an animal model (namely, rodents), a shorter AGD is a well-documented sign that something was amiss during the masculin-ization process *in utero,* that this process wasn't completed.

Research conducted by Swan and her colleagues in 2019 found that a reduced AGD in eighteen-year-old men predicted poorer fertility and semen quality, including a lower percentage of mor-phologically normal sperm, sperm concentration, and count.[60] (Conversely, a longer AGD is associated with lower reproductive success in women.)

Normally shaped sperm, characterized by an oval head and a long, uncoiled tail, are better equipped for swimming in a straight line, the skill needed to reach their final destination and fertilize the egg. Possessing a greater number and percentage of these healthy-shaped sperm increases the likelihood of a man success-fully impregnating his spouse or partner. As mentioned, low sperm count (also known as *oligospermia,* defined as fewer than fifteen million sperm for every milliliter of semen) is the most common explanation for male infertility. *Azoospermia* is a medical term that refers to semen that contains no sperm. About one percent of all men have azoospermia, as do 10 percent of infertile men.[61]

In my view, this suggests that something is happening during the prenatal developmental process that is shaping men's future reproductive trajectory. A mother's exposure to phthalates during pregnancy has been associated with shortened AGD in newborn baby boys.[62]

Of men who manage to successfully partner up in today's sex-less climate, they may nevertheless be unable to reproduce, which can lead to mental health distress,[63] less enjoyment of sexual ac-tivity, more frequent erectile dysfunction, social isolation from embarrassment, marital strain, conflict, and potentially divorce. Research on male-factor infertility and relationship dissolution has been sparse, but a Danish study found that nearly one-third of couples experiencing female-factor infertility divorced or ended cohabitation within ten years.[64]

The Food and Drug Administration has acknowledged these risks and stated it is reviewing the ongoing scientific discussion while at the same time maintaining that the use of phthalates in food preparation[65] and cosmetics[66] is diminishing.

Fertility has also been declining in younger females, documented as far back as the 1980s, suggesting that it isn't solely advanced age or a lack of access to desirable male partners that is affecting women's ability to have children. Microplastics, which contain endocrine-disrupting chemicals, have been found in human placenta, which may have an impact on the prenatal environment and the outcome of a pregnancy.[67] Since baby girls have all the eggs they will ever have at birth, this prenatal exposure has the ability to harm not only a vulnerable fetus (along with the mother) but also a third generation and possibly others into the future.

As for the widespread indifference toward sex, both depression and the use of antidepressants may be playing a role. Prominent symptoms of depression are *anhedonia* (loss of motivation and interest in pleasurable activities), which can involve less interest in sex, and low self-esteem, which can negatively affect how a person views themselves and how they evaluate romantic partners. Five percent of people worldwide are currently depressed. In America, about one in five currently has or is being treated for depression, with greater prevalence among adults aged eighteen to twenty-nine (Gen Z, 25 percent) and those aged thirty to forty-four (Millennials, 21 percent), than those aged forty-five to sixty-four (Gen X and younger Boomers, 16 percent).[68]

One in five American college students is using antidepressants. Like hormonal contraception's effects on women's sex drive, antidepressants can lower libido and inhibit orgasm. Could this be why Gen Z prefers depictions of platonic friendships over sex in the entertainment they consume?[69] When sex is no longer forbidden, it loses its allure and becomes overbearing, akin to a chore. It's also possible that an overabundance of extraneous hormonal signaling has tampered with our ability to properly appraise and respond to sexual cues.

An astounding statistic from the CDC estimated that autism affects 1 in 36 children, or more specifically, 4 percent of boys, and 1 percent of girls.[70] Autism spectrum disorder (ASD) is characterized by deficits in socioemotional communication, difficulty making eye contact, intense interests, and rigid adherence to routines. It has historically been attributed to familial genetics, extreme masculinization of the prenatal brain,[71] maternal obesity, and older parental age (as touched upon earlier), but it's worth asking to what extent additional, environmental factors have come into play.[72] Maternal exposure to a common herbicide, glyphosate, has been connected to autism.[73] Glyphosate has also been found in human sperm.[74]

This is relevant to the decline in sexual activity because people, and particularly men, on the autism spectrum prefer alone time and find social environments over-stimulating. Difficulties with communication and understanding social rules can create a challenging dynamic for those with ASD who are in a relationship with someone who isn't on the autism spectrum. Non-ASD individuals will express feeling lonely and not having their needs met by a partner with ASD.[75] It is possible to work through these issues but requires extra effort, which may deter those who are already feeling tepid about relationships, whether they have ASD or are considering dating someone who does.

Let's return to study results discussed earlier that revealed lower rates of masturbation in adolescents[76] and similar levels of reported happiness between sexless and sexually active people.[77] Could these phenomena be the product of silent, external forces damping down young people's sex drives without their knowledge or awareness?

We can proactively make changes to avoid these toxins and live a healthier lifestyle, but this isn't fully possible if we aren't aware of all the ways our bodies and minds are being affected. If we can't reproduce, it will be the end of our species. No matter how much we advance with each ingenious invention, we will always be at the mercy of our biology.

Reconnecting

I thought a lot about what I wanted to say in this final chapter. It feels in some ways as though I'm sending you all on your way to fend for yourselves in this strange simulation.

While writing this book, I heard from so many of you that an unshakable loneliness follows you every moment of the day. Dating has become a nightmare, and you feel hopeless about ever finding someone. Although the issues discussed in this book have certainly made the romantic process more challenging, here are my words of tough love: It isn't enough to say that dating is impossible and civilization is doomed.

To the men who are struggling, I say, treat your mind and body with respect and the rest will follow. Eat healthy, unprocessed food,* go to the gym, train in martial arts, get a haircut, shower daily, and invest in an iron (women appreciate the small details). Get your driver's license, learn to cook, and pursue hobbies besides

---

* I would never recommend something to my audience without trying it first. Eliminating processed food has been life-changing for me.

video games. Practice making small talk with strangers to improve your social skills.

Even a few small changes can make a difference. These habits will make you well-rounded, independent, and interesting. They will inspire a sense of mastery and self-esteem. A side bonus is that romantic rejection, if and when it happens, will be easier to tolerate.

If you've lost motivation or a sense of purpose, figure out what it is that you're really good at and pursue that fully. Work ruthlessly hard, be willing to delay gratification,[1] and you will be successful. When I look at the people around me who are self-made, what they have in common is how they chased after and eventually achieved their dreams. When you reach that day, the world really will be your oyster because the sex ratio is skewed so heavily in your favor.

Surround yourself with friends who are on a similar mission to better themselves. Most important, stop—or at the very least, cut down on—self-medicating through distractions like alcohol, drugs, doomscrolling, online gambling,[2] and porn. Have a positive mindset, because negativity will send most well-adjusted women running for the hills, no matter how tall, rich, or handsome you are.

For the ladies, I could throw out platitudes like "Love is all that matters," but the reality is that in a shortage of suitable mates, your options are: (1) compete for the high-status men; (2) date someone who is lesser in status than you (and that's perfectly fine); or (3) stay single. Whichever strategy you choose, I'd suggest positioning yourself so that when the right person comes along, there's a higher chance it will work.

Men tend to hesitate about approaching a woman unless they

sense she will be receptive to it. #MeToo has amplified this anxiety to the point of almost no return. I'm not a fan of women asking men out, as you know.[3] So, to increase a woman's opportunities, there are a number of things she can do.

The next time you see someone whom you find attractive, look him directly in the eyes and smile *very obviously* at him. (If you're like me and suffer from resting b*tch face, you may need to practice doing this in the mirror until it looks less like you're grimacing in pain and more like you're radiating inner joy.)

A region of the brain called the medial orbitofrontal cortex activates in response to seeing an attractive face, and this activation is even stronger if that face is smiling.[4] People are naturally drawn to happy, friendly faces. A smile operates like a giant high beam, signaling to the other person that they should approach instead of avoid.

Men are also biologically programmed to pick up on flirtatious mannerisms, like touching your face or hair, tilting your head to the side, showing coyness by gazing downward, and speaking in a slightly higher-pitched voice. (Ladies, if you aren't convinced, ask the men in your lives. They will agree.)[5]

Don't try to compete with men at being men. It's okay to be feminine, nurturing, and to show a softer side. When you're in a relationship, make him feel wanted, compliment him, be generous with physical affection, and wear sexy outfits every once in a while. If you want children, put this at the top of your priority list, because you may contend with forces outside your control that will make finding a partner and starting a family more challenging than you had anticipated. Once the biological window of opportunity has passed, you can't get it back.

As a larger suggestion for everyone, text conversations may

be the gold standard for communicating, but they aren't a replacement for the real thing. Human beings, as a species, need face-to-face interaction, to gaze into one another's eyes, and to hear each other's voices. Nothing can replace our hardwired need for community and interpersonal closeness. We are not meant to be hiding behind screens. Feeling lonely is a sign you should be around people, not burying deeper into technological stand-ins that simulate human connection.

When we are in each other's company, we should spend more time listening than talking and invest more effort in compromising instead of being right. Let's return to an earlier time of decorum by putting our phones away. If you are married or in a long-term relationship, don't take your partner for granted, because today's culture gives them every incentive to leave.

It will take at least a decade for the current dating imbalance to turn around. The sooner young men get back on track, the better off both sexes will be. Men and women must help each other if they want to succeed. At the end of the day, most of us yearn for the same thing, to be understood and appreciated. The more we try to deny this or displace it with glittering distractions, the worse it will backfire. Repercussions built into our biology will haunt us tenfold.

Honest conversations about sex are difficult, and solutions to the problems we are facing are no easier. We should want the best for our partners, as much as we wish it for ourselves. Falling in love isn't a zero-sum game. The opposite sex isn't your enemy.

Acknowledgments

Writing *Sextinction* was an absolute dream.

Thank you, Matt Carlini, for your representation, guidance, and vital insights every step of the way. I couldn't have done it without you. Many thanks to Keith Urbahn and everyone at Javelin for inspiration and feedback during the early stages of writing.

I am extremely grateful to Natasha Simons for believing in this project from its inception. A very big thank-you to Paul Choix—your edits and encouragement helped me shape *Sextinction* into a story that will resonate with every reader. Thank you to Patty Romanowski and Sarah Wright, whose copyediting fine-tuned the manuscript beautifully.

A special thank-you to Drs. David Buss and Michael Shermer for many brilliant, thought-provoking conversations. Fascinating discussions with Dr. John Canady; "Alex," the AI companion programmer; the expert in sexual robotics; Dr. Erik Wibowo; and Marcus Dib helped me gain a nuanced perspective on many issues throughout these pages.

I am indebted to Joe Rogan, Jamie Vernon, and Matt Staggs

for helping me with this endeavor. Thank you to the *Joe Rogan Experience* audience—I received thousands of messages from you, all over the world, in response to my third appearance on the show (#2082). I hope this book helps you navigate the confusing times we're in and feel less alone.

Notes

Chapter 1: The New Contraception

1. Jean M. Twenge, Ryne A. Sherman, and Brooke E. Wells, "Sexual Inactivity During Young Adulthood Is More Common Among US Millennials and iGen: Age, Period, and Cohort Effects on Having No Sexual Partners After Age 18," *Archives of Sexual Behavior* 46, no. 2 (2016): 433–40, https://doi.org/10.1007/s10508-016-0798-z.

2. The years documenting the beginning and end of a generation are defined somewhat arbitrarily, as generational trends tend to be gradual, as opposed to discrete. The years listed in this book follow a general consensus. Stacy M. Campbell, Jean M. Twenge, and W. Keith Campbell, "Fuzzy But Useful Constructs: Making Sense of the Differences Between Generations," *Work, Aging and Retirement* 3, no. 2 (2017): 130–39, https://doi.org/10.1093/workar/wax001.

3. Kate Julian, "Why Are Young People Having So Little Sex?," *The Atlantic*, December 15, 2018.

4. Christopher Ingraham, "The Share of Americans Not Having Sex Has Reached a Record High," *Washington Post*, March 29, 2019, https://www.washingtonpost.com/business/2019/03/29/share-americans-not-having-sex-has-reached-record-high/.

5. Peter Ueda et al., "Trends in Frequency of Sexual Activity and Number of Sexual Partners Among Adults Aged 18 to 44 Years in the US,

2000–2018," *JAMA Network Open* 3, no. 6 (2020): 1–15, https://doi
.org/10.1001/jamanetworkopen.2020.3833.

6. Michael Rosenfeld, "Are Tinder and Dating Apps Changing Dating and
    Mating in the USA?," in eds. Jennifer Van Hook, Susan M. McHale, and
    Valarie King, *Families and Technology*, vol. 9, National Symposium on
    Family Issues (Springer, Cham, 2018), 103–17, https://doi.org/10.1007
    /978-3-319-95540-7_6.

7. Michaeleen Doucleff, "The Truth About Teens, Social Media and the
    Mental Health Crisis," NPR, April 25, 2023, https://www.npr.org
    /sections/health-shots/2023/04/25/1171773181/social-media-teens
    -mental-health.

8. For more information on how hypergamy influences mating behavior,
    see Debra Soh, *The End of Gender: Debunking the Myths About Sex
    and Identity in Our Society* (Threshold Editions, 2020), 226.

9. "Table 318.10. Degrees Conferred by Postsecondary Institutions, by
    Level of Degree and Sex of Student: Selected Years, 1869–70 Through
    2029–30," National Center for Education Statistics, 2020, https://nces
    .ed.gov/programs/digest/d20/tables/dt20_318.10.asp.

10. Richard Fry, "Women Now Outnumber Men in the US College-
    Educated Labor Force," Pew Research Center, September 26, 2022,
    https://www.pewresearch.org/short-reads/2022/09/26/women-now-out
    number-men-in-the-u-s-college-educated-labor-force/.

11. David M. Buss, "The Mating Crisis Among Educated Women," *Edge*,
    2016, https://www.edge.org/response-detail/26747.

12. Kathleen E. Kiernan, "Who Remains Celibate?," *Journal of Bio-
    social Science* 20, no. 3 (1988): 253–63, https://doi.org/10.1017
    /S0021932000006593.

13. Gerard Baker, "The Decline of Men in the Workforce," *Wall Street Jour-
    nal Opinion: Free Expression*, August 22, 2022, https://www.wsj.com/
    podcasts/opinion-free-expression/the-decline-of-men-in-the-workforce/
    b2e11b0d-5ec6-4652-a974-5a2ede320760.

14. "Happy 80th Birthday Gloria Steinem: 8 of Her Funniest Quips," *Time*,
    March 25, 2014, https://time.com/36046/gloria-steinem-8-funny-quotes
    -80-birthday.

15. Bruce King, "Average-Size Erect Penis: Fiction, Fact, and the Need for Counseling," *Journal of Sex & Marital Therapy* 47, no. 1 (2021): 80–89, https://doi.org/10.1080/0092623X.2020.1787279.

16. Russell Eisenman, "Penis Size: Survey of Female Perceptions of Sexual Satisfaction," *BMC Women's Health* 1, no. 1 (2001): 1–2, https://doi.org/10.1186/1472-6874-1-1.

17. Michael D. Botwin, David M. Buss, and Todd K. Shackelford, "Personality and Mate Preferences: Five Factors in Mate Selection and Marital Satisfaction," *Journal of Personality* 65, no. 1 (1997): 107–36, https://doi.org/10.1111/j.1467-6494.1997.tb00531.x.

18. Samantha Joel et al., "Machine Learning Uncovers the Most Robust Self-Report Predictors of Relationship Quality Across 43 Longitudinal Couples Studies," *Proceedings of the National Academy of Sciences* 117, no. 32 (2020): 19061–071, https://www.pnas.org/doi/10.1073/pnas.1917036117.

19. Kathrin Boerner, Daniela S. Jopp, Deborah Carr, Laura Sosinsky, and Se-Kang Kim, "'His' and 'Her' Marriage? The Role of Positive and Negative Marital Characteristics in Global Marital Satisfaction Among Older Adults," *Journals of Gerontology: Series B, Psychological Sciences & Social Sciences* 69, no. 4 (2014): 579–89, https://doi.org/10.1093/geronb/gbu032.

20. For example, see American College of Cardiology, "Lifelong Bachelors Face Poorest Prognosis with Heart Failure," ACC.org, February 23, 2023, https://www.acc.org/About-ACC/Press-Releases/2023/02/22/21/23/Lifelong-Bachelors-Face-Poorest-Prognosis-with-Heart-Failure.

21. Clare Ansberry, "Should Your Spouse Be Your Best Friend?," *Wall Street Journal*, September 17, 2023, https://www.wsj.com/lifestyle/relationships/should-your-spouse-be-your-best-friend-473ce00a.

22. Laurel Thomas, "Exactly How Much Housework Does a Husband Create?," University of Michigan, April 3, 2008, https://news.umich.edu/exactly-how-much-housework-does-a-husband-create/.

23. Amelia Karraker and Kenzie Latham, "In Sickness and in Health? Physical Illness as a Risk Factor for Marital Dissolution in Later Life," *Journal of Health and Social Behavior* 56, no. 3 (2015): 420–35, https://doi.org/10.1177/0022146515596354.

24. For example, see Leah Bitsky, "Jana Kramer Felt 'Resentment' Paying Mike Caussin Child Support After He Cheated," *Page Six*, October 19, 2022, https://pagesix.com/2022/10/19/jana-kramer-felt-resentment-pay ing-mike-caussin-child-support/.

25. Marianne Bertrand, Emir Kamenica, and Jessica Pan, "Gender Identity and Relative Income Within Households," *Quarterly Journal of Economics* 130, no. 2 (2015): 571–614, https://www.jstor.org/stable /26372609.

26. Soh, *The End of Gender*, 238–40.

27. "Relationships in 2023 Take Many Forms, Tinder Daters Are Saying 'Yes' to All the Possibilities," Tinder, March 14, 2023, https://www .tinderpressroom.com/2023-03-16-RELATIONSHIPS-IN-2023-TAKE -MANY-FORMS,-TINDER-DATERS-ARE-SAYING-YES-TO-ALL -THE-POSSIBILITIES.

28. Legislation exists in some states to recognize polyamorous parentage. For example, see Lesley McClurg, "Polyamorous Families Are Recognized and Protected in Oakland, CA," NPR, May 31, 2024, https:// www.npr.org/2024/05/31/nx-s1-4966296/polyamorous-families-are -recognized-and-protected-in-oakland-ca.

29. David M. Buss, *When Men Behave Badly: The Hidden Roots of Sexual Deception, Harassment, and Assault* (New York: Little, Brown Spark, 2021), 243.

30. Ueda et al., "Trends in Frequency of Sexual Activity and Number of Sexual Partners Among Adults Aged 18 to 44 Years in the US, 2000–2018," 2020.

31. Sabino Kornrich, Julie Brines, and Katrina Leupp, "Egalitarianism, Housework, and Sexual Frequency in Marriage," *American Sociological Review* 78, no. 1 (2012): 26–50, https://doi.org/10.1177 /0003122412472340.

32. Alice Garnett, "'I'd Snogged Him Before I Even Knew His Name': Why I Ditched Dating Apps," *The Telegraph*, August 18, 2024, https://www .telegraph.co.uk/family/relationships/hinge-tinder-bumble-delete-dating -apps.

33. Sheena S. Iyengar and Mark R. Lepper, "When Choice Is Demotivating: Can One Desire Too Much of a Good Thing?," *Personality Processes*

and Individual Differences 79, no. 6 (2000): 995–1006, https://doi.org
/10.1037/0022-3514.79.6.995.

34. Gábor Orosz, István Tóth-Király, Beáta Bőthe, and Dóra Melher, "Too Many Swipes for Today: The Development of the Problematic Tinder Use Scale (PTUS)," *Journal of Behavioral Addictions* 5, no. 3 (2016): 518–23, https://doi.org/10.1556/2006.5.2016.016.

35. Nina Harren, Vera Walburg, and Henri Chabrol, "Studying the Relationship of Problematic Online Dating, Social Media Use and Online Sexual Behaviors with Body Esteem and Sexuality," *Sexuality & Culture* 25 (2021): 2264–91, https://doi.org/10.1007/s12119-021-09876-z.

36. "State of Gen Z Mental Health," Harmony Healthcare IT, September 15, 2022, https://www.harmonyhit.com/state-of-gen-z-mental-health/.

37. "1 in 2 Gen Z with Anxiety Struggle Daily," Harmony Healthcare IT, October 7, 2023, https://www.harmonyhit.com/gen-z-anxiety-statistics/.

38. Patti M. Valkenburg and Jochen Peter, "Who Visits Online Dating Sites? Exploring Some Characteristics of Online Daters," *Cyberpsychology & Behavior* 10, no. 6 (2007): 849–52, https://doi.org/10.1089/cpb.2007.9941.

39. Ginette C. Blackhart, Jennifer Fitzpatrick, and Jessica Williamson, "Dispositional Factors Predicting Use of Online Dating Sites and Behaviors Related to Online Dating," *Computers in Human Behavior* 33 (2014): 113–18, https://doi.org/10.1016/j.chb.2014.01.022.

40. "Call Declined! A Quarter of 18–24s Refuse to Pick Up the Phone Says New Research," Sky, October 12, 2023, https://www.skygroup.sky /article/call-declined.

41. Jean M. Twenge and Heejung Park, "The Decline in Adult Activities Among US Adolescents, 1976–2016," *Child Development* 90, no. 2 (2017): 638–54, https://doi.org/10.1111/cdev.12930.

42. Aditi Paul, "Is Online Better Than Offline for Meeting Partners? Depends: Are You Looking to Marry or to Date?," *Cyberpsychology, Behavior, and Social Networking* 17, no. 10 (2014): 664–67, https://doi .org/10.1089/cyber.2014.0302.

43. "Is Screen Time Damaging Your Sex Life?," Lloyds Pharmacy Online Doctor, April 24, 2023, https://onlinedoctor.lloydspharmacy.com /uk/sexual-health-advice/sex-and-screen-time.

44. Debra Soh, host, *The Dr. Debra Soh Podcast*, "Episode 9, David Buss: Sexual Conflict and Deception," May 25, 2021.

45. John Burn-Murdoch, "A New Global Gender Divide is Emerging," *Financial Times*, January 26, 2024, https://www.ft.com/content/29fd9b5c-2f35-41bf-9d4c-994db4e12998.

Chapter 2: Permanent Bachelors

1. Jean M. Twenge and Heejung Park, "The Decline in Adult Activities Among US Adolescents, 1976–2016," *Child Development* 90, no. 2 (2017): 638–54, https://doi.org/10.1111/cdev.12930.

2. "GSS 1972–2021 Cumulative Datafile," General Social Survey, February 11, 2022, https://www.docdroid.net/Ow9GtjA/tables-sda3-pdf.

3. Risa Gelles-Watnick, "For Valentine's Day, 5 Facts About Single Americans," Pew Research Center, February 8, 2023, https://www.pew research.org/short-reads/2023/02/08/for-valentines-day-5-facts-about -single-americans/.

4. Rachelle Hampton and Sarah Marshall, "What Everyone Gets Wrong about Gen Z and the Sex It's Allegedly Not Having," *Slate*, April 30, 2022, https://slate.com/human-interest/2022/04/gen-z-generation-sex -abstience-puriteen-research-studies.html.

5. For the original conceptualization of intersectional theory, see Kimberlé Crenshaw, "Mapping the Margins: Intersectionality, Identity Politics, and Violence Against Women of Color," *Stanford Law Review* 43, no. 6 (1991): 1241–99, https://doi.org/10.2307/1229039.

6. This has been disputed by some researchers, but there remains a consensus in the field; for example, see Roy F. Baumeister, Kathleen R. Catanese, and Kathleen D. Vohs, "Is There a Gender Difference in Strength of Sex Drive? Theoretical Views, Conceptual Distinctions, and a Review of Relevant Evidence," *Personality and Social Psychology Review* 5, no. 3 (2001): 242–73, https://doi.org/10.1207/S15327957PSPR0503_5.

7. Judith A. Easton, Jaime C. Confer, Cari D. Goetz, and David M. Buss, "Reproduction Expediting: Sexual Motivations, Fantasies, and the Ticking Biological Clock," *Personality and Individual Differences* 49, no. 5 (2010): 516–20, https://doi.org/10.1016/j.paid.2010.05.018.

8. Russell D. Clark and Elaine Hatfield, "Gender Differences in Receptivity to Sexual Offers," *Journal of Psychology & Human Sexuality* 2, no. 1 (1989): 39–55, https://doi.org/10.1300/J056v02n01_04.

9. For example, see Kimberly R. McBride, Stephanie A. Sanders, Brandon J. Hill, and June M. Reinisch, "Heterosexual Women's and Men's Labeling of Anal Behaviors as Having 'Had Sex,'" *Journal of Sex Research* 54, no. 9 (2017): 1166–70, https://doi.org/10.1080 /00224499.2017.1289362.

10. Twenge and Park, "The Decline in Adult Activities Among US Adolescents, 1976–2016," 2017.

11. David M. Buss et al., "Human Status Criteria: Sex Differences and Similarities Across 14 Nations," *Journal of Personality and Social Psychology* 119, no. 5 (2020): 979–98, https://doi.org/10.1037/pspa0000206.

12. David M. Buss, *When Men Behave Badly: The Hidden Roots of Sexual Deception, Harassment, and Assault* (Little, Brown Spark, 2021), 169.

13. Robert Bozick, "Is There Really a Sex Recession? Period and Cohort Effects on Sexual Inactivity Among American Men, 2006–2019," *American Journal of Men's Health* 15, no. 6 (2021): 1–11, https://doi.org /10.1177/15579883211057710.

14. Debby Herbenick et al., "Changes in Penile-Vaginal Intercourse Frequency and Sexual Repertoire from 2009 to 2018: Findings from the National Survey of Sexual Health and Behavior," *Archives of Sexual Behavior* 51, no. 3 (2022): 1419–33, https://doi.org/10.1007/s10508-021-02125-2.

15. Mike Stobbe, "Pandemic Sent High School Sex to New Low, Survey Finds," Associated Press, April 27, 2023, https://apnews.com/article /teen-sex-survey-high-school-3d45d0441f531d1da9f5b44373becee4.

16. Mary Kekatos, "Teenage Birth Rates in the US Reached Historic Lows in 2022, CDC Report Finds," ABC News, June 1, 2023, https://abc news.go.com/Health/teenage-birth-rates-us-reached-historic-lows-2022 /story?id=99720479.

17. Centers for Disease Control and Prevention, "Reported STDs in the United States, 2021," April 11, 2023, https://www.cdc.gov/nchhstp /newsroom/fact-sheets/std/std-us-2021.html.

18. Debra Soh, "Safer Sex Means Less Promiscuity, Not More," *Washington Examiner*, October 10, 2023, https://www.washingtonexaminer.com/opinion/beltway-confidential/2713019/safer-sex-means-less-promiscuity-not-more/.

19. Herbenick et al., "Changes in Penile-Vaginal Intercourse Frequency and Sexual Repertoire from 2009 to 2018: Findings from the National Survey of Sexual Health and Behavior," 2022.

20. Jean H. Kim et al., "Sociodemographic Correlates of Sexlessness Among American Adults and Associations with Self-Reported Happiness Levels: Evidence from the US General Social Survey," *Archives of Sexual Behavior* 46, no. 8 (2017): 2403–15, https://doi.org/10.1007/s10508-017-0968-7.

21. Nancy Jo Sales, "Tinder and the Dawn of the 'Dating Apocalypse,'" *Vanity Fair*, August 6, 2015, https://www.vanityfair.com/culture/2015/08/tinder-hook-up-culture-end-of-dating.

22. "Relationships in 2023 Take Many Forms, Tinder Daters Are Saying 'Yes' to All the Possibilities," Tinder, March 14, 2023.

23. "Tinder Takes on the Skeptics, Claiming Dating App Fatigue Is 'Overstated,'" *Adweek*, March 14, 2023, https://www.adweek.com/brand-marketing/tinder-takes-on-the-skeptics-claiming-dating-app-fatigue-is-overstated/.

24. Michael Rosenfeld, "Are Tinder and Dating Apps Changing Dating and Mating in the USA?" *Families and Technology*, vol. 9, National Symposium on Family Issues (Springer, Cham, 2018), 103–17, https://doi.org/10.1007/978-3-319-95540-7_6.

25. Worst-online-dater, "Tinder Experiments II: Guys, Unless You Are Really Hot You Are Probably Better Off Not Wasting Your Time on Tinder—A Quantitative Socio-Economic Study," Medium, March 24, 2015, https://medium.com/@worstonlinedater/tinder-experiments-ii-guys-unless-you-are-really-hot-you-are-probably-better-off-not-wasting-your-2ddf370a6e9a.

26. Elizabeth A. Armstrong, Paula England, and Alison C. K. Fogarty, "Accounting for Women's Orgasm and Sexual Enjoyment in College Hookups and Relationships," *American Sociological Review* 77, no. 3 (2012): 435–62, https://doi.org/10.1177/0003122412445802.

27. Stuart Brody, "Blood Pressure Reactivity to Stress Is Better for People Who Recently Had Penile-Vaginal Intercourse Than for People Who Had Other or No Sexual Activity," *Biological Psychology* 71, no. 2 (2006): 214–22, https://doi.org/10.1016/j.biopsycho.2005.03.005.

28. Susan A. Hall, Rebecca Shackelton, Raymond C. Rosen, and Andre B. Araujo, "Sexual Activity, Erectile Dysfunction, and Incident Cardiovascular Events," *American Journal of Cardiology* 105, no. 2 (2010): 192–97, https://doi.org/10.1016/j.amjcard.2009.08.671.

29. Jong-In Kim et al., "Sexual Activity Counteracts the Suppressive Effects of Chronic Stress on Adult Hippocampal Neurogenesis and Recognition Memory," *Brain Research* 1538 no. 13 (2013): 26–40, https://doi.org/10.1016/j.brainres.2013.09.007.

30. Carl J. Charnetski and Francis X. Brennan, "Sexual Frequency and Salivary Immunoglobulin A (IgA)," *Psychological Reports* 94, no. 3 (2004): 839–44, https://doi.org/10.2466/pr0.94.3.839-844.

31. Keith Leavitt et al., "From the Bedroom to the Office: Workplace Spillover Effects of Sexual Activity at Home," *Journal of Management* 45, no. 3 (2017): 1173–92, https://doi.org/10.1177/0149206317698022.

32. Stuart Brody, "The Relative Health Benefits of Different Sexual Activities," *Journal of Sexual Medicine* 7, no. 4 (2010): 1336–61, https://doi.org/10.1111/j.1743-6109.2009.01677.x.

33. Megan Arnot and Ruth Mace, "Sexual Frequency Is Associated with Age of Natural Menopause: Results from the Study of Women's Health Across the Nation," *Royal Society Open Science* 7, no. 1 (2020): 1–10, https://doi.org/10.1098/rsos.191020.

34. Justin R. Garcia et al., "Variation in Orgasm Occurrence by Sexual Orientation in a Sample of US Singles," *Journal of Sexual Medicine* 11, no. 11 (2014): 2645–52, https://doi.org/10.1111/jsm.12669.

35. David A. Frederick et al., "Differences in Orgasm Frequency Among Gay, Lesbian, Bisexual, and Heterosexual Men and Women in a US National Sample," *Archives of Sexual Behavior* 47, no. 1 (2018): 273–88, https://doi.org/10.1007/s10508-017-0939-z.

36. Juha Koskimäki et al., "Regular Intercourse Protects Against Erectile Dysfunction: Tampere Aging Male Urologic Study," *American Journal*

of Medicine 121, no. 7 (2008): 592–96, https://doi.org/10.1016 /j.amjmed.2008.02.042.

37. Jennifer R. Rider et al., "Ejaculation Frequency and Risk of Prostate Cancer: Updated Results with an Additional Decade of Follow-Up," *European Urology* 70, no. 6 (2016): 974–82. https://doi.org/10.1016 /j.eururo.2016.03.027.

38. Anne Campbell, "The Morning After the Night Before: Affective Reactions to One-Night Stands Among Mated and Unmated Women and Men," *Human Nature* 19, no. 2 (2008): 157–73, https://doi.org/10.1007 /s12110-008-9036-2.

39. Amy Muise, Ulrich Schimmack, and Emily A. Impett, "Sexual Frequency Predicts Greater Well-Being, But More Is Not Always Better," *Social Psychological and Personality Science* 7, no. 4 (2016): 295–302, https:// doi.org/10.1177/1948550615616462.

40. Denise Donnelly et al., "Involuntary Celibacy: A Life Course Analysis," *Journal of Sex Research* 38, no. 2 (2001): 159–69, https://doi.org /10.1080/00224490109552083.

41. Vanessa Friedman, "What Does It Mean to Dress like a Zillennial?" *New York Times*, July 15, 2024, https://www.nytimes.com/2024/07/15 /style/gen-z-millennial-young-fashion.html.

42. "Census Bureau Releases New Estimates on America's Families and Living Arrangements," United States Census Bureau, November 17, 2022, https://www.census.gov/newsroom/press-releases/2022/americas-families -and-living-arrangements.html.

43. Richard Fry, "A Record-High Share of 40-Year-Olds in the US Have Never Been Married," Pew Research Center, June 28, 2023, https:// www.pewresearch.org/short-reads/2023/06/28/a-record-high-share-of -40-year-olds-in-the-us-have-never-been-married/.

44. Paulina Cachero and Claire Ballentine, "Nearly Half of All Young Adults Live with Mom and Dad—and They Like It," *Bloomberg*, September 20, 2023, https://www.bloomberg.com/news/articles/2023-09-20 /nearly-half-of-young-adults-are-living-back-home-with-parents.

45. Caitlin Tilley, "Doctors Warn US Is Barreling Towards Same Fertility Crisis as Japan—Where One in 10 Men in Their 30s Are Virgins and [Sic] Third of Women Will Be Childless," *Daily Mail* (UK), September 1,

2023, https://www.dailymail.co.uk/health/article-12461821/Doctors
-warn-barreling-fertility-crisis-Japan-one-10-men-30s-VIRGINS-women
-childless.html.

46. "Rise of the SHEconomy," Morgan Stanley, September 23, 2019,
     https://www.morganstanley.com/ideas/womens-impact-on-the-economy.

47. Tilley, "Doctors Warn US Is Barreling Towards Same Fertility Crisis as
     Japan—Where One in 10 Men in Their 30s Are Virgins and [Sic] Third
     of Women Will Be Childless," 2023.

48. "Country Comparisons—Total Fertility Rate," The World Factbook,
     n.d., accessed June 25, 2025, https://www.cia.gov/the-world-factbook
     /field/total-fertility-rate/country-comparison/.

49. Caroline Crawford, "Niger's Approach to Child Marriage: A Violation
     of Children's Right to Health?," *Health and Human Rights Journal* 24,
     no. 2 (2022): 101–9.

50. Rachel Minkin, Juliana Menasce Horowitz, and Carolina Aragão, "The
     Experiences of US Adults Who Don't Have Children," Pew Research
     Center, July 25, 2024, https://www.pewresearch.org/social-trends/2024
     /07/25/the-experiences-of-u-s-adults-who-dont-have-children/.

51. Andrew Van Dam, "Millennials Aren't Having Kids. Here's Why,"
     Washington Post, November 3, 2023, https://www.washingtonpost.com
     /business/2023/11/03/millennials-only-children/.

52. Carolina Aragão, "Among Young Adults Without Children, Men
     Are More Likely Than Women to Say They Want to Be Parents
     Someday," Pew Research Center, February 15, 2024, https://www
     .pewresearch.org/short-reads/2024/02/15/among-young-adults-with
     out-children-men-are-more-likely-than-women-to-say-they-want-to
     -be-parents-someday/.

53. Kim Parker and Rachel Minkin, "What Makes for a Fulfilling Life?,"
     Pew Research Center, September 14, 2023, https://www.pewresearch.org
     /social-trends/2023/09/14/what-makes-for-a-fulfilling-life/.

54. Mark Banschick, "The High Failure Rate of Second and Third Mar-
     riages," *Psychology Today*, February 6, 2012, https://www.psy
     chologytoday.com/ca/blog/the-intelligent-divorce/201202/the-high
     -failure-rate-of-second-and-third-marriages.

55. Shelby B. Scott et al., "Reasons for Divorce and Recollections of Premarital Intervention: Implications for Improving Relationship Education," *Couple and Family Psychology: Research and Practice* 2, no. 2 (2013): 131–45, https://doi.org/10.1037/a0032025.

56. "I Do Not: Gen Z, Millennials Shifting Expectations About Marriage in 2023," Thriving Center of Psychology, June 23, 2023, https://thriving centerofpsych.com/blog/millennials-gen-z-marriage-expectations-statistics/.

57. Rosenfeld, "Are Tinder and Dating Apps Changing Dating and Mating in the USA?," 2018.

58. For example, see Melissa S. Kearney, Phillip B. Levine, and Luke Pardue, "The Puzzle of Falling US Birth Rates Since the Great Recession," *Journal of Economic Perspectives* 36, no. 1 (2022): 151–76, https://doi.org /10.1257/jep.36.1.151.

59. Faith Karimi, "These Women Wanted a Symbolic Expression of Self-Love. So They Married Themselves," CNN, May 31, 2023, https://www .cnn.com/2023/05/28/us/sologamy-self-marriage-women-cec/index.html.

60. "Tinder's Year in Swipe™ 2023," Tinder, December 6, 2023, https:// www.tinderpressroom.com/Year-in-Swipe-US.

61. Thriving Center of Psychology, June 23, 2023. The remaining 7 percent of respondents identified as "nonbinary" or left the question unanswered. You all know what I think about that; see Soh, *The End of Gender*, 67–96.

62. Catherine Turvey, "Women More Likely Than Men to Initiate Divorces, but Not Non-Marital Breakups," *American Sociological Association*, September 28, 2022, https://www.asanet.org/women-more-likely-men -initiate-divorces-not-non-marital-breakups/.

63. Augustine J. Kposowa, "Divorce and Suicide Risk," *Journal of Epidemiology and Community Health* 57, no. 12 (2003): 993, https://doi.org /10.1136/jech.57.12.993.

64. Rhoshel K. Lenroot and Jay N. Giedd, "Sex Differences in the Adolescent Brain," *Brain and Cognition* 72, no. 1 (2010): 1–19, https://doi.org /10.1016/j.bandc.2009.10.008.

65. Mark Olfson et al., "Treatment of US Children with Attention-Deficit/ Hyperactivity Disorder in the Adolescent Brain Cognitive Development

Study," *JAMA Network Open* 6, no. 4 (2023): e2310999, https://doi.org/10.1001/jamanetworkopen.2023.10999.

66. Marianne Bertrand and Jessica Pan, "The Trouble with Boys: Social Influences and the Gender Gap in Disruptive Behavior," *American Economic Journal: Applied Economics* 5, no. 1 (2013): 32–64, https://doi.org/10.1257/app.5.1.32.

67. Jack Brewer, "Issue Brief: Fatherlessness and Its Effects on American Society," America First Policy Institute, May 15, 2023, https://americafirstpolicy.com/issues/issue-brief-fatherlessness-and-its-effects-on-american-society.

68. Kelly Dore, "Affirmative Action Is Ending—But Holistic Admissions Can Still Allow Higher Education to Better Reflect Society," *Fortune*, June 30, 2023, https://fortune.com/2023/06/30/affirmative-action-end-holistic-admissions-can-still-allow-higher-education-to-better-reflect-society-supreme-court-politics-universities/.

69. Debra Soh, "Diversity, Equity, and Inclusion Initiatives Do Not Belong in Academia," *Globe and Mail* (Canada), May 4, 2021, https://www.theglobeandmail.com/opinion/article-diversity-equity-and-inclusion-initiatives-do-not-belong-in-academia/.

70. Debra Soh, "The US Supreme Court Must End Affirmative Action, Once and for All," *Globe and Mail* (Canada), October 29, 2022, https://www.theglobeandmail.com/opinion/article-us-supreme-court-affirmative-action/.

71. Zack Stanton, "2020 Has Been Miserable. Is Extreme Masculinity to Blame?," *Politico*, November 19, 2020, https://www.politico.com/news/magazine/2020/11/19/masculinity-coronavirus-masks-pandemic-2020-trump-biden-438413.

72. Laura Kiesel, "Don't Blame Mental Illness for Mass Shootings; Blame Men," *Politico*, January 17, 2018, https://www.politico.com/magazine/story/2018/01/17/gun-violence-masculinity-216321/.

73. Emily Tomasik and Jeffrey Gottfried, "US Journalists' Beats Vary Widely by Gender and Other Factors," Pew Research Center, April 4, 2023, https://www.pewresearch.org/short-reads/2023/04/04/us-journalists-beats-vary-widely-by-gender-and-other-factors/.

74. Sandra J. Berg and Kenneth E. Wynne-Edwards, "Changes in Testosterone, Cortisol, and Estradiol Levels in Men Becoming Fathers," *Mayo*

Clinic Proceedings 76, no. 6 (2001): 582–92, https://doi.org/10.4065 /76.6.582.

75. Alan Teo and Arthur Gaw, "Hikikomori, a Japanese Culture-Bound Syndrome of Social Withdrawal? A Proposal for DSM-V," *Journal of Nervous and Mental Disease* 198, no. 6 (2010): 444–49. https://doi.org /10.1097/NMD.0b013e3181e086b1.

76. "Prevalence of Mental Illness 2024," Mental Health America, https:// mhanational.org/issues/2024/mental-health-america-prevalence-data.

77. Daniel A. Cox, "Men's Social Circles Are Shrinking," *AEI Survey Center on American Life*, June 29, 2021, https://www.americansurveycenter.org /why-mens-social-circles-are-shrinking/.

78. Lisa O'Mary, "'Deaths of Despair' Among Men Fueling Life Expectancy Gap," WebMD, November 14, 2023, https://www.webmd.com/men /news/20231114/cm/deaths-among-men-fueling-life-expectancy-gap.

Chapter 3: Imaginary Girlfriends

1. For an example, see "The Earliest Pornography?," *Science*, May 13, 2009, https://www.science.org/content/article/earliest-pornography.

2. Peter Ueda et al., "Trends in Frequency of Sexual Activity and Number of Sexual Partners Among Adults Aged 18 to 44 Years in the US, 2000–2018," *JAMA Network Open* 3, no. 6 (2020): 1–15, https://doi .org/10.1001/jamanetworkopen.2020.3833.

3. Ibid.

4. Jean M. Twenge, Ryne A. Sherman, and Brooke E. Wells. "Declines in Sexual Frequency among American Adults, 1989–2014," *Archives of Sexual Behavior* 46, no. 8 (2017): 2389–2401, https://doi.org/10.1007 /s10508-017-0953-1.

5. Michael B. Robb and Sarah Mann, "Teens and Pornography," *Common Sense*, 2023, https://www.commonsensemedia.org/research/teens-and -pornography.

6. Harold Mouras et al., "Activation of Mirror-Neuron System by Erotic Video Clips Predicts Degree of Induced Erection: An fMRI Study," *NeuroImage* 42, no. 3 (2008): 1142–50, https://doi.org/10.1016 /j.neuroimage.2008.05.051.

7. Risa Gelles-Watnick, "For Valentine's Day, 5 Facts About Single Americans," Pew Research Center, February 8, 2023, https://www.pew research.org/short-reads/2023/02/08/for-valentines-day-5-facts-about -single-americans/.

8. Beáta Bőthe et al., "Problematic Pornography Use Across Countries, Genders, and Sexual Orientations: Insights From the International Sex Survey and Comparison of Different Assessment Tools," *Addiction* 119, no. 5 (2024): 928–50, https://doi.org/10.1111/add.16431.

9. "AASECT Position on Sex Addiction," American Association of Sexuality Educators, Counselors and Therapists, https://www.aasect.org /position-sex-addiction.

10. For example, see Valerie Voon et al., "Neural Correlates of Sexual Cue Reactivity in Individuals with and without Compulsive Sexual Behaviours," *PLOS One* 9, no. 7 (2014): 1–10, https://doi.org/10.1371 /journal.pone.0102419.

11. Christian C. Joyal, Amélie Cossette, and Vanessa Lapierre, "What Exactly Is an Unusual Sexual Fantasy?," *Journal of Sexual Medicine* 12, no. 2 (2015): 328–40, https://doi.org/10.1111/jsm.12734.

12. James W. Antony et al., "Behavioral, Physiological, and Neural Signatures of Surprise During Naturalistic Sports Viewing," *Neuron* 109, no. 2 (2021): 377–390.e7, https://doi.org/10.1016/j.neuron.2020.10.029.

13. Valorie N. Salimpoor et al., "Anatomically Distinct Dopamine Release During Anticipation and Experience of Peak Emotion to Music," *Nature Neuroscience* 14, no. 2 (2011): 257–62, https://doi.org/10.1038/nn.2726.

14. Nicholas Longpré, Courtney Burdis Galiano, and Jean-Pierre Guay, "The Impact of Childhood Trauma, Personality, and Sexuality on the Development of Paraphilias," *Journal of Criminal Justice* 82 (2022): 1–11, https://doi.org/10.1016/j.jcrimjus.2022.101981.

15. "About Child Sexual Abuse," Centers for Disease Control and Prevention, May 16, 2024, https://www.cdc.gov/child-abuse-neglect/about /about-child-sexual-abuse.html?CDC_AAref_Val=https://www.cdc.gov /violenceprevention/childsexualabuse/fastfact.html.

16. Rory C. Reid, Sheila Garos, and Bruce N. Carpenter, "Reliability, Validity, and Psychometric Development of the Hypersexual Behavior Inventory in an Outpatient Sample of Men," *Sexual Addiction &*

Compulsivity: The Journal of Treatment & Prevention 18, no. 1 (2011): 30–51, https://doi.org/10.1080/10720162.2011.555709.

17. Andrew B. Moynihan, Eric R. Igou, and Wijnand A. P. van Tilburg, "Pornography Consumption as Existential Escape from Boredom," *Personality and Individual Differences* 198, no. 9 (2022): 1–6, https://doi.org/10.1016/j.paid.2022.111802.

18. Vlad Burtăverde et al., "Why Do People Watch Porn? An Evolutionary Perspective on the Reasons for Pornography Consumption," *Evolutionary Psychology* 19, no. 2 (2021): 1–15, https://doi.org/10.1177/14747049211028798.

19. John M. Kuzma and Donald W. Black, "Epidemiology, Prevalence, and Natural History of Compulsive Sexual Behavior," *Psychiatric Clinics of North America* 31, no. 4 (2008): 603–11, https://doi.org/10.1016/j.psc.2008.06.005.

20. Moynihan et al., "Pornography Consumption as Existential Escape from Boredom," 2022.

21. Justin M. Dubin et al., "The Broad Reach and Inaccuracy of Men's Health Information on Social Media: Analysis of TikTok and Instagram," *International Journal of Impotence Research* 36 (2022): 256–60, https://doi.org/10.1038/s41443-022-00645-6.

22. Adrienne Santos-Longhurst, "Too Much, Too Fast: Death Grip Syndrome," *Healthline*, January 7, 2020, https://www.healthline.com/health/death-grip-syndrome.

23. Joshua B. Grubbs and Mateusz Gola, "Is Pornography Use Related to Erectile Functioning? Results from Cross-Sectional and Latent Growth Curve Analyses," *Journal of Sexual Medicine* 16, no. 1 (2019): 111–25, https://doi.org/10.1016/j.jsxm.2018.11.004.

24. Jordan Sculley and Christopher D. Watkins, "The Great Porn Experiment v2.0: Sexual Arousal Reduces the Salience of Familiar Women When Heterosexual Men Judge Their Attractiveness," *Archives of Sexual Behavior* 51 (2022): 3071–82, https://doi.org/10.1007/s10508-022-02317-4.

25. Zoltan Varadi, "Why Online Porn Is a Public Health Issue for Kids," *University of Calgary News*, September 24, 2021, https://www.ucalgary.ca/news/why-online-porn-public-health-issue-kids.

26. "Children See Pornography as Young as Seven, New Report Finds," British Board of Film Classification, September 26, 2019, https://www .bbfc.co.uk/about-us/news/children-see-pornography-as-young-as-seven -new-report-finds.

27. Debra Soh, "Britain Is Going to Ban Porn for Kids Under 18. Here's Why It Won't Work," *Globe and Mail* (Canada), 2019, https://www .theglobeandmail.com/opinion/article-britain-is-going-to-ban-porn-for -kids-under-18-heres-why-it-wont/.

28. Belén Sanz-Barbero et al., "Pornography, Sexual Orientation, and Ambivalent Sexism in Young Adults in Spain," *BMC Public Health* 24, no. 374 (2024): 1–14, https://doi.org/10.1186/s12889-024-17853-y.

29. Melinda Tankard Reist, "Early Sexualisation and Pornography Expo-sure: The Detrimental Impacts on Children," Australian Childhood Foundation, *Prosody*, July 6, 2016, https://professionals.childhood.org .au/prosody/2016/07/melinda-tankard-reist/.

30. Gail Hornor, "Child and Adolescent Pornography Exposure," *Journal of Pediatric Health Care* 34, no. 2 (2020): 191–99, https://doi.org/10.1016 /j.pedhc.2019.10.001.

31. Joanne Upton et al., "The Relationship Between Pornography Use and Harmful Sexual Behaviours," Government Equalities Office, January 15, 2021, https://www.gov.uk/government/publications/the -relationship-between-pornography-use-and-harmful-sexual-behaviours /the-relationship-between-pornography-use-and-harmful-sexual-behav iours.

32. Anne J. Maheux, Savannah R. Roberts, Reina Evans, Laura Widman, and Sophia Choukas-Bradley, "Associations Between Adolescents' Por-nography Consumption and Self-Objectification, Body Comparison, and Body Shame," *Body Image* 37, (2021): 89–93, https://doi.org/10.1016 /j.bodyim.2021.01.014.

33. Elena Martellozzo et al., "'I Wasn't Sure It Was Normal to Watch It,'" National Society for the Prevention of Cruelty to Children, 2016, https:// doi.org/10.6084/m9.figshare.3382393.

34. L. Monique Ward, "Media and Sexualization: State of Empirical Research, 1995–2015," *Journal of Sex Research* 53, nos. 4–5 (2016): 560–77, https://doi.org/10.1080/00224499.2016.1142496.

35. Debra K. Braun-Courville and Mary Rojas, "Exposure to Sexually Explicit Web Sites and Adolescent Sexual Attitudes and Behaviors," *Journal of Adolescent Health* 45, no. 2 (2009): 156–62, https://doi.org/10.1016/j.jadohealth.2008.12.004.

36. Kimberly J. Mitchell, David Finkelhor, and Janis Wolak, "The Exposure of Youth to Unwanted Sexual Material on the Internet: A National Survey of Risk, Impact, and Prevention," *Youth & Society* 34, no. 3 (2003): 330–58, https://doi.org/10.1177/0044118X02250123.

37. Anna Moore and Coco Khan, "The Fatal, Hateful Rise of Choking During Sex," *The Guardian* (UK), July 25, 2019, https://www.theguardian.com/society/2019/jul/25/fatal-hateful-rise-of-choking-during-sex.

38. Debby Herbenick et al., "#ChokeMeDaddy: A Content Analysis of Memes Related to Choking/Strangulation During Sex," *Archives of Sexual Behavior* 52, no. 3 (2022): 1299–315, https://doi.org/10.1007/s10508-022-02502-5.

39. Debby Herbenick et al., "Frequency, Method, Intensity, and Health Sequelae of Sexual Choking Among US Undergraduate and Graduate Students," *Archives of Sexual Behavior* 51, no. 6 (2022): 3121–39, https://doi.org/10.1007/s10508-022-02347-y.

40. Debby Herbenick et al., "Prevalence and Characteristics of Choking/Strangulation During Sex: Findings from a Probability Survey of Undergraduate Students," *Journal of American College Health* 71, no. 4 (2021): 1059–73, https://doi.org/10.1080/07448481.2021.1920599.

41. Herbenick et al., "Frequency, Method, Intensity, and Health Sequelae of Sexual Choking Among US Undergraduate and Graduate Students," 2022.

42. Ibid.

43. Mike Abrams, Agatha Chronos, and M. Milisavljevic Grdinic, "Childhood Abuse and Sadomasochism: New Insights," *Sexologies* 31, no. 3 (2022): 240–59, https://doi.org/10.1016/j.sexol.2021.10.004.

44. Christian C. Joyal and Julie Carpentier, "The Prevalence of Paraphilic Interests and Behaviors in the General Population: A Provincial Survey," *Journal of Sex Research* 54, no. 2 (2016): 161–71, https://doi.org/10.1080/00224499.2016.1139034.

45. Monica M. Moore, "Courtship Communication and Perception," *Perceptual and Motor Skills* 94, no. 1 (2002): 97–105, https://doi.org /10.2466/PMS.94.1.97-105.

46. Longpré et al., "The Impact of Childhood Trauma, Personality, and Sexuality on the Development of Paraphilias," 2022.

47. Abrams et al., "Childhood Abuse and Sadomasochism: New Insights," 2022.

48. Rosa Walling-Wefelmeyer and Tully O'Neill, "'There Are a Lot of Bad Dominants, Mostly Men, Where It's Basically Abuse Dressed Up as a Kink': Victim-Survivors' Everyday Navigation of BDSM, Kink and Fetish," *Child and Family Law Quarterly* 33, no. 4 (2021): 363–78, https://plus.lexis.com/api/permalink/5f255b30-342d-46b4-89d5 -1ddeb521add8/?context=1001073.

49. Mary-Anne Kate, Graham Jamieson, and Warwick Middleton, "Childhood Sexual, Emotional, and Physical Abuse as Predictors of Dissociation in Adulthood," *Journal of Child Sexual Abuse* 30, no. 8 (2021): 953–976, https://doi.org/10.1080/10538712.2021.1955789.

50. Lucas J. H. Lim, Roger C. M. Ho, and Cyrus S. H. Ho, "Dangers of Mixed Martial Arts in the Development of Chronic Traumatic Encephalopathy," *International Journal of Environmental Research and Public Health* 16, no. 2 (2019): 254–61, https://doi.org/10.3390 /ijerph16020254.

51. Paul McCrory, Tsharni Zazryn, and Peter Cameron, "The Evidence for Chronic Traumatic Encephalopathy in Boxing," *Sports Medicine* 37, no. 6 (2007): 467–76, https://doi.org/10.2165/00007256 -200737060-00001.

52. David A. Frederick et al., "Differences in Orgasm Frequency Among Gay, Lesbian, Bisexual, and Heterosexual Men and Women in a US National Sample," *Archives of Sexual Behavior* 47, no. 1 (2018): 273–88, https://doi.org/10.1007/s10508-017-0939-z.

53. Eva Elmerstig, Barbro Wijma, and Katarina Swahnberg, "Prioritizing the Partner's Enjoyment: A Population-Based Study on Young Swedish Women with Experience of Pain During Vaginal Intercourse," *Journal of Psychosomatic Obstetrics & Gynecology* 34, no. 2 (2013): 82–89, https://doi.org/10.3109/0167482X.2013.793665.

Chapter 4: Digital Love

1. Although OnlyFans has explicitly prohibited its creators from using chatbot technology, it turns out some paying subscribers may be chatting with AI software unknowingly. See Andrew R. C. Marshall, Jason Szep, and Linda So, "AI Bots Talk Dirty So OnlyFans Stars Don't Have To," Reuters, July 30, 2024, https://www.reuters.com/technology/artificial-intelligence/ai-bots-talk-dirty-so-onlyfans-stars-dont-have-2024-07-30/.

2. David de Visé, "A Record Share of Americans Is Living Alone," *The Hill*, July 10, 2023, https://thehill.com/policy/healthcare/4085828-a-record-share-of-americans-are-living-alone/.

3. American Psychiatric Association, "New APA Poll: One in Three Americans Feels Lonely Every Week," January 30, 2024, https://www.psychiatry.org/news-room/news-releases/new-apa-poll-one-in-three-americans-feels-lonely-e.

4. Richard Weissbourd et al., "Loneliness in America: How the Pandemic Has Deepened an Epidemic of Loneliness and What We Can Do About It," Making Caring Common Project, February 2021, https://mcc.gse.harvard.edu/reports/loneliness-in-america.

5. American Psychiatric Association, "New APA Poll," January 30, 2024.

6. Stacy Jo Dixon, "Daily Time Spent on Social Networking by Internet Users Worldwide from 2012 to 2024," Statista, April 10, 2024, https://www.statista.com/statistics/433871/daily-social-media-usage-worldwide/.

7. American Psychiatric Association, "Media Advisory: As a Third of Americans Spend Four or More Hours a Day on Social Media, APA Offers New Polling, Resources on Technology Use," April 10, 2024, https://www.psychiatry.org/News-room/News-Releases/Media-Advisory-Resources-on-Technology-Use.

8. "Our Epidemic of Loneliness and Isolation: The US Surgeon General's Advisory on the Healing Effects of Social Connection and Community," US Department of Health and Human Services, 2023, https://www.hhs.gov/sites/default/files/surgeon-general-social-connection-advisory.pdf.

9. "Are You Addicted to Your Phone? American Phone Usage & Screen Time Statistics," Harmony Healthcare IT, January 8, 2025, https://www.harmonyhit.com/phone-screen-time-statistics/.

10. Colin Hesse and Kory Floyd, "Affection Substitution: The Effect of Pornography Consumption on Close Relationships," *Journal of Social and Personal Relationships* 36, nos. 11–12 (2019): 3887–907, https://doi.org/10.1177/0265407519841719.

11. Achim Haettich, Comment on "Trends in Frequency of Sexual Activity and Number of Sexual Partners Among Adults Aged 18 to 44 Years in the US, 2000–2018," *JAMA Network Open*, July 1, 2020, https://jamanetwork.com/journals/jamanetworkopen/fullarticle/2767066.

12. Joshua Zitser, "A Woman Is Marrying an AI Hologram, Ushering in a Weird New Era for Human-Robot Relationships," *Business Insider*, February 22, 2024, https://www.businessinsider.com/woman-marrying-ai-hologram-trained-it-on-past-relationships-2024-2.

13. Ben Dooley and Hisako Ueno, "This Man Married a Fictional Character. He'd Like You to Hear Him Out," *New York Times*, April 24, 2022, https://www.nytimes.com/2022/04/24/business/akihiko-kondo-fictional-character-relationships.html.

14. Casey Newton, "Speak, Memory," *The Verge*, https://www.theverge.com/a/luka-artificial-intelligence-memorial-roman-mazurenko-bot.

15. Tianling Xie and Iryna Pentina, "Attachment Theory as a Framework to Understand Relationships with Social Chatbots: A Case Study of Replika," *Hawaii International Conference on System Sciences*, January 2022, https://doi.org/10.24251/HICSS.2022.258.

16. Linnea Laestadius et al., "Too Human and Not Human Enough: A Grounded Theory Analysis of Mental Health Harms from Emotional Dependence on the Social Chatbot Replika," *New Media & Society* 26, no. 10 (2022): 5923–41, https://doi.org/10.1177/14614448221142007.

17. James Purtill, "Replika Users Fell in Love with Their AI Chatbot Companions. Then They Lost Them," Australian Broadcasting Corporation, February 28, 2023, https://www.abc.net.au/news/science/2023-03-01/replika-users-fell-in-love-with-their-ai-chatbot-companion/102028196.

18. The interview has been lightly edited for clarity. Interview with programmer, 2/28/24.

19. Alexandra Del Rosario, "Those Explicit Taylor Swift Deepfakes Are 'Sexual Exploitation,' Lawmakers Say," *Los Angeles Times*, January 25,

2024, https://www.latimes.com/entertainment-arts/music/story/2024-01 -25/taylor-swift-fans-slam-spread-nsfw-ai-images.

20. "Generative AI CSAM Is CSAM," National Center for Missing & Exploited Children, March 11, 2024, https://www.missingkids.org/blog /2024/generative-ai-csam-is-csam.

21. Leslie J. Seltzer et al., "Instant Messages vs. Speech: Hormones and Why We Still Need to Hear Each Other," *Evolution and Human Behavior* 33, no. 1 (2012): 42–45, https://doi.org/10.1016 /j.evolhumbehav.2011.05.004.

22. Xia Song, Bo Xu, and Zhenzhen Zhao, "Can People Experience Romantic Love for Artificial Intelligence? An Empirical Study of Intelligent Assistants," *Information & Management* 59, no. 2 (2022): 1–10, https:// doi.org/10.1016/j.im.2022.103595.

23. Xie and Pentina, "Attachment Theory as a Framework to Understand Relationships with Social Chatbots: A Case Study of Replika," 2022.

24. David M. Buss, Randy J. Larsen, Drew Westen, and Jennifer Semmel-roth, "Sex Differences in Jealousy: Evolution, Physiology, and Psychology," *Psychological Science* 3, no. 4 (1992): 251–55, https://doi.org /10.1111/j.1467-9280.1992.tb00038.x.

25. Maria Kraxenberger, Christine A. Knoop, and Winfried Menninghaus, "Who Reads Contemporary Erotic Novels and Why?," *Humanities and Social Sciences Communications* 8, no. 96 (2021): 1–13, https://doi.org /10.1057/s41599-021-00764-3.

Chapter 5: The Two-Track Mind

1. Henry Moore, "Revealed: Sleazy Adverts Used to Entice Models to Become Cannes 'Yacht Girl' Escorts Offering Sex to Arab, Russian and US Billionaires Throughout the Famous Film Festival," *Daily Mail* (UK), May 24, 2024, https://www.dailymail.co.uk/news/article-13456185 /Sseazy-adverts-models-cannes-film-festival-yacht-girl-escorts.html.

2. "The Sick Things IG Models Do in Dubai," December 22, 2021, Tunde, YouTube, https://www.youtube.com/watch?v=272HMOiTCgE.

3. For example, see Inez Stepman, "Hey, *Teen Vogue*. On Career Day, No Young Girl Should Say 'I Want to Be a Prostitute,'" *USA*

Today, June 20, 2019, https://www.usatoday.com/story/opinion/2019/06/20/teen-vogue-sex-trafficking-work-minors-column/1502109001/.

4. Naomi K. Muggleton, Sarah R. Tarran, and Corey L. Fincher, "Who Punishes Promiscuous Women? Both Women and Men Are Prejudiced Towards Sexually-Accessible Women, but Only Women Inflict Costly Punishment," *Evolution and Human Behavior* 40, no. 3 (2018): 259–68, https://doi.org/10.1016/j.evolhumbehav.2018.12.003.

5. Matthew Smith, "What Does Britain Think of Sex Work and Sex Workers?," YouGov, February 28, 2024, https://yougov.co.uk/society/articles/48773-what-does-britain-think-of-sex-work-and-sex-workers.

6. Tom Hollands, "The Economics of OnlyFans," XSRUS, April 24, 2020, https://xsrus.com/the-economics-of-onlyfans.

7. Fortesa Latifi, "I Regret Doing OnlyFans When I Turned 18. My Subscribers Pushed My Boundaries, Sent Degrading Messages, and Treated Me Like an Object," *Business Insider*, n.d. Accessed June 25, 2025, https://www.businessinsider.com/downsides-and-regrets-of-doing-onlyfans-2023-9.

8. Bernadette Barton, "Managing the Toll of Stripping: Boundary Setting Among Exotic Dancers," *Journal of Contemporary Ethnography* 36, no. 5 (2007): 571–96, https://doi.org/10.1177/0891241607301971.

9. Holly Baxter, "They Thought They Were Chatting with OnlyFans Models, Not Men Being Paid to Pretend," *The Independent* (UK), March 5, 2025, https://www.independent.co.uk/news/world/americas/onlyfans-models-chatters-reddit-class-action-lawsuit-b2710675.html.

10. Grishma Patel et al., "Undergraduate Students Sugar Dating in the US Demonstrate Increased Financial Need and a History of Severe Adverse Childhood Experiences," *Research Square*, 2023, https://doi.org/10.21203/rs.3.rs-3171711/v1.

11. Felix Betzler, Stephan Köhler, and Ludwig Schlemm, "Sex Work Among Students of Higher Education: A Survey-Based, Cross-Sectional Study," *Archives of Sexual Behavior* 44, no. 3 (2015): 525–28, https://doi.org/10.1007/s10508-014-0476-y.

12. Kate B. Metcalfe et al., "'I Was Worshiped and in Control': Sugar Arrangements Involving Transactional Sex from the Perspective of Both Sugar Babies and Sugar Benefactors," *Journal of Sex Research* 61, no. 7 (2023): 1013–25, https://doi.org/10.1080/00224499.2023.2293888.

13. Ibid.

14. For example, see Ranjani Utpala-Kumar and Frank P. Deane, "Heavy Episodic Drinking Among University Students: Drinking Status and Perceived Normative Comparisons," *Substance Use & Misuse* 47, no. 3 (2012): 278–85, https://doi.org/10.3109/10826084.2011.636134.

15. "Logan Paul: I Couldn't Believe She Was a Prostitute," July 29, 2021, Impaulsive Clips, YouTube, https://www.youtube.com/watch?v=jtZcmoMXHR0.

16. Melissa Farley, "Prostitution and the Invisibility of Harm," *Women & Therapy* 26, nos. 3–4 (2003): 247–80, https://doi.org/10.1300/J015v26n03_06.

17. Debra Soh, *The End of Gender: Debunking the Myths About Sex and Identity in Our Society* (Threshold Editions, 2020), 219–45.

18. David M. Buss and David P. Schmitt, "Sexual Strategies Theory: An Evolutionary Perspective on Human Mating," *Psychological Review* 100, no. 2 (1993): 204–32, https://doi.org/10.1037/0033-295x.100.2.204.

19. Béla Birkás et al., "Providing Sexual Companionship for Resources: Development, Validation, and Personality Correlates of the Acceptance of Sugar Relationships in Young Women and Men Scale (ASR-YWMS)," *Frontiers in Psychology* 11 (2020): 1–15, https://doi.org/10.3389/fpsyg.2020.01135.

20. Jade Butterworth, Sam Pearson, and William von Hippel, "Dual Mating Strategies Observed in Male Clients of Female Sex Workers," *Human Nature* 34, no. 1 (2023): 46–63, https://doi.org/10.1007/s12110-023-09439-1.

21. "Infidelity Statistics," Couples Academy, https://couplesacademy.org/infidelity-statistics/.

22. Melissa Farley, Julie Bindel, and Jacqueline M. Golding, "Men Who Buy Sex: Who They Buy and What They Know," *Eaves*, December 2009, https://i1.cmsfiles.com/eaves/2012/04/MenWhoBuySex-89396b.pdf.

23. Corita R. Grudzen et al., "Comparison of the Mental Health of Female Adult Film Performers and Other Young Women in California," *Psychiatric Services* 62, no. 6 (2011): 639–45, https://doi.org/10.1176/appi.ps.62.6.639.

24. Brian Willis et al., "Causes of mortality among female sex workers: Results of a multi-country study," *eClinicalMedicine* 52 (2022): 1–11, https://doi.org/10.1016/j.eclinm.2022.101658.

25. Patel et al., "Undergraduate Students Sugar Dating in the US Demonstrate Increased Financial Need and a History of Severe Adverse Childhood Experiences," 2023.

26. Judith K. Inazu and Greer L. Fox, "Maternal Influence on the Sexual Behavior of Teen-Age Daughters: Direct and Indirect Sources," *Journal of Family Issues* 1, no. 1 (1980): 81–102, https://doi.org/10.1177/0192513X8000100105.

27. Danielle J. DelPriore, Gabriel L. Schlomer, and Bruce J. Ellis, "Impact of Fathers on Parental Monitoring of Daughters and Their Affiliation with Sexually Promiscuous Peers," *Developmental Psychology* 53, no. 7 (2017): 1330–43, https://doi.org/10.1037/dev0000327.

28. "Sky Bri's Craziest Fan Interactions," December 15, 2023, MommyDaddyTalk, YouTube, https://www.youtube.com/shorts/Dul15bTF2e0.

29. Chris Morris, "Banks to Porn Stars: Your Money's Not Welcome," NBC News, May 17, 2013, https://www.nbcnews.com/business/business-news/banks-porn-stars-your-moneys-not-welcome-flna1c9.

30. David M. Buss et al., "Sex Differences in Jealousy: Evolution, Physiology, and Psychology," *Psychological Science* 3, no. 4 (1992): 251–55, https://doi.org/10.1111/j.1467-9280.1992.tb00038.x.

31. "OnlyFans Dating Survey," XF Hub, n.d., accessed June 25, 2025, https://xfanshub.com/onlyfans-dating-survey/.

32. For example, see Farley, "Prostitution and the Invisibility of Harm," 2003.

33. Matthew Smith, "Women Unwilling to Date OnlyFans Users," YouGov, March 18, 2024, https://yougov.co.uk/society/articles/48949-women-unwilling-to-date-onlyfans-users.

34. Stacey D. A. Litam, Megan Speciale, and Richard S. Balkin, "Sexual Attitudes and Characteristics of OnlyFans Users," *Archives of Sexual Behavior* 51 (2022): 3093–103, https://doi.org/10.1007/s10508-022-02329-0.

35. "Who Has the Wealthiest Sugar Daddy?," December 7, 2022, Jubilee, YouTube, https://www.youtube.com/watch?v=JsJLISvY-C0.

Chapter 6: Life in Plastic

1. "Chinese Man Sues Wife for Being Ugly, Wins $120,000," FOX31 KDVR and Channel 2 KWGN, October 26, 2012, https://kdvr.com/news/chinese-man-sues-wins-120000/.

2. David A. Frederick and Martie G. Haselton, "Why Is Muscularity Sexy? Tests of the Fitness Indicator Hypothesis," *Personality and Social Psychology Bulletin* 33, no. 8 (2007): 1167–83, https://doi.org/10.1177/0146167207303022.

3. American Society of Plastic Surgeons, 2023 ASPS Procedural Statistics Release (2023).

4. American Academy of Facial Plastic and Reconstructive Surgery, "As Americans Return to the Office, AAFPRS Unveils Aesthetic Trends from Annual Facial Plastic Surgery Survey," February 13, 2023, https://www.aafprs.org/Media/Press_Releases/New-Trends-in-Facial-Plastic-Surgery.aspx.

5. Callie Holtermann, "Why Does Gen Z Believe It's 'Aging Like Milk'?," *New York Times*, January 23, 2024, https://www.nytimes.com/2024/01/23/style/gen-z-aging.html.

6. David M. Buss, "Sex Differences in Human Mate Preferences: Evolutionary Hypotheses Tested in 37 Cultures," *Behavioral and Brain Sciences* 12, no. 1 (1989): 1–49, https://doi.org/10.1017/S0140525X00023992.

7. Douglas T. Kenrick et al., "Adolescents' Age Preferences for Dating Partners: Support for an Evolutionary Model of Life-History Strategies," *Child Development* 67, no. 4 (1996): 1499–511, https://doi.org/1131714.

8. Madison Freeman, "Lip Flips May Have Been Trending on TikTok, But Is It the Right Choice for You?," *American Society of Plastic Surgeons*, September 6, 2022, https://www.plasticsurgery.org/news/articles/lip-flips-may-have-been-trending-on-tiktok-but-is-it-the-right-choice-for-you.

9. Ayman D'Souza and Chew L. Ng, "Applied Anatomy for Botulinum Toxin Injection in Cosmetic Interventions," *Current Otorhinolaryngol-*

ogy Reports 8 (2020): 336–43, https://doi.org/10.1007/s40136-020
-00308-4.

10. Charles Trepany, "'Barbie Botox' Trend Has People Breaking the Bank to Make Necks Longer. Is It Worth It?," *USA Today*, August 2, 2023, https://www.usatoday.com/story/life/health-wellness/2023/08/02/barbie-botox-trend-has-tiktokers-trying-to-make-necks-look-longer/70509754007/.

11. Lauren Valenti, Chloe Atkins, and Audrey Noble, "Why Preventative Botox Injections Could Be Aging You," *Vogue*, January 15, 2025, https://www.vogue.com/article/preventative-botox-injections-twenty-somethings-expert-guide-wrinkles-fine-lines-eyes-lips-forehead.

12. Lauren Burwell, "How Young Is Too Young for 'Baby Botox' and Fillers?," *Huffington Post*, February 5, 2024, https://www.huffpost.com/entry/how-young-botox-fillers_l_65ba7543e4b01c5c3a395d91.

13. "I Got Surgery to Look Like a Snapchat Filter," July 17, 2021, Refinery29, YouTube, https://www.youtube.com/watch?v=FfJ_wSowVfM.

14. Mounir Bashour, "History and Current Concepts in the Analysis of Facial Attractiveness," *Plastic and Reconstructive Surgery* 118, no. 3 (2006): 741–56, https://doi.org/10.1097/01.prs.0000233051.61512.65.

15. Vinet Coetzee et al., "Cross-Cultural Agreement in Facial Attractiveness Preferences: The Role of Ethnicity and Gender," *PLOS One* 9, no. 7 (2014): 1–17, https://doi.org/10.1371/journal.pone.0099629.

16. Judith H. Langlois et al., "Infant Preferences for Attractive Faces: Rudiments of a Stereotype?," *Developmental Psychology* 23, no. 3 (1987): 363–69, https://doi.org/10.1037/0012-1649.23.3.363.

17. Karel Kleisner, Veronika Chvátalová, and Jaroslav Flegr, "Perceived Intelligence Is Associated with Measured Intelligence in Men but Not Women," *PLOS One* 9, no. 3 (2014): 1–7, https://doi.org/10.1371/journal.pone.0081237.

18. Jason M. Fletcher, "Beauty vs. Brains: Early Labor Market Outcomes of High School Graduates," *Economics Letters* 105 (2009): 321–25, https://doi.org/10.1016/j.econlet.2009.09.006.

19. Satoshi Kanazana and Jody L. Kovar, "Why Beautiful People Are More Intelligent," *Intelligence* 32, no. 3 (2004): 227–43, https://doi.org/10.1016/j.intell.2004.03.003.

20. Kaitlin Lenoir and Eric Stocks, "Attractiveness Norm Violations and the Halo Effect," *Undergraduate Journal of Psychology* 31, no. 1 (2019): 54–61, https://journals.charlotte.edu/ujop/article/view/906.

21. Markus Jokela, "Physical Attractiveness and Reproductive Success in Humans: Evidence from the Late 20th Century United States," *Evolution and Human Behavior* 30, no. 5 (2009): 342–50, https://doi.org/10.1016/j.evolhumbehav.2009.03.006.

22. David M. Buss, *Evolutionary Psychology: The New Science of the Mind* (Routledge, 2019).

23. Steven W. Gangestad and David M. Buss, "Pathogen Prevalence and Human Mate Preferences," *Ethology & Sociobiology* 14, no. 2 (1993): 89–96, https://doi.org/10.1016/0162-3095(93)90009-7.

24. David C. Geary, Jacob Vigil, and Jennifer Byrd-Craven, "Evolution of Human Mate Choice," *Journal of Sex Research* 41, no. 1 (2004): 27–42, https://doi.org/10.1080/00224490409552211.

25. David I. Perrett et al., "Effects of Sexual Dimorphism on Facial Attractiveness," *Nature* 394, no. 6696 (1998): 884–87, https://doi.org/10.1038/29772.

26. Vojtěch Fiala et al., "Facial Attractiveness and Preference of Sexual Dimorphism: A Comparison Across Five Populations," *Evolutionary Human Sciences* 3 (2021): 1–24, https://doi.org/10.1017/ehs.2021.33.

27. Gillian Rhodes, "The Evolutionary Psychology of Facial Beauty," *Annual Review of Psychology* 57, no. 1 (2006): 199–226, https://doi.org/10.1146/annurev.psych.57.102904.190208.

28. Siân A. McLean et al., "Photoshopping the Selfie: Self Photo Editing and Photo Investment Are Associated with Body Dissatisfaction in Adolescent Girls," *International Journal of Eating Disorders* 48, no. 8 (2015): 1132–40, https://doi.org/10.1002/eat.22449.

29. Susruthi Rajanala, Mayra B. C. Maymone, and Neelam A. Vashi, "Selfies—Living in the Era of Filtered Photographs," *JAMA Facial Plastic Surgery* 20, no. 6 (2018): 443–44, https://doi.org/10.1001/jamafacial.2018.0486.

30. American Academy of Facial Plastic and Reconstructive Surgery, Inc., "AAFPRS Survey Says the Selfie Endures and Is Stronger Than Ever,"

February 27, 2020, https://www.aafprs.org/Media/Press_Releases/Self
ies%20Endure%20February%2027,%202020.aspx.

31. Mariska Kleemans et al., "Picture Perfect: The Direct Effect of Ma-
     nipulated Instagram Photos on Body Image in Adolescent Girls,"
     Media Psychology 21 (2018): 93–110, https://doi.org/10.1080
     /15213269.2016.1257392.

32. Jacqueline Nesi and Mitchell J. Prinstein, "Using Social Media for Social
     Comparison and Feedback-Seeking," *Journal of Abnormal Child Psy-
     chology* 43, no. 8 (2015): 1427–38, https://doi.org/10.1007/s10802-015
     -0020-0.

33. American Society of Plastic Surgeons, *Plastic Surgery Statistics Report*
     (2020), https://www.plasticsurgery.org/documents/news/statistics/2020
     /plastic-surgery-statistics-full-report-2020.pdf.

34. Aria Bendix and Berkeley Lovelace Jr., "What It's Like to Take the
     Blockbuster Drugs Ozempic and Wegovy, from Severe Side Effects to
     Losing 50 Pounds," NBC News, January 29, 2023, https://www.nb
     cnews.com/health/health-news/ozempic-wegovy-diabetes-weight-loss
     -side-effects-rcna66493.

35. Kathleen Hou, "Is Plastic Surgery Having a Vibe Shift?," *Elle*,
     January 10, 2025, https://www.elle.com/beauty/makeup-skin-care/a6
     3267441/undetectable-plastic-surgery-trend-2025-explained/.

36. Mayo Clinic, "Screen Time and Children: How to Guide Your Child,"
     June 19, 2024, https://www.mayoclinic.org/healthy-lifestyle/childrens
     -health/in-depth/screen-time/art-20047952.

37. Maria T. Maza, Kara A. Fox, and Seh-Joo Kwon, "Association of Ha-
     bitual Checking Behaviors on Social Media with Longitudinal Func-
     tional Brain Development," *JAMA Pediatrics* 117, no. 2 (2023): 160–67,
     https://doi.org/10.1001/jamapediatrics.2022.4924.

38. "Get the Facts," National Organization for Women, https://now.org
     /now-foundation/love-your-body/love-your-body-whats-it-all-about/get
     -the-facts/.

39. Francesca Chloe Ryding and Daria J. Kuss, "The Use of Social Network-
     ing Sites, Body Image Dissatisfaction, and Body Dysmorphic Disorder:
     A Systematic Review of Psychological Research," *Psychology of Popular
     Media* 9, no. 4 (2020): 412–35, https://doi.org/10.1037/ppm0000264.

40. Mingli Liu et al., "Time Spent on Social Media and Risk of Depression in Adolescents: A Dose-Response Meta-Analysis," *International Journal of Environmental Research and Public Health* 19, no. 9 (2022): 1–17, https://doi.org/10.3390/ijerph19095164.

41. Juan Zhang et al., "The Relationship Between SNS Usage and Disordered Eating Behaviors: A Meta-Analysis," *Frontiers in Psychology* 12 (2021): 1–16, https://doi.org/10.3389/fpsyg.2021.641919.

42. Zachary Rausch and Jonathan Haidt, "The Teen Mental Health Crisis Is International, Part 1: The Anglosphere," After Babel, March 29, 2023, https://www.afterbabel.com/p/international-mental-illness-part-one.

43. Zachary Rausch and Jonathan Haidt, "Suicide Rates Are Up for Gen Z Across the Anglosphere, Especially for Girls," After Babel, October 30, 2023, https://www.afterbabel.com/p/anglo-teen-suicide.

44. Georgia Wells, Jeff Horwitz, and Deepa Seetharaman, "Facebook Knows Instagram Is Toxic for Teen Girls, Company Documents Show," *Wall Street Journal*, September 14, 2021, https://www.wsj.com/articles/facebook-knows-instagram-is-toxic-for-teen-girls-company-documents-show-11631620739.

45. Adrian Furnham and James Levitas, "Factors That Motivate People to Undergo Cosmetic Surgery," *Canadian Journal of Plastic Surgery* 20, no. 4 (2012): e47–e50, https://doi.org/10.4172/plastic-surgery.1000777.

46. Debra Soh, "The Backlash Against Australia's Ban on Social Media for Children Is Misguided," *Globe and Mail* (Canada), November 26, 2024, https://www.theglobeandmail.com/opinion/article-the-backlash-against-australias-ban-on-social-media-for-children-is.

47. Scott J. Fatt, Jasmine Fardouly, and Ronald M. Rapee, "#MaleFitspo: Links Between Viewing Fitspiration Posts, Muscular-Ideal Internalisation, Appearance Comparisons, Body Satisfaction, and Exercise Motivation in Men," *New Media & Society* 21, no. 6 (2019): 1311–25, https://doi.org/10.1177/1461444818821064.

48. David Veale et al., "Body Dysmorphic Disorder in Different Settings: A Systematic Review and Estimated Weighted Prevalence," *Body Image* 18 (2016): 168–86, https://doi.org/10.1016/j.bodyim.2016.07.003.

49. Mohammed Alsaidan et al., "The Prevalence and Determinants of Body Dysmorphic Disorder Among Young Social Media Users: A Cross-

Sectional Study," *Dermatology Reports* 12, no. 3 (2020): 70–76, https://doi.org/10.4081/dr.2020.8774.

50. Ryding and Kuss, "The Use of Social Networking Sites, Body Image Dissatisfaction, and Body Dysmorphic Disorder: A Systematic Review of Psychological Research," 2020.

51. Rajanala et al., "Selfies—Living in the Era of Filtered Photographs," 2018.

52. Payal Shah et al., "Cosmetic Procedure Use as a Type of Substance-Related Disorder," *Journal of the American Academy of Dermatology* 84, no. 1 (2020): 86–91, https://doi.org/10.1016/j.jaad.2020.08.123.

53. Mair Underwood and Richard Olivardia, "'The Day You Start Lifting Is the Day You Become Forever Small': Bodybuilders Explain Muscle Dysmorphia," *Health* 27, no. 6 (2022): 998–1018, https://doi.org/10.1177/13634593221093494.

54. Alex Hawgood, "What Is 'Bigorexia'?," *New York Times*, March 5, 2022, https://www.nytimes.com/2022/03/05/style/teen-bodybuilding-bigorexia-tiktok.html.

55. Karen M. Skemp, Renae Elwood, and David M. Reineke, "Adolescent Boys Are at Risk for Body Image Dissatisfaction and Muscle Dysmorphia," *Californian Journal of Health Promotion* 17, no. 1 (2019): 61–70, https://doi.org/10.32398/cjhp.v17i1.2224.

56. Kimberly Glazer et al., "The Course of Weight/Shape Concerns and Disordered Eating Symptoms Among Adolescent and Young Adult Males," *Journal of Adolescent Health* 69, no. 4 (2021): 615–21, https://doi.org/10.1016/j.jadohealth.2021.03.036.

57. "Dr. Mike Mew's Ultimate Mewing Guide: Beginner," December 27, 2023, Mewing By Mike Mew, YouTube, https://www.youtube.com/watch?v=3Z_Fp9lGrGY.

58. For example, see J. R. C. Mew, "Orthodontics: Mandibular Advancement Appliances," *British Dental Journal* 225, no. 2 (2018): 95–96, https://doi.org/10.1038/sj.bdj.2018.597.

59. r/Howtolooksmax. Reddit. https://www.reddit.com/r/Howtolooksmax/.

60. Vivek Kaul, "The Necktie Syndrome: Why CEOs Tend to Be Significantly Taller Than the Average Male," *Economic Times*, September 30,

2011, https://economictimes.indiatimes.com/the-necktie-syndrome-why
-ceos-tend-to-be-significantly-taller-than-the-average-male/articleshow
/10178115.cms.

61. Adjusted for inflation, $166,000 would be worth approximately
$276,000 today. See Timothy A. Judge and Daniel M. Cable, "The Ef-
fect of Physical Height on Workplace Success and Income: Preliminary
Test of a Theoretical Model," *Journal of Applied Psychology*, 89(3)
(2004): 428–41, https://doi.org/10.1037/0021-9010.89.3.428.

62. Laura Forman, "Online Dating Is Great—for Investors. For Customers,
It's Complicated," *Wall Street Journal*, July 15, 2022, https://www.wsj
.com/articles/online-dating-investing-match-tinder-bumble-11657890982.

63. BBC News, "The Price of a Bigger Penis," *BBC Reel*, January 23, 2019,
https://www.bbc.com/reel/playlist/the-future-of-sex?vpid=p06q922c.

64. Lucy Johnston, Tracey McLellan, and Audrey McKinlay, "(Perceived)
Size Really Does Matter: Male Dissatisfaction with Penis Size," *Psychology of Men & Masculinity* 15, no. 2 (2014): 225–28, https://doi.org
/10.1037/a0033264.

65. Pornhub, "2024 Year in Review," December 5, 2024.

66. Sammy Sinno et al., "An Assessment of Gender Differences in Plastic
Surgery Patient Education and Information in the United States: Are We
Neglecting Our Male Patients?," *Aesthetic Surgery Journal* 36, no. 1
(2016): 107–10, https://doi.org/10.1093/asj/sjv100.

67. Morgan Sloss, "'I Vowed to Keep This My Secret Forever': 13 Famous
Men Who've Opened Up About Their Cosmetic Procedures," *BuzzFeed*,
April 2, 2024, https://www.buzzfeed.com/morgansloss1/male-celebrities
-cosmetic-procedures.

Chapter 7: At Your Command

1. Debra Soh, "No, the Google Manifesto Isn't Sexist or Anti-Diversity.
It's Science," *Globe and Mail* (Canada), August 8, 2017, https://www
.theglobeandmail.com/opinion/no-the-google-manifesto-isnt-sexist-or
-anti-diversity-its-science/article35903359/.

2. Debra Soh, *The End of Gender: Debunking the Myths About Sex and
Identity in Our Society* (Threshold Editions, 2020), 139–88.

3. "Sex Neuroscientist on the Scary Future of Sex Robots," January 3, 2024, PowerfulJRE, YouTube, https://www.youtube.com/watch?v=WJH90hziZS4.

4. Debra Soh, "The Sex Robots Are Coming. Do Not Fear Them," *Globe and Mail* (Canada), July 18, 2017, A9, https://www.theglobeandmail.com/opinion/the-sex-robots-are-coming-do-not-fear-them/article35698109/.

5. Debra Soh, "Sex Robots Provide a Glimpse into the Future of Intimacy," *Globe and Mail* (Canada), December 8, 2017, A12, https://www.theglobeandmail.com/opinion/sex-robots-provide-glimpse-into-the-future-of-intimacy/article37274005/.

6. Michael Phelan, "Expert Predicts Women Will Be Having More Sex with Robots Than Men Next Year," *Daily Mail* (UK), December 27, 2024, https://www.dailymail.co.uk/sciencetech/article-14230313/Expert-predicts-women-having-sex-robots-men-year.html.

7. For example, see Craig A. Harper, Rebecca Lievesley, and Katie Wanless, "Exploring the Psychological Characteristics and Risk-Related Cognitions of Individuals Who Own Sex Dolls," *Journal of Sex Research* 60, no. 2 (2023): 190–205, https://doi.org/10.1080/00224499.2022.2031848.

8. Ibid.

9. International Society for Sexual Medicine, "What Is the 'Normal' Frequency of Masturbation?," n.d., accessed June 25, 2025, https://www.issm.info/sexual-health-qa/what-is-the normal-frequency-of-masturbation.

10. Jeanne C. Desbuleux and Johannes Fuss, "Is the Anthropomorphization of Sex Dolls Associated with Objectification and Hostility Toward Women? A Mixed Method Study Among Doll Users," *Journal of Sex Research* 60, no. 2 (2022): 206–20, https://doi.org/10.1080/00224499.2022.2103071.

11. Gordon B. Forbes et al., "First- and Second-Generation Measures of Sexism, Rape Myths and Related Beliefs, and Hostility Toward Women: Their Interrelationships and Association with College Students' Experiences with Dating Aggression and Sexual Coercion," *Violence Against Women* 10, no. 3 (2004): 236–61, https://doi.org/10.1177/1077801203256002.

12. Krupa Samji and Eduardo A. Vasquez, "The Link between Myths About Sexual Aggression and Sexual Objectification via Hostile Attitudes Toward Women," *Journal of Sexual Aggression* 26, no. 3 (2020): 385–93, https://doi.org/10.1080/13552600.2019.1676924.

13. Harper, Lievesley, and Wanless, "Exploring the Psychological Characteristics and Risk-Related Cognitions of Individuals Who Own Sex Dolls," 2023.

14. Jeanne C. Desbuleux and Johannes Fuss, "The Self-Reported Sexual Real-World Consequences of Sex Doll Use," *Journal of Sex Research* 61, no. 8 (2023): 1261–1275. https://doi.org/10.1080/00224499.2023.2199727.

15. Ibid.

16. Jonathan Turley, "Sex Robots Go to Court: Testing the Limits of Privacy and Sexual Freedom," *The Hill*, January 27, 2024, https://thehill.com/opinion/technology/4432313-sex-robots-go-to-court-testing-the-limits-of-privacy-and-sexual-freedom/.

17. Markus Appel, Caroline Marker, and Martina Mara, "Otakuism and the Appeal of Sex Robots," *Frontiers in Psychology* 10 (2019): 1–11, https://doi.org/10.3389/fpsyg.2019.00569.

18. Jessica M. Szczuka and Nicole C. Krämer, "Not Only the Lonely—How Men Explicitly and Implicitly Evaluate the Attractiveness of Sex Robots in Comparison to the Attractiveness of Women, and Personal Characteristics Influencing This Evaluation," *Multimodal Technologies and Interaction* 1, no. 3 (2017): 1–18, https://doi.org/10.3390/mti1010003.

19. Emily Fippen and George Gaither, "Prevalence, Comfort with, and Characteristics of Sex Toy Use in a US Convenience Sample Using Reddit.com," *Graduate Student Journal of Psychology* 20 (2023): 1–21, https://doi.org/10.52214/gsjp.v20i1.10143.

20. Christiane Eichenberg, Marwa Khamis, and Lisa Hübner, "The Attitudes of Therapists and Physicians on the Use of Sex Robots in Sexual Therapy: Online Survey and Interview Study," *Journal of Medical Internet Research* 21, no. 8 (2019): 1–28, https://doi.org/10.2196/13853.

21. Wendy Wang and Michael Toscano, "More Scrolling, More Marital Problems," Institute for Family Studies, July 26, 2023, https://ifstudies.org/blog/more-scrolling-more-marital-problems-.

22. Nina J. Rothstein et al., "Perceptions of Infidelity with Sex Robots," *Proceedings of the 2021 ACM/IEEE International Conference on Human-Robot Interaction*, Boulder, CO, March 9, 2021.

23. "Japanese Scientists Develop 'Living Human Skin' on Robotic Finger," June 10, 2022, Reuters, YouTube, https://www.youtube.com/watch?v=1fvlYZ0zwa0.

24. Holly McKenzie-Sutter, "Newfoundland Man Found Not Guilty of Possessing Child Pornography in Sex Doll Trial," *The Globe and Mail* (Canada), May 23, 2019, https://www.theglobeandmail.com/canada/article-newfoundland-man-found-not-guilty-of-possessing-child-pornography-in/.

25. Alex Matthews, "'I Was Lonely': Man Who Bought Sex Doll Online Hoping It Would 'Make Him Happier' Ends Up in Court Because It Was a Child-Sized Version," *The Sun*, September 13, 2018, https://www.thesun.co.uk/news/7252935/nathan-watts-sex-doll-child-version-china/.

26. Caitlin Roper, "Child Sex Abuse Dolls Are Being Made in the Likeness of Real Children," Reduxx, July 15, 2022, https://reduxx.info/child-sex-abuse-dolls-are-being-made-from-photographs-of-real-children/.

27. Elizabeth Letourneau, "The Economic Burden of Child Sexual Abuse in the United States," *Child Abuse & Neglect* 79 (2018): 413–22, https://doi.org/10.1016/j.chiabu.2018.02.020.

28. Ray Blanchard et al., "IQ, Handedness, and Pedophilia in Adult Male Patients Stratified by Referral Source," *Sexual Abuse* 19, no. 3 (2007): 285–309, https://doi.org/10.1177/107906320701900307.

29. Ray Blanchard et al., "Self-Reported Head Injuries Before and After Age 13 in Pedophilic and Nonpedophilic Men Referred for Clinical Assessment," *Archives of Sexual Behavior* 32, no. 6 (2003): 573–81, https://doi.org/10.1023/a:1026093612434.

30. Charlotte Gibbels et al., "Two Sides of One Coin: A Comparison of Clinical and Neurobiological Characteristics of Convicted and Non-Convicted Pedophilic Child Sexual Offenders," *Journal of Clinical Medicine* 8, no. 7 (2019): 947–59, https://doi.org/10.3390/jcm8070947.

31. "About Child Sexual Abuse," Centers for Disease Control and Prevention, May 16, 2024, https://www.cdc.gov/child-abuse-neglect/about/about-child-sexual-abuse.html?CDC_AAref_Val=https://www.cdc.gov/violenceprevention/childsexualabuse/fastfact.html.

32. Craig A. Harper and Rebecca Lievesley, 2022. "Exploring the Ownership of Child-Like Sex Dolls," *Archives of Sexual Behavior* 51 (2022): 4141–56, https://doi.org/10.1007/s10508-022-02422-4.

33. Desbuleux and Fuss, "The Self-Reported Sexual Real-World Consequences of Sex Doll Use," 2023.

34. Michael C. Seto, K. Hanson, and Kelly M. Babchishin, "Contact Sexual Offending by Men with Online Sexual Offenses," *Sexual Abuse* 23, no. 1 (2011): 124–45, https://doi.org/10.1177/1079063210369013.

35. For more information on sexual grooming and prevention of child sexual abuse, see Debra Soh, host, *The Dr. Debra Soh Podcast*, "Episode 43, Grooming—Beware These Predatory Warning Signs (Solo Episode)," May 3, 2022.

36. Friedrich Lösel and Martin Schmucker, "The Effectiveness of Treatment for Sexual Offenders: A Comprehensive Meta-Analysis," *Journal of Experimental Criminology* 1, no. 1 (2005): 117–46, https://doi.org/10.1007/s11292-004-6466-7.

37. David Thornton, "Evidence Regarding the Need for a Diagnostic Category for a Coercive Paraphilia," *Archives of Sexual Behavior* 39, no. 2 (2010): 411–18, https://doi.org/10.1007/s10508-009-9583-6.

Chapter 8: Pregnancy Procrastination and Society-Wide Sterilization

1. For example, see Alison Venn et al., "Risk of Cancer After Use of Fertility Drugs with In-Vitro Fertilisation," *Lancet* 354, no. 9190 (1999): 1586–90, https://doi.org/10.1016/S0140-6736(99)05203-4.

2. National Health Service, "Risks," October 18, 2021, https://www.nhs.uk/conditions/ivf/risks/.

3. Michelle J. K. Osterman et al., "Births: Final Data for 2022," *National Vital Statistics Reports* 73, no. 2 (2024): 1–56, https://www.cdc.gov/nchs/data/nvsr/nvsr73/nvsr73-02.pdf.

4. Malinee Laopaiboon et al., "Advanced Maternal Age and Pregnancy Outcomes: A Multicountry Assessment," *BJOG: An International Journal of Obstetrics & Gynaecology* 121, no. s1 (2014): 49–56, https://doi.org/10.1111/1471-0528.12659.

5. Christi Clarridge and Cindy Mallenbaum, "Not 'Geriatric' Anymore: Pregnancy at 35 Has Its Pluses," *Axios Seattle*, April 10, 2024, https://www.axios.com/local/seattle/2024/04/10/pregnant-35-older-age-advanced-geriatric-seattle-washington.

6. Hannah Devlin, "'A Lottery Ticket, Not a Guarantee': Fertility Experts on the Rise of Egg Freezing," *Guardian* (UK), November 11, 2022, https://www.theguardian.com/society/2022/11/11/not-a-guarantee-why-freezing-your-eggs-shouldnt-be-an-insurance-policy.

7. Aimee Picchi, "The Cost of Raising a Child Is Almost $240,000—and That's Before College," CBS News, September 14, 2023, https://www.cbsnews.com/news/how-much-does-it-cost-to-raise-a-child-240000/.

8. Kate A. Ratliff and Shigehiro Oishi, "Gender Differences in Implicit Self-Esteem Following a Romantic Partner's Success or Failure," *Journal of Personality and Social Psychology* 105, no. 4 (2013): 688–702, https://doi.org/10.1037/a0033769.

9. Marianne Bertrand, Emir Kemenica, and Jessica Pan, "Gender Identity and Relative Income Within Households," *Quarterly Journal of Economics* 130, no. 2 (2015): 571–614, https://www.jstor.org/stable/26372609.

10. Yinjunjie Zhang and Robert Breunig, "Female Breadwinning and Domestic Abuse: Evidence from Australia," *Journal of Population Economics* 36 (2023): 2925–65, https://doi.org/10.1007/s00148-023-00975-9.

11. Christin L. Munsch, "Her Support, His Support: Money, Masculinity, and Marital Infidelity," *American Sociological Review* 80, no. 3 (2015): 469–95, https://doi.org/10.1177/0003122415579989.

12. Lisa Kailai Han, "'Too Few College-Educated Men': A Look at Why Many Women Undergo Egg Freezing, and the Costs Associated with It," CNBC, March 30, 2024, https://www.cnbc.com/2024/03/30/a-look-at-why-many-women-undergo-egg-freezing-and-the-costs-associated-with-it.html.

13. Sarah Druckenmiller Cascante et al., "Fifteen Years of Autologous Oocyte Thaw Outcomes from a Large University-Based Fertility Center," *Fertility and Sterility* 118, no. 1 (2022): 158–66, https://doi.org/10.1016/j.fertnstert.2022.04.013.

14. Gina Kolata, "'Sobering' Study Shows Challenges of Egg Freezing," *New York Times*, September 23, 2022, https://www.nytimes.com/2022/09/23/health/egg-freezing-age-pregnancy.amp.html.

15. Susan Golombok et al., "Single Mothers by Choice: Parenting and Child Adjustment in Middle Childhood," *Journal of Family Psychology* 35, no. 2 (2021): 192–202, https://doi.org/10.1037/fam0000797.

16. Jack Brewer, "Issue Brief: Fatherlessness and Its Effects on American Society," *America First Policy Institute*, May 15, 2023, https://americafirstpolicy.com/issues/issue-brief-fatherlessness-and-its-effects-on-american-society.

17. For example, see Joseph O. Doyle et al., "Successful Elective and Medically Indicated Oocyte Vitrification and Warming for Autologous in Vitro Fertilization, with Predicted Birth Probabilities for Fertility Preservation According to Number of Cryopreserved Oocytes and Age at Retrieval," *Fertility and Sterility* 105, no. 2 (2016): 459–66.e2, https://doi.org/10.1016/j.fertnstert.2015.10.026.

18. Emma Brockes, "Single at 38? Have That Baby," *New York Times*, June 23, 2018, https://www.nytimes.com/2018/06/23/opinion/sunday/single-at-38-have-that-baby.html.

19. National Institute on Aging, "Census Bureau Releases Report on Childless Older Americans," NIA News, September 1, 2021, https://www.nia.nih.gov/news/census-bureau-releases-report-childless-older-americans.

20. Amelia Hill, "'I Just Assumed It Would Happen': The Unspoken Grief of Childless Men," *The Guardian* (UK), August 28, 2023, https://www.theguardian.com/society/2023/aug/28/unspoken-grief-childless-men.

21. JuJu Kim, "World's Oldest Dad, 96, Fathers Another Child," *Time*, October 18, 2012, https://newsfeed.time.com/2012/10/18/worlds-oldest-dad-96-fathers-another-child/.

22. Magdalena Janecka et al., "Advanced Paternal Age Effects in Neurodevelopmental Disorders—Review of Potential Underlying Mechanisms," *Translational Psychiatry* 7 (2017): 1–9, https://doi.org/10.1038/tp.2016.294.

23. Judith A. Easton, Jaime C. Confer, Cari D. Goetz, and David M. Buss, "Reproduction Expediting: Sexual Motivations, Fantasies, and the Ticking Biological Clock," *Personality and Individual Differences* 49, no. 5 (2010): 516–20, https://doi.org/10.1016/j.paid.2010.05.018.

24. Wade N. Hazel et al., "An Age-Dependent Ovulatory Strategy Explains the Evolution of Dizygotic Twinning in Humans," *Nature Ecology & Evolution* 4 (2020): 987–92, https://doi.org/10.1038/s41559-020-1173-y.

25. Debra Soh, "Womb Transplants Will Soon Allow Transgender Women to Become Pregnant," *Washington Examiner*, August 29, 2023, https://www.washingtonexaminer.com/opinion/beltway-confidential/2730271/womb-transplants-will-soon-allow-transgender-women-to-become-pregnant.

26. Jacqueline Mroz, "Their Mothers Chose Donor Sperm. The Doctors Used Their Own," *New York Times*, August 21, 2019, https://www.nytimes.com/2019/08/21/health/sperm-donors-fraud-doctors.html.

27. For example, see Jacqueline Mroz, "Their Children Were Conceived with Donated Sperm. It Was the Wrong Sperm," *New York Times*, June 3, 2019, https://www.nytimes.com/2019/06/03/health/sperm-banks-fertility-artificial-insemination.html.

28. Carolina Aragão, "Among Young Adults Without Children, Men Are More Likely Than Women to Say They Want to Be Parents Someday," Pew Research Center, February 15, 2024, https://www.pewresearch.org/short-reads/2024/02/15/among-young-adults-without-children-men-are-more-likely-than-women-to-say-they-want-to-be-parents-someday/.

29. Sabrina Tavernise et al., "Why American Women Everywhere Are Delaying Motherhood," *New York Times*, June 16, 2021, https://www.nytimes.com/2021/06/16/us/declining-birthrate-motherhood.html.

30. Rachel Minkin, Juliana Menasce Horowitz, and Carolina Aragão, "The Experiences of US Adults Who Don't Have Children," Pew Research Center, July 25, 2024, https://www.pewresearch.org/social-trends/2024/07/25/the-experiences-of-u-s-adults-who-dont-have-children/.

31. Sammy Jenkins, "'I Felt Like a Freak Because I Didn't Want Children,'" BBC, April 26, 2024, https://www.bbc.com/news/articles/c72pnllv8nko.

32. Anthony C. Little et al., "Oral Contraceptive Use in Women Changes Preferences for Male Facial Masculinity and Is Associated with Partner Facial Masculinity," *Psychoneuroendocrinology* 38, no. 9 (2013): 1777–85, https://doi.org/10.1016/j.psyneuen.2013.02.014.

33. S. Craig Roberts et al., "MHC-Correlated Odour Preferences in Humans and the Use of Oral Contraceptives," *Proceedings of the Royal*

Society B 275, no. 1652 (2008): 2715–22, https://doi.org/10.1098/rs
pb.2008.0825.

34. Kimberly Daniels and Joyce C. Abma, "Current Contraceptive Status
    Among Women Aged 15–49: United States, 2017–2019," National
    Center for Health Statistics, October 2020, https://www.cdc.gov/nchs
    /products/databriefs/db388.htm.

35. Belinda A. Pletzer and Hubert H. Kerschbaum, "50 Years of Hormonal
    Contraception—Time to Find Out, What It Does to Our Brain," *Fron-
    tiers in Neuroscience* 8, no. 256 (2014): 1–6, https://doi.org/10.3389
    /fnins.2014.00256.

36. Rachel K. Jones, "Beyond Birth Control: The Overlooked Benefits
    of Oral Contraceptive Pills," Guttmacher Institute, November 2011,
    https://www.guttmacher.org/sites/default/files/pdfs/pubs/Beyond-Birth
    -Control.pdf.

37. Niklas Zethraeus et al., "Combined Oral Contraceptives and Sexual
    Function in Women—A Double-Blind, Randomized, Placebo-Controlled
    Trial," *Journal of Clinical Endocrinology & Metabolism* 101, no. 11
    (2016): 4046–53, https://doi.org/10.1210/jc.2016-2032.

38. S. Craig Roberts et al., "Female Facial Attractiveness Increases During
    the Fertile Phase of the Menstrual Cycle," *Proceedings of the Royal Soci-
    ety B* 271 (2004): S270–S272, https://doi.org/10.1098/rsbl.2004.0174.

39. Martie G. Haselton et al., "Ovulatory Shifts in Human Female Ornamen-
    tation: Near Ovulation, Women Dress to Impress," *Hormones and Behav-
    ior* 51, no. 1 (2007): 40–45, https://doi.org/10.1016/j.yhbeh.2006.07.007.

40. Devendra Singh and P. Matthew Bronstad, "Female Body Odour Is a
    Potential Cue to Ovulation," *Proceedings of the Royal Society B* 268,
    no. 1469 (2001): 797–801, https://doi.org/10.1098/rspb.2001.1589.

41. Summer Mengelkoch et al., "Hormonal Contraceptive Use Is Associated
    with Differences in Women's Inflammatory and Psychological Reactivity
    to an Acute Social Stressor," *Brain, Behavior, and Immunity* 115 (2023):
    747–57, https://doi.org/10.1016/j.bbi.2023.10.033.

42. Nicole Petersen et al., "Oral Contraceptive Pill Use and Menstrual
    Cycle Phase Are Associated with Altered Resting State Functional
    Connectivity," *Neuroimage* 90 (2014): 24–32, https://doi.org/10.1016
    /j.neuroimage.2013.12.016.

43. Soum D. Lokeshwar et al., "Decline in Serum Testosterone Levels Among Adolescent and Young Adult Men in the USA," *European Urology Focus* 7, no. 4 (2021): 886–89, https://doi.org/10.1016 /j.euf.2020.02.006.

44. Magdalena Natalia Wojtas et al., "Interplay Between Hippocampal TACR3 and Systemic Testosterone in Regulating Anxiety-Associated Synaptic Plasticity," *Molecular Psychiatry* 29 (2024): 686–703, https:// doi.org/10.1038/s41380-023-02361-z.

45. Wenshan Lv, Na Du, Ying Liu, et al., "Low Testosterone Level and Risk of Alzheimer's Disease in the Elderly Men: A Systematic Review and Meta-Analysis," *Molecular Neurobiology* 53, no. 4 (2016): 2679–84, https://doi.org/10.1007/s12035-015-9315-y.

46. Courtney Kube and Molly Boigon, "Every Branch of the Military Is Struggling to Make Its 2022 Recruiting Goals, Officials Say," NBC News, June 27, 2022, https://www.nbcnews.com/news/military/every -branch-us-military-struggling-meet-2022-recruiting-goals-officia-rcna 35078.

47. Robert C. Kolodny et al., "Depression of Plasma Testosterone Levels After Chronic Intensive Marihuana [Sic] Use," *New England Journal of Medicine* 290, no. 16 (1974): 872–74, https://doi.org/10.1056 /NEJM197404182901602.

48. Thomas G. Travison et al., "A Population-Level Decline in Serum Testosterone Levels in American Men," *Journal of Clinical Endocrinology & Metabolism* 92, no. 1 (2007): 196–202, https://doi.org/10.1210 /jc.2006-1375.

49. Julene Argaluza et al., "Environmental Pollution with Psychiatric Drugs," *World Journal of Psychiatry* 11, no. 10 (2021): 791–804, https://doi.org/10.5498/wjp.v11.i10.791.

50. A meta-analysis from 2011 found that birth control pills are only a small contribution to overall estrogenicity of drinking water, but more research needs to be done to determine the effects of this contamination on human health. Amber Wise, Kacie O'Brien, and Tracey Woodruff, "Are Oral Contraceptives a Significant Contributor to the Estrogenicity of Drinking Water?," *Environmental Science & Technology Journal* 45, no. 1 (2011): 51–60, https://doi.org/10.1021/es1014482.

51. Wilfried Sanchez et al., "Adverse Effects in Wild Fish Living Downstream from Pharmaceutical Manufacture Discharges," *Environment International* 37, no. 8 (2011): 1342–48, https://doi.org/10.1016/j.en vint.2011.06.002.

52. Sijing Wang et al., "Bioconcentration and Behavioral Interference Effect of Diazepam on Adult Japanese Medaka (*Oryzias Latipes*)," *Journal of the Faculty of Agriculture*, Kyushu University 68, no. 2 (2023): 135–41, https://doi.org/10.5109/6796256.

53. Alex T. Ford, "From Gender Benders to Brain Benders (and Beyond!)," *Aquatic Toxicology* 151 (2014): 1–3, https://doi.org/10.1016 /j.aquatox.2014.02.005.

54. Tyrone B. Hayes et al., "Atrazine Induces Complete Feminization and Chemical Castration in Male African Clawed Frogs (*Xenopus Laevis*)," *Proceedings of the National Academy of Sciences* 107, no. 10 (2010): 4612–17, https://doi.org/10.1073/pnas.0909519107.

55. Ramji K. Bhandari, Frederick S. vom Saal, and Donald E. Tillitt, "Transgenerational Effects from Early Developmental Exposures to Bisphenol A or 17α-Ethinylestradiol in Medaka, Oryzias Latipes," *Scientific Reports* 5 (2015): 1–5, https://doi.org/10.1038/srep09303.

56. Hiroyuki Inaba et al., "Soy Isoflavones Induce Feminization of Japanese Eel (*Anguilla Japonica*)," *International Journal of Molecular Science* 24, no. 1 (2022): 1–12, https://doi.org/10.3390/ijms24010396.

57. Neal G. Simon et al., "Increased Aggressive Behavior and Decreased Affiliative Behavior in Adult Male Monkeys After Long-Term Consumption of Diets Rich in Soy Protein and Isoflavones," *Hormones and Behavior* 45, no. 4 (2004): 278–84, https://doi.org/10.1016/j.yh beh.2003.12.005.

58. Jorge E. Chavarro et al., "Soy Food and Isoflavone Intake in Relation to Semen Quality Parameters Among Men from an Infertility Clinic," *Human Reproduction* 23, no. 11 (2008): 2584–90, https://doi.org /10.1093/humrep/den243.

59. György Csaba, "The Present and Future of Human Sexuality: Impact of Faulty Perinatal Hormonal Imprinting," *Sexual Medicine Reviews* 5, no. 2 (2017): 163–69, https://doi.org/10.1016/j.sxmr.2016.10.002.

60. Lærke Priskorn et al., "Anogenital Distance Is Associated with Semen Quality but Not Reproductive Hormones in 1,106 Young Men from the General Population," *Human Reproduction* 34, no. 1 (2019): 12–24, https://doi.org/10.1093/humrep/dey326.

61. "Azoospermia," Johns Hopkins Medicine, https://www.hopkinsmedi cine.org/health/conditions-and-diseases/azoospermia.

62. Shanna H. Swan et al., "First Trimester Phthalate Exposure and Anogenital Distance in Newborns," *Human Reproduction* 30, no. 4 (2015): 963–72, https://doi.org/10.1093/humrep/deu363.

63. James F. Smith et al., "Sexual, Marital, and Social Impact of a Man's Perceived Infertility Diagnosis," *Journal of Sexual Medicine* 6, no. 9 (2009): 2505–15, https://doi.org/10.1111/j.1743-6109.2009.01383.x.

64. See Trille Kjaer et al., "Divorce or End of Cohabitation Among Danish Women Evaluated for Fertility Problems," *Acta Obstetricia et Gynecologica Scandinavica* 93, no. 3 (2015): 269–76, https://doi.org/10.1111/aogs.12317.

65. US Food and Drug Administration, "Phthalates in Food Packaging and Food Contact Applications," October 29, 2024, https://www.fda.gov/food/food-additives-and-gras-ingredients-information-consumers/phthalates-food-packaging-and-food-contact-applications.

66. US Food and Drug Administration, "Phthalates in Cosmetics," May 19, 2022, https://www.fda.gov/cosmetics/cosmetic-ingredients/phthalates-cosmetics.

67. Marcus A. Garcia et al., "Quantitation and Identification of Microplastics Accumulation in Human Placental Specimens Using Pyrolysis Gas Chromatography Mass Spectrometry," *Toxicological Sciences* 199, no. 1 (2024): 81–88, https://doi.org/10.1093/toxsci/kfae021.

68. Dan Witters, "US Depression Rates Reach New Highs," Gallup, May 17, 2023, https://news.gallup.com/poll/505745/depression-rates-reach-new-highs.aspx.

69. Elizabeth Kivowitz, "Romance or Nomance? Adolescents Prefer to See Less Sex, More Friendships, Platonic Relationships on Screen," *UCLA Newsroom*, October 25, 2023, https://newsroom.ucla.edu/releases/adolescents-prefer-less-sex-more-friendships-on-screen.

70. Matthew J. Maenner et al., "Prevalence and Characteristics of Autism Spectrum Disorder Among Children Aged 8 Years—Autism and Developmental Disabilities Monitoring Network, 11 Sites, United States, 2020," *Surveillance Summaries* 72, no. 2 (2023): 1–14, https://www.cdc.gov/mmwr/volumes/72/ss/ss7202a1.htm?s_cid=ss7202a1_w.

71. Simon Baron-Cohen, "The Extreme Male Brain Theory of Autism," *Trends in Cognitive Sciences* 6, no. 6 (2002): 248–54, https://doi.org/10.1016/s1364-6613(02)01904-6.

72. "Fauci, Vaccines, and Big Pharma's Power: Robert F. Kennedy, Jr. Interview, Part 1," March 21, 2022, Megyn Kelly, YouTube, https://www.youtube.com/watch?v=e3w8hzZIVZk.

73. Kenji Hashimoto and Bruce D. Hammock, "Reply to Reeves and Dunn: Risk for Autism in Offspring After Maternal Glyphosate Exposure," *Proceedings of the National Academy of Sciences* 118, no. 2 (2021): 1–2, https://doi.org/10.1073/pnas.2016496118.

74. Claudine Vasseur et al., "Glyphosate Presence in Human Sperm: First Report and Positive Correlation with Oxidative Stress in an Infertile French Population," *Ecotoxicology and Environmental Safety* 278 (2024): 1–11, https://doi.org/10.1016/j.ecoenv.2024.116410.

75. Laura F. Lewis, "We Will Never Be Normal: The Experience of Discovering a Partner Has Autism Spectrum Disorder," *Journal of Marital and Family Therapy* 43, no. 4 (2017): 631–43, https://doi.org/10.1111/jmft.12231.

76. Debby Herbenick et al., "Changes in Penile-Vaginal Intercourse Frequency and Sexual Repertoire from 2009 to 2018: Findings from the National Survey of Sexual Health and Behavior," *Archives of Sexual Behavior* 51, no. 3 (2022): 1419–33, https://doi.org/10.1007/s10508-021-02125-2.

77. Jean H. Kim et al., "Sociodemographic Correlates of Sexlessness Among American Adults and Associations with Self-Reported Happiness Levels: Evidence from the US General Social Survey," *Archives of Sexual Behavior* 46, no. 8 (2017): 2403–15, https://doi.org/10.1007/s10508-017-0968-7.

Conclusion: Reconnecting

1. Yuichi Shoda, Walter Mischel, and Philip K. Peake, "Predicting Adolescent Cognitive and Self-Regulatory Competencies from Preschool Delay

of Gratification: Identifying Diagnostic Conditions," *Developmental Psychology* 26, no. 6 (1990): 978–86, https://doi.org/10.1037/0012 -1649.26.6.978.

2. Sasha Rogelberg, "Americans Are Draining Stock Portfolios to Shovel More Money into Sports Betting," *Fortune*, August 27, 2024, https:// fortune.com/2024/08/27/sports-betting-gambling-investment-stock-bank ruptcy-gen-z-men/.

3. Debra Soh, *The End of Gender: Debunking the Myths About Sex and Identity in Our Society* (Threshold Editions, 2020), 238–40.

4. John O'Doherty et al., "Beauty in a Smile: The Role of Medial Orbito-frontal Cortex in Facial Attractiveness," *Neuropsychologia* 41, no. 2 (2003): 147–55, https://doi.org/10.1016/S0028-3932(02)00145-8.

5. David B. Givens, "The Nonverbal Basis of Attraction: Flirtation, Court-ship, and Seduction," *Psychiatry* 41, no. 4 (1978): 346–59, https://doi .org/10.1080/00332747.1978.11023994.